WOO,
WOW,
and
WIN

BY THOMAS A. STEWART

Intellectual Capital: The New Wealth of Organizations

The Wealth of Knowledge: Intellectual Capital and the Twenty-First-Century Organization

BY NEIL SMITH AND PATRICIA O'CONNELL

*How Excellent Companies Avoid Dumb Things:
Breaking the 8 Hidden Barriers That Plague Even the Best Businesses*

WOO, WOW, AND WIN

SERVICE DESIGN, STRATEGY, AND THE ART OF CUSTOMER DELIGHT

···

Thomas A. Stewart and Patricia O'Connell

**HARPER
BUSINESS**

An Imprint of HarperCollinsPublishers

HarperCollins books may be purchased for educational, business, or sales promotional use. For information, please email the Special Markets Department at SPsales@harpercollins.com.

FIRST EDITION

Library of Congress Cataloging-in-Publication Data

Names: Stewart, Thomas A., 1948- author. | O'Connell, Patricia (Business writer), author.
Title: Woo, wow, and win : service design, strategy, and the art of customer delight / Thomas A. Stewart and Patricia O'Connell.
Description: First edition. | New York, NY : HarperBusiness, [2016] | Includes index.
Identifiers: LCCN 2016028812 | ISBN 9780062415691 (hardcover : alk. paper)
Subjects: LCSH: Customer services. | Customer relations. | Service industries.
Classification: LCC HF5415.5 .S744 2016 | DDC 658.8/12—dc23
LC record available at https://lccn.loc.gov/2016028812

16 17 18 19 20   RRD   10 9 8 7 6 5 4 3 2 1

To Amanda, Pamela, and Patrick, and to William J. Boyd, who bent this twig—TAS

To John A. Byrne, my own Red Pollard and Tom Smith, and the memory of Thomas Augustine—PO'C

Contents

WOO,
WOW,
and
WIN

Introduction

The purpose of a business is to create and keep a customer.
—PETER F. DRUCKER

G reat service is not just a consequence of good intentions, attentive management, and a supportive culture. In fact, cause and effect are reversed: Service needs to be laid into the company's keel, the way performance is built into a BMW or intuitiveness designed into an iPad. A company designed for service will naturally display the behaviors—the intentions, attention, and culture—good service requires. If service isn't built in, no amount of goodwill can deliver it reliably, and no effort can compensate for the lack of it. Trying to satisfy customers will be like canoeing into a headwind: The effort will eventually exhaust even the most determined team.

The surprising fact is, most companies are not, actually, designed for service—to provide an experience that matches a customer's expectations, and to deliver it time and again. The reasons for this are complex and partly historical, as we will explain in the pages that follow. For now, accept our premise that providing superior service is unnatural in most organizations.

Addressing that problem is what this book is about. In the last few years, a handful of progressive thinkers, pioneering executives, and scholars have begun to develop ideas and experiments in *service design.* Their thesis and ours is simple: Services should be designed with as much care as products are. We include service *delivery* in the concept, too, because artistry without execution is meaningless, in business at least. Service design and delivery involve reimagining, re-creating, and rethinking the execution of every stage and aspect of customer and company interaction, regardless of what is being sold and regardless of whether a transaction actually occurs, to satisfy that customer and advance your strategic goals.

Put another way, service design and delivery—what we call SD^2—is what you do so your customers get the experience you want them to have—every time. Three ideas are embedded in that sentence. First, service design is proactive, not reactive; it involves choices, actions, and consequences. Second, service design starts with what you, the seller, want; it is about delivering on your promise to customers in accordance with your strategy, not about acceding to everything a customer asks. Third, service design creates consistency, and consistency is no accident.

*   *   *

After scores of interviews, thousands of hours spent, and tens of thousands of miles traveled, we have come to hold four propositions about service design almost as tenets of faith.

* We believe that the design of a service—what it does and does not do, the experience it creates, the value it delivers—should be an essential element of the go-to-market strategy of every service business, from a coffee shop (Starbucks is a brilliant example of service design), to top-of-the-line personal and professional services like Singapore Airlines or Goldman Sachs.

* We believe that excellence in service, like quality in manufactured goods, needs to be built in, not painted on at the end.

* We believe that great service should be free, also like quality—that is, that well-designed service pays for itself and then some,

by saving you and your customers time and money, including the cost of making up for errors.

∗ We have learned and believe that excellence in service design and delivery is the best way—a sustainable, repeatable way—to differentiate your company from your rivals, and profitably woo, wow, and win not just customers, but the right customers for you.

Companies that embrace SD² are bringing new thinking, new actions, and new effectiveness to running businesses by applying design thinking and sound strategy to services. *Woo, Wow, and Win* shows how, by explaining the what, why, and how of service design and delivery, the principles that should guide it, the results it can produce, and the tools you will need.

Our focus is on the vast portion of the economy known as the "service sector"—basically everything that is not mining, agriculture, or manufacturing. But the benefits of SD² accrue to those sectors, too. Economists like to separate goods-producing companies from those that deliver services, but customers do not. They care about the total experience they have with a company. Understanding service design helps all companies interact with customers in ways that augment the value of what they do. Think of Apple Stores, for example, where the act of shopping has been imagined and designed with the same attentiveness and concern for experience that Apple applies to its phones and computers. Whether it is about customer or user, it is the *experience* that matters.

It is said that luck is the residue of design. So is great service. SD² is in part a sophisticated application of "design thinking." Tim Brown, president and CEO of design firm IDEO, describes design thinking as "a human-centered approach to innovation that uses the designer's toolkit to integrate the needs of people, the possibilities of technology, and the requirements for business success." Service design pulls from that toolkit not only for innovation but to ensure excellence, elegance, and empathy wherever a service company interacts with customers. It can help every company, because there is no business where the customer does not matter.

*   *   *

Executives know—as Peter Drucker put it—that their most important job is to create and keep customers; yet management science and practice are less advanced in service industries and in customer-facing functions than in practically any others. We have a century or so during which industrial and product design have been studied and applied—but just a generation of service design. In business functions, we have much more solid knowledge of finance, operations, technology, and even HR than we do of sales, customer service, or even marketing.

Lacking design and the knowledge of it, executives lurch from tactic to tactic, sometimes trying to attract and retain customers with sales and promotions, then with loyalty programs, then with extras for preferred customers, then by giving more decision-making authority to frontline employees. Some of these techniques will work on some of the people some of the time, but there is little if any insight into why or how.

Without a design-oriented approach, companies pursue customer-centricity, as eager to please as puppies but with no clear sense of their unique identity or what they can do better than anyone else. Without service design and delivery—without being able to plan and execute in a way that is repeatable, predictable, scalable, and profitable—companies cannot set customers' expectations, let alone meet them. They cannot support their strategy. They cannot offer reliable results to stakeholders. Like rubes in a casino, they will win occasionally, but will lose far more often.

*   *   *

We know this because we have seen it. In our careers we have witnessed, chronicled, and analyzed management at its best and worst. You have seen it, too, as a businessperson and as someone who consumes services both in your personal life and at work. Tom had a less than satisfying service experience not long ago, checking into a hotel at Walt Disney World in Orlando, Florida. Tired after a long flight, he was delighted to find no line at registration and relieved that the woman behind the counter was professional rather than artificially and aggressively cheerful. He got his key and directions to his "casita" in the sprawling resort, and headed happily along the path prescribed.

Then he spent the next twenty minutes walking in circles, increasingly flustered because he could see signs for buildings 1, 2, and 4, but not for building 3, where his room awaited. Nor could he find any employee to help him find his way. "Call me spatially challenged," Tom admits. Accustomed to Manhattan's orderly grid, he gets lost on the looping pathways of resorts. That is his problem (but probably not his alone).

What might Disney's solution have been? A luxury resort would have golf carts and drivers: They would be part of the design and factored into the price. But Disney, catering to Mouseketeers and conventioneers, cannot make a profit if it hires armies of navvies. Nor would it make sense to have bottles of bubbly and boxes of chocolates on hand to soothe the souls of grumpy guests: That would be off-brand.

A couple of standard tools, customer service and customer care—both of which amount to throwing money at a problem, often after the fact—should not have been pulled out here. But service design would have prevented the problem in the first place: better maps and more signs, to be sure, but also interactive maps, like the kind you find at science museums and the Paris Metro, where you push a button for your destination and are shown the route to take. Something like that would be affordable, on-brand (kids would love it), and useful (even to Tom). More to the point, a customer-centric solution would likely occur to you only if you approached your service with the mindset and toolkit of a designer and with your customer's experience in mind.

Clearly Tom's story is not about customer service—and neither is this book. The world does not need another book saying that customer service is important (of course it is), extolling the (obvious) importance of frontline employees, calculating the value of loyalty, or any of the other topics that fill literally thousands of volumes about customer service, most of which, frankly, are long on exhortation and short on value. The people with whom Tom interacted in Orlando gave him exemplary service, yet his experience was unsatisfactory because it wasn't well designed. In Tom's mind, Disney came up short for not walking, literally, in customers' shoes.

*   *   *

We're drawn to this topic for three reasons. The first is that service design itself is a relatively new idea, only starting to be studied and beginning to be embraced, ready for the synthesis and call to action we propose. This approach is grounded in the realities of business today, attuned to the impact of technology on how companies and customers interact. It is charged with the intellectual excitement and practical insight that come from looking at old problems through new eyes and having new tools with which to solve them. When old mindsets are replaced by a service-dominant logic (to use the phrase of a pair of influential thinkers), valuable insights tumble out.

Second, it is an important idea: Service design and delivery carry the potential to transform your company and many industries for the better—retail, banking, travel, and tourism, to be sure, but also health care, IT services, and government functions as critical as fire, police, and public health, as well as activities as mundane as renewing a driver's license. Third, that transformation can eliminate waste for companies while also improving outcomes for customers. It has the same win-win potential as Total Quality Management, and on an equally large scale.

Till now, the concept of service design has been embraced mostly by marketing executives and people with trendy titles like Chief Experience Officer. While marketing is a big beneficiary, the value of

SD² reaches high into the strategy sphere and deep into companies' operational core. It is equally critical for the C-suite and frontline employees, as useful in business-to-business transactions as it is in B2C.

As we tell the stories of companies that have begun to take this journey, we will share what we have learned about:

* The "Ahhh" moment. In every business, there is a moment when the customer makes a judgment about you—when she decides she is in good hands, relaxes, and gives you the chance to capture her loyalty. The *Ahhh* moment might be as simple as when an 800-number phone tree gets her to where she wants quickly. It could be as complex as the confidence a B2B customer has that everyone on your team understands how individual activities fit into the big picture of your business together.

* The "Ow"—the equal and opposite of an *Ahhh*. At the *Ow* moment, customers draw away from the possibility of commitment. They may complete the deal or transaction, may even come back, but something is broken. They are ready to shop around, leave your store, abandon an online shopping cart, vow never to do business with you again, or, God forbid, take to social media to vent their frustration.

* The "Aha" moment. This happens on the other side of the relationship—when you and your colleagues recognize the implications and opportunity offered by your customer's *Ahhh*s and *Ow*s. It is when you understand what you've got to do— every time—to capture and keep your customer's business. The *Aha* moment is when discovery feeds into strategy. These moments allow you to mobilize your organization to act on what customers tell you, with specific interventions that create more value for them.

*   *   *

Service "fit" is an increasingly important element of strategy—and a key concept of SD². Singapore Airlines and Southwest Airlines consistently rank near the top in customer satisfaction surveys in their industry. One is famous for luxury; the other is a low-cost, few-frills carrier. The comparison illustrates the point that service design and business design must fit together.

Every company's strategy is (or should be) unique, but as we will see, these strategies map to certain archetypes of SD². What's great design for a trendsetting company like Warby Parker is unlikely to work for a neighborhood optometrist or a chain like Pearle Vision; Goldman Sachs should design its approach to customers differently from TD Bank. But whatever a company's strategy, its service design will follow the same principles and be aimed at the same result: a customer experience that is reliably delightful for the customers you want and produces value for them and profits for you.

The goals of companies and consumers haven't changed since the first market was established: Companies have always wanted to make a profit by meeting customers' needs; customers have always wanted their needs sufficiently and efficiently met. But what has changed is how customers define "sufficiently" and "efficiently." Thanks in part to globalization and the Internet, a customer's choice is no longer constrained by distance, whether it is for books or consulting services; selection no longer sets a company apart—another choice is a couple of clicks away. Even price is less of a differentiator; not at the low end (where rivals compete to offer rock-bottom prices) or in the middle (where customers can easily compare), or the high end (where price barely matters). So how does a consumer decide?

Study after study has shown that the nature of consumers' *experience with* a company is a key deciding factor in how they choose to spend their money. Poor customer experience results from a lack of consideration for every step and aspect of the customer's journey and poor decisions about those steps. Poor customer experience results in poor word of mouth, which is amplified online to a wider audience than ever before.

Providing a superior service experience is the gateway to success. And SD² is the key that unlocks it.

* * *

This book is in three main parts, each of which is a stage in what we hope will be a journey of discovery for you, followed by an appendix with tools.

The first part of the book—"Setting Out"—is designed to orient you for the journey ahead. We will discuss how managing services and customer experiences differs from much of what you learned in school or on the job about managing. We will place service design and delivery in three contexts—economic, historical, and strategic—to help you understand how it can be most valuable to you. We will discuss the most important elements of well-designed, well-delivered service—ten indicators that you can use to create a baseline of your strengths and weaknesses and plan progress.

In this section, we will also introduce the concept of the "service journey"—a metaphor that can help you map a service design and manage its delivery. This is a visualization of your customer's journeys and of what you do behind the scenes to make the experience work for them. We will then zero in on the most important parts of the journey, the critical customer interactions that have the potential to make or break your strategy.

In part two, "The Principles of Service Design," you will apply those insights to your interactions with customers and to the backstage activities you need to perform. We will work through five principles that apply to SD² in every company: finding the right customers, delivering what delights them, eliminating heroic efforts and waste from your work and theirs, providing a coherent experience on all platforms and at all times, and continuous innovation. You cannot execute your strategy if you do not get these principles right. Understanding them will reveal real tensions in your organization that get in the way of designing and delivering coherent, excellent experiences. As you work through these tensions, you will be able to set priorities for progress and make plans for change.

In part three, "Service Design in Action," we will widen our perspective again, putting the pieces of what we have learned into a framework for action. The principles of SD^2 come to life in various archetypes of service design. Based on nine fundamental value propositions—from Trendsetter to Bargain, from Specialist to Utility—these archetypes are *the expression of strategy as your customer experiences it.* These archetypes will give you a clearer understanding of how to fit strategy to design. We will talk about how touchpoints—the moments of interaction you have with customers—come together into a continuous journey, and how to manage not just the touchpoints but the journey as a whole.

We will take some time to talk about the customer's side of service design and in particular how to work with customers to co-create their experience, adding more value for them—and for you, creating customer capital. We will also bring in the critical topic of culture. Most services are delivered by people, whether it is a frontline employee asking, "Want fries with that?" or a lawyer working through a contract, which makes culture as important a part of service fit as strategy.

The Appendix, titled "Tools for the Journey," begins by showing how to create a report card to assess your SD^2 grade point average—a baseline measurement for when you begin to put these ideas into practice. Also here you will find an introduction to mapping service journeys and creating service blueprints—showing you how to take the concept of a service journey map, which you read about periodically through the text, and apply it to your business. With these two fundamental tools—a report card and a map—you can embark on a series of projects to strengthen your design and enhance your delivery capabilities. We propose seven of them. These are projects that you can run over and over in a cycle of continuous improvement. The section concludes with a number of specific how-tos: instructions for measuring the value of customers, tracking the effectiveness of service innovation, and so on.

* * *

Throughout this book, you will see vignettes about great examples of service design and delivery, including those that illustrate the five principles that we identified as key to excellence in SD². Rather than focus on just one or two companies of the dozens we researched, visited, and studied, we have used a broad sample to show the breadth of service design and delivery's impact. We've written about companies old and new, those that cater to consumers, those that work with clients, and we have ensured that each archetype is represented. Some companies will be household names; others are not—at least not yet.

Our selection of these companies does not suggest they are the only ones in their sector or industry who are SD²-adept, or frankly that they have done everything right. Like us, these companies understand that excellence in service design and delivery is a journey, a goal that always seems just out of reach. Achieving excellence in service design and delivery is like catching a soap bubble; you have it in your hand for a brief moment only. And that is not a bad thing. If good is the enemy of great, complacency is the enemy of excellence.

Stumbles, losing one's way, and switching course are all part of any journey. For the most part, our goal has been to focus on the triumphs. That is not to paint an overly optimistic or misleading picture or to pretend obstacles do not exist. Our goal is to inspire you to think about how your company can identify critical moments in your customers' journeys—and your own—so that you can better woo, wow, and win customers.

We do not pretend to have discovered fire with this book. Rather, it is about reminding you of the power of fire, and how to harness it.

PART I

Setting Out

....

CHAPTER 1

The Road to *"Ahhh!"*

Membership has its privileges," according to one well-known charge card company. To Jeff Potter, CEO of membership-based commuter airline Surf Air, those privileges are convenience, comfort, camaraderie, and connections. He learned the value of membership as CEO of Exclusive Resorts, a luxury vacation club. "Membership gives people something in common from the very start. It makes people more invested in your product or service," he says.

Surf Air subscribers pay a monthly fee (currently $1,950, plus a one-time membership fee) for unlimited flights between any cities on its system in California and Nevada. That is a great deal for many business customers: a Los Angeles lawyer who needs to be in Sacramento several times a month; a tech mogul who weekends in Tahoe; consultants with clients scattered around California; a restaurateur with properties in different cities. It is an even better deal because of the ingenious (a word we do not use lightly) aspects of the carrier's service design.

Surf Air flies only Pilatus PC-12 NG aircraft—nine-passenger craft that have the feel of a private plane. That eliminates security screening and a lengthy check-in process, because Transportation Security Administration rules exempt planes carrying fewer than ten passengers from the time-consuming checks. Surf Air's use of the membership-based revenue model and small, largely underutilized regional airports means passengers waste almost no time on the ground; the economics of the business are so attractive that the airline can make a profit on a flight just 60 percent full. It can—and will—fly scheduled flights with even one passenger.

A stint as CEO of Frontier Airlines gave Potter insight into the issues that bedevil both commercial airlines and their passengers—issues that he and his partners sought to resolve when designing Surf Air. "Airlines ranked 36 out of 40 industries in the Net Promoter Score, yet domestic travel was booming," Potter recalls. "We saw an opportunity to cater to the frequent traveler, to be the equivalent of high-speed rail: addressing local markets, people who need to travel a small corridor quickly at an affordable cost."

Flying Surf Air is indeed a different experience: The airline has practically eliminated the airport. You can arrive just fifteen minutes before flight time; free snacks and beverages await passengers in the preflight area; you do not need a boarding pass; there is no security check; there is no boarding group scrum at the gate; luggage is taken from you planeside and delivered moments after you walk off. "When our members first come in, they're very confused," says Potter. "They're used to loudspeakers and bright lights and being corralled."

The radically simplified customer journey eliminates backstage hassle, too. Surf Air needs no baggage-handling system and employs no flight attendants. Because it is a subscription model, it needs no algorithms to set fares, has no tickets to process—the whole IT system is much simpler.

For all that members enjoy the luxury, convenience, and relative economy that Surf Air offers, those are not the most important things to members. "People constantly point out that flying commercially between LAX and SFO—a ninety-minute flight—actually takes three to four hours more because of all the things we have eliminated," says Potter. "Our surveys show the number-one thing people value is time. We like to think we're not saving them time—we're giving it back to them."

*   *   *

"The number-one thing people value is time." That is the crux of the Surf Air experience—and its design. Think about the last customer satisfaction survey you received. (We know better than to ask about your last flight.) Did that survey seek to capture what was important to you? If it was from a hotel, it probably asked you to evaluate check-in and checkout, the cleanliness of your room, the promptness of room service, and a number of similar items, on a scale of 1 to 5 or 1 to 7, then asked if you would be likely to return or recommend the place to others.

And, if you're like us, you felt that the survey had little to do with your stay. Check-in? Sure, it was fine, no problems. The room? Sure, it was clean, no problems. Return? Sure, next time I'm in Atlanta and depending on where my meetings are. But the survey missed the point: It should have been about your *experience*: how you felt about the stay, if you got what you expected, whether it was distinctive or special, or just another night in another hotel in another city—fine, no problem.

That survey wasn't really gauging your satisfaction or experience. It was measuring whether the employees did what they were supposed to do—smiled at check-in, vacuumed the room, delivered breakfast on time. The survey was headquarters's way of measuring how well managers and their teams complied with instructions.

Those not-about-you surveys are a symptom of a surprising fact: Most companies are not actually designed to serve. In large part, service industry operating models—their org charts, processes, incentives—have been adapted from manufacturing, where measures are based on quantity and quality of output: how many widgets, how few defects. These models are designed from production out, not from customer back.

The result of our industrial legacy: Company after company is underwhelming its customers and leaving money on the table. Not just services businesses; industrial companies—makers of things—underperform, too, because they do not make the most of opportunities to create great customer experience as well as great products. Services, the most important sector of the economy, the biggest employer and creator of wealth, are too much managed by guess and by gosh.

Now think about your last memorable interaction with a company—via their website, in person, on the phone, through social media. Maybe you bought something online, tried a new restaurant, had your car serviced, or patronized a local store. It could be a professional experience—working with a supplier or distributor, dealing with an advertising agency.

How would you rate your experience? Was it great? So good you have become a Loyalist or Evangelist? Was it lousy? So bad you'll never return? Or was it *meh*—not bad but not distinctive? Perhaps most important of all—was it what you expected?

Now imagine your customers' interactions with your own company's services, products, or personnel. What are their experiences like? What matters to them? Do you know? Or are you only imagining or reciting meaningless stats like the ones on that hotel survey?

The key that unlocks meaningful service is *design*—the deliberate laying out and execution of a plan to create and deliver the experience you want your customer to get, every time. Understanding experience from the customer's perspective is where the Road to *Ahhh* begins. The road takes you to where you can deliver superior customer experience, but it takes you beyond that. We believe that companies that apply the principles of service design will create not just satisfied customers but *strategic* strength: that the road to *Ahhh* leads to a competitive position others will be unable to match or attack.

Most of the time, most companies treat most customers reasonably well. Sure, sometimes something goes drastically wrong; sometimes something goes spectacularly right—usually when an employee steps forward in a special effort. But overall, companies deserve a grade of B or B minus. That is not good enough. We think grade-A service experiences should be the norm, and we believe they can be. How? By understanding and applying the principles of service design, to ensure that a great customer experience is reliably, replicably, scalably delivered, time and again, in a way that satisfies you and your customer.

Experiences matter. Experiences are journeys. Journeys are designed. These statements are fundamental to understanding service design and delivery. A large and growing management and psychological literature shows that people derive more happiness from new experiences—a day by the sea, a night at the opera—than from new things. Moreover, the pleasure of a new object diminishes over time (as every child knows on December 26), while the pleasure of experience grows (as every adult knows, enjoying those warm holiday memories). But an experience is rarely about one thing. Experiences happen over time and often over space: They are journeys, whether physical (like a flight from Dallas to Detroit) or temporal (like a relationship with an insurance company) or intellectual (like a six-week consulting engagement). For customers, these journeys involve need, planning, anticipation, embarkation, the event itself, disembarkation, and a memory. Companies need to analyze, design, and deliver at every stage of the journey, and at every point of contact—every touchpoint—because every moment is an opportunity to engage or alienate your customer.

You need to imagine and shape your customer's experience of the journey as a whole. Though a problem at any stage can damage the experience, it is not enough just to fix the parts. Journeys are not just linear; they are complex adaptive systems. The experience of the whole affects each stage and vice versa; something that happens at the third stage not only influences the fourth but causes your customer to reevaluate what came before. And—since you want your customer to come back—each journey affects subsequent journeys.

When service is designed well and delivered expertly, it is because there is alignment among your strategic goals, your customer's wants and needs, and what actually happens between you. That alignment is a function of ten things:

* **Empathy:** Developing products, services, and experiences from the customer's point of view; taking full account of how your customers use and interact with you

* **Expectation:** Ensuring that customers know what to expect from their interaction with you

* **Emotion:** Knowing the emotions your customer brings to your relationship, and guiding customers to a satisfied feeling about working with you

* **Elegance:** Providing offerings that are clean, simple, easy to work with, and complete—nothing superfluous, nothing omitted

* **Engagement:** Communicating with customers—and they with you—at every point of contact, to understand their experience and how to improve it

* **Execution:** Reliably meeting all the expectations you have set

* **Engineering:** Possessing technical excellence (for example, compared to peers, but also to general business standards) and eliminating waste of materials, time, and effort, so that no extraneous effort is necessary on the part of you or your customer

* **Economics:** Pricing your services appropriately, so that the customer gets value for money and you the profit you expect

* **Experimentation:** Building processes for improvement and innovation into the daily work of your business; developing capabilities to develop and roll out new offerings

* **Equivalence:** Managing the customer, your team, and partner organizations so that you, the seller/service provider, are satisfied, too.

The first five of these emphasize the customer's side of the relationship; the second five are mostly about you, the provider. These ten elements form the basis for an *SD² Report Card* that helps you measure how successful your company, department, or function is in creating a superior experience with and for your customers. It also allows you to benchmark yourself against your goals and your competitors, or to compare business units within a company. (We show you how to construct your report card in part four, p. 244.)

Together, these ten elements constitute a system—they work together. To what end? Relationships, according to Victor Ermoli, who leads the service design department at the prestigious Savannah College of Art and Design. "Service design is a system for *developing the relationship* between an entity—a bank, a law firm, a health care system, a store, a church—and its customers," says Ermoli.

It is difficult to think of a transaction between a buyer and a seller that cannot be made more valuable to both parties by adding at least the possibility of a relationship beyond the transaction itself. Even the act of filling a gas tank on an interstate presents the possibility of additional value—the decision to stop *here* (because you like Sunoco) or drive on to *there* (because you prefer Shell) or buy a Coke, coffee, or candy bar. In an economy that is 80 percent services, service design is front and center: "The touchpoint is the product," Ermoli says. And the selling of products is heavily influenced by the experiences and services that surround it, whether those are Web pages or credit card processing or retail display or after-sales service or even the outfits salespeople wear.

Service design is a discipline that recognizes that services can and should be designed as thoughtfully as products are, taking into account the customer experience at every possible point of interaction between customer and company, and regardless of whether a transaction actually occurs. Born in Europe—its roots are in Germany and Scandinavia—service design is spreading rapidly among advanced businesses worldwide.

The topic of SD² couldn't be more timely or important, but till now the subject has been addressed primarily in technical or scholarly publications or mentioned in passing in books about design thinking. The service sector accounts for about 80 percent of U.S. economic output and employment, yet the principles of managing these organizations are less known, less studied, and less widely practiced than those of manufacturing. At the same time, the task of managing services has become immeasurably more difficult. Web and mobile devices have multiplied the number of channels, touchpoints, and opportunities for interaction between companies and customers. All these mean more complexity, less control, more ways to screw things up, and increased competition. Yet they also mean more ways for customers to find you and opportunities for you to woo, wow, and win them.

Retailers, for example, once had to design and manage just one type of customer experience: shopping in a store. Where to shop was largely determined by proximity and price. Then came mail-order catalogues, and ordering by phone. Those eliminated the proximity factor and broadened the range of experiences a customer could have, but customers were already committed to you by the time they mailed off their order or picked up the phone.

Now the same customer might order via a website—yours or someone else's—after having first learned about you and your offerings from Pinterest, Yelp, Instagram, or other social media, as well as traditional sources like catalogues, word of mouth, face-to-face shopping, or old-fashioned advertising. Not only that: Your customer might share her experience not with a handful of friends, but with hundreds on Facebook and Instagram. And she will judge you not just in comparison with your direct competitors but with other service providers she patronizes. It is not enough for a bank to design an online experience that is the best in the industry if its customers—fairly or not—are comparing it to Amazon.com.

Great service design and delivery are challenging for another reason. The customer is an active participant in most service transactions, as Frances Frei and Anne Morriss point out in their book,

Uncommon Service. An automobile assembly plant is a massive and intricate place, but at least the customer is not on the factory floor barking orders, changing his mind, and generally misbehaving. In a hospital, on an airline website, in a restaurant, the customer is right there, letting you know what he or she expects from the experience. Consequently, practices and lessons from product design and design thinking cannot simply be portaged over to services.

Nevertheless—and importantly—service design is vital to manufacturers, government agencies, and others whose business is not in the services sector per se. Toyota developed an entirely new dealership network for its premium Lexus marque, precisely to be able to design and deliver a level of service that complemented the promise of the brand. Is it possible even to imagine IKEA furniture without the experience of the retail environment—including the restaurants serving Swedish meatballs and the challenge of wedging all your purchases into your car—and the subsequent experience of assembling the stuff when you get it back home?

Great service design, like great industrial design, is elegant in the sense that its goal is to achieve excellence and efficiency at the same time. Service design sees customer satisfaction and cost management as complementary, not contradictory, the way product design transcends trade-offs among form, function, and price. When you, as a seller, do not have a good design, you are more likely to base decisions on cost rather than value, because you cannot tell the difference between spending money and investing it. To take just one piece of evidence, commercial airlines spend more than $10 billion a year on information technology, most of it, they say, directed to customer-facing activities like mobile apps and websites. But does any frequent flyer believe that the experience of air travel has improved?

At the heart of *Woo, Wow, and Win* is our identification of the five essential principles of service design and delivery. Derived from our combined experience working with and analyzing the characteristics of successful companies, innovative cultures, and effective leaders, the principles are a way for senior leaders to shape service design initiatives, evaluate proposals and programs, and, above all, bring coherence to service strategy.

1. THE CUSTOMER IS ALWAYS RIGHT—PROVIDED THE CUSTOMER IS RIGHT FOR YOU.

You have to decide which customers you want, and which you do not. A customer who demands a level of service, a type of product, or prices that you are not designed and willing to deliver is the wrong customer for you. Deciding which customers you engage with and what you are willing to do for them is a powerful exercise in defining your brand. That isn't to say you cannot segment customers—you should. This is not about discriminating against classes of customers, which is of course illegal. It is a strategic determination of what your business is about.

2. DON'T SURPRISE AND DELIGHT YOUR CUSTOMERS—JUST DELIGHT THEM.

A well-designed service is predictably excellent. You delight your customers by meeting their needs within the expectations they have for whatever you are offering, whether those expectations are high or low. If they do not know what to expect from you, why will they come? If their expectations are not met, why will they stay or return?

3. GREAT SERVICE MUST NOT REQUIRE HEROIC EFFORTS ON THE PART OF THE PROVIDER OR THE CUSTOMER.

SD^2 should be efficient, effective, scalable, and if not error-proof, error-resistant. That is what makes it reliable—the delightful nonsurprise of the Second Principle. Employees should not need to be superheroes, bend the rules, or take shortcuts to give customers a great experience. By the same token, saving time and money is just as important for customers as it is for you. The realization that customers' time and money are as important as your own is a critical aspect of the co-creating partnership we write about in Chapter 10.

4. SERVICE DESIGN MUST DELIVER A COHERENT EXPERIENCE ACROSS ALL CHANNELS AND TOUCHPOINTS.

Simply put, any place you choose to play, you have to play well. And anything you are going to do, you have to do well in every way. A company that provides a fabulous customer experience in the store but has a website that frustrates and annoys customers will confuse and lose them.

A corollary to this principle is that partners that provide complementary services are as much a part of the service value chain as your own touchpoints, platforms, and channels are; a rental car company is helped by a well-designed, well-run airport, and hurt by the opposite. Customers open one wallet to you; you should present one face to them. They do not care about your internal organizational problems or the problems you have with your partners. Overcoming such problems can be the single biggest impediment to turning a service design blueprint into reality.

5. YOU'RE NEVER DONE: ANTICIPATE, CREATE, INNOVATE, ITERATE—AND REPEAT AS NEEDED.

Much was learned in the twentieth century about research and development in manufacturing. Compared to products, services innovation is in its infancy, but best practices are starting to emerge, and foundational knowledge about what constitutes good research is being laid. One lesson: The life cycle of a service needs to be managed as carefully as the life cycle of a product. And by managed, we mean treated as nonstatic, organic, and constantly open to change and improvement.

Looking through the lens of service design, and bearing these principles in mind, it is easy to see how whole industries could be enormously improved by better service design and delivery.

Health care, for example: The United States boasts of offering the best medical care in the world, but getting it can be a nightmare. The tortuous politics of American health care are no excuse for the fact that the annual cost of *unnecessary* paperwork and administrative activity in the United States is an enormous $190 billion, according to the Institute of Medicine, and that the annual cost of medical error, much of it preventable by good design, is $29 billion—and 400,000 lives. Overall, the institute estimates, one-third of the money spent on health care has nothing to do with improving health—and that is not counting the $1.5 billion worth of time that patients waste cooling their heels in doctors' offices and otherwise waiting for care.

The consequences of bad design in health care are felt by providers as well as patients. New Medicare policies are reducing reimbursement to hospitals that fail to meet standards for medical treatment and also for hospitals that receive low scores for patient experience. Most hospitals find it difficult to improve on both dimensions at once—unless they apply the principles of service design.

In the *hotel industry*, lives are not at stake, but plenty of money is. Hotels trying to attract business travelers—the most profitable customer segment—walk a thin line. In this as in any industry, the ability to command loyalty or higher prices comes from having a differentiated offering—something customers value that their rivals cannot match. But business travelers also demand a fairly uniform set of features in terms of comfort, technology, amenities, and even location.

How can you be both different and the same? That is a challenge Hyatt, Marriott, and others are meeting through service design, studying every aspect of every interaction so that a guest can check in, stay, and check out with a consistent, hassle-free experience. More broadly, the travel and tourism industry has begun to work with academics and local tourism authorities to design the interaction among interdependent players in the industry—airlines, airports, transportation companies, hotels, and destinations like theme parks. They recognize that a family's memories of a trip to Disney World are strongly affected by the moments when they move from one provider to another—from the airline to the hotel to a restaurant to the amusement park.

Government services: Long before the kludgy debut of the Affordable Care website in 2013, it was evident that government services are often delivered in ways that frustrate both citizens and employees. It is also clear that the problem isn't the people but design (or the lack of it), as this unedited Yelp review of a visit to a New York State Department of Motor Vehicles office shows:

> I'm not exactly sure how their serving system works. depending on what service you need you can find yourself waiting for a really long time.
>
> I needed to get my license renewed so i went in with my application printed and filled out so that i wouldn't have to waste any time.
>
> haha what a joke . . .
>
> When i went to the information desk, i received my "number" F661. just wait for your number to be called . . . ok cool.
>
> i look to see what was the last "F" number called? F612. What the heck? that cannot be right. well . . . with just 1 person working on "F" i knew i was going to be waiting for a long time . . . 2 hours later . . . finally . . .
>
> one thing to be said . . . once my number was called the person who helped me was pretty nice.

"The person was pretty nice"—the design was at fault. Similar design flaws inhibit the work of policemen in Britain, where sergeants spend 45 percent of their time filling out paperwork, according to Her Majesty's Inspectorate of Constabulary. Wasting cops' time and taxpayer money is a bad enough consequence of poorly designed service, but with policing—as with any other service—the value side of the equation is more important than the cost side.

Cops filling out forms are not tracking down crooks or building up relationships with the communities they serve. The revolution in police work that began in New York City in 1994 when William Bratton first became police commissioner is at its core an early application of the principles of service design, with spectacular results. The New York City Police Department's focus on providing information to precincts in real time and getting more cops out of their cars and onto the streets is one reason New York became the safest big city in the United States. The unexpectedly huge margins demonstrate that the reason has been how the NYPD is managed rather than other factors: There is almost three times more murder per capita in Columbus, Ohio, for example.

*   *   *

So how does all this relate to you, as a seller?

Consider a hammer. Nothing is more utilitarian than a hammer; but it is also a consciously designed object, and in some cases, a beautiful one. Pick one up, or imagine one in your hand. Feel its weight and balance and how the grip fits in your hand; look at the shape of the claw, the polish of the head. As you look at the hammer, you can see that its design and its value are inseparable. And so it is in the act of selling that hammer. Customers might buy hammers online at Amazon, at a big-box store such as Home Depot, at a traditional hardware store, or from the small hardware section at a place like Walgreens.

Each of these shopping environments is and should be designed differently, depending on what kind of experience you want the customer to have. The classic hardware store offers a big selection— claw, ball peen, framing—in different weights; it provides expert sales help, and, perhaps, sets the whole thing in a masculine environment, with wooden store fittings and slowly turning ceiling fans.

Online you would make different design choices. You'd offer a big selection, too, but not the sales help or the handsome environment; instead, you would invest in providing clear and helpful product descriptions, a convenient, efficient, secure checkout process, and capabilities to ensure prompt delivery and, if necessary, returns. If you were Walgreens, your customer would expect to find just one inexpensive hammer suitable for routine home uses, like hanging a picture, displayed alongside blister packs of nails and picture hooks. As for sales help, you'd provide none, except someone to tell you to look on the left-hand side of aisle three.

With those elements—venue, selection, setup, and staff—you, the seller, have made design choices that send a clear message to your customer about what the experience of buying a hammer will be like. The consumer can make a choice based on what is important to him or her: price, convenience, selection, expert help.

Okay, give the hammer to us, and we will drive home a few points:

* What is being sold here is not just a product, but an experience. You decide what that experience will be and how it relates to your value proposition. The engineering of this experience began well before your customer walked into the store or came to your website, and has to take into account all that could happen after he or she left. Experiences involve emotions as much as they do reason. "A momentary positive experience does not do much," says Ermoli. "But a momentary positive experience brought to the level of emotional connection does." That is service design.

* To effectively design a service and be able to deliver it, you must sort through a seemingly infinite number of variables. Who's your buyer? Professional, hobbyist, suburban dad with a workbench, apartment dweller who stashes a few tools in a cardboard box at the back of her closet? Is she doing carpentry or just hanging pictures? How does he want to pay? What if he wanted to return it? What else do you sell that you'd like the customer to pick up on this visit? You cannot just think about a customer—you have to be the customer and walk in his shoes.

* You cannot satisfy a customer if you do not also satisfy yourself. The value of SD^2 is that it allows you to manage your needs and your customer's not as a conflict but as a collaboration—to make intelligent, deliberate decisions about where to invest and how to pay for it, and to do so strategically, and not by happen-

stance. It does not matter whether you're selling a hammer, a five-star meal, consulting expertise, or the ability for someone to get in and out of the DMV without going insane.

* Service design is not complex. Indeed, it is the opposite: Like all good design, it is elegant. There's nothing extra, nothing left out. But every designer—and every businessperson—knows that simplicity is hard to achieve and difficult to maintain. Simplicity takes vision, discipline, and tools. It has many enemies, most of them well-intentioned: the attractive new market that, in your heart of hearts, you know you should resist; the valuable old customer whose requests pull you away from what you do best; and all the centrifugal forces that cause functional and business unit leaders to build capabilities or chase opportunities outside the core of the business.

As we will see in the next chapter, most services were not designed in the first place; while engineers and industrial designers were applying their skills to factories and manufactured goods, services just sort of happened. Where services have been designed, the ordinary course of business has tended to clutter them with distractions and detractions. You have only to think of how Starbucks—one of the best-designed service companies ever—lost its way in the first decade of the twenty-first century and had to be put right by its returning founder, Howard Schultz, who cleaned out the company's offerings and let its design once again show profitably through.

But it is possible to offer and to maintain excellent service design and delivery, whether you're running a hotel or selling investment banking services. Done right, you can woo and wow your customer—and win for your business. And in a time when too many companies feel they are at the mercy of technological change they cannot control or quarrelsome customers who take to social media to vent their frustration, excellence in SD^2 is essential for creating superior service experiences. Our job is to help you nail it.

CHAPTER 2

The Service Design Revolution

The story of Blockbuster and Netflix is usually told in terms of disruptive innovation, a triumph of agile clicks over complacent bricks. It is actually a tale of service design. Both companies provided *exactly the same* service: They rented recorded movies for people to play at home. Blockbuster itself was no slouch in the service design department: It became a wild success by rolling up mom-and-pop video rentals, developing a standard store format with bright lighting and a family-friendly environment (no dirty movies in a back room), and, modeling itself on bestseller-oriented chain bookstores like Waldenbooks and B. Dalton, loading its shelves with current hit movies. It was a coherent, clever design that worked brilliantly for a time.

But no design is perfect forever, and Blockbuster's included inherent flaws that alienated customers and cost money:

* Because a customer could rent only what was on the shelf at the time, the company had to buy hit movies in massive quantity to minimize stockouts (which were nonetheless inevitable at the store level regardless of the situation regionally or nationally)—a failure of execution.

* All that inventory became all but worthless when a film cooled off—a failure of elegance and economics.

* To get movies back to rent them to the next customer, Blockbuster needed to impose late fees. These fees came to account for more than 10 percent of its revenue, every dollar of which decreased customer satisfaction—a failure of empathy. (U.S. airlines generated about 11.3 percent of revenue from ancillary fees in 2015, up from 9.3 percent the year before: a dangerous addiction.)

* As the company expanded to more than five thousand retail outlets, every new store increased fixed costs and the law of diminishing returns inevitably came into play—a problem of economics.

If Blockbuster was Waldenbooks, Netflix was Amazon. Netflix, before broadband made streaming possible, was a mail-order house. It created an all-you-can-watch subscription model, in which your next movie was shipped when you returned the one you had; it thus rewarded you for returning a movie quickly, rather than penalizing you for returning one late. Plus, a "recommendation engine"—software that suggested movies based on your past choices—allowed Netflix to shift demand away from hits. This not only reduced stockouts but created a mechanism by which Netflix could learn directly about individual customers. By contrast, Blockbuster could learn only about aggregated customer preferences.

Further, Netflix could manage inventory and back-office functions nationally, enjoying economies of scale rather than enduring diminishing returns. Instead of paying rent and buying fixtures, it leveraged the postal service. And, of course, Netflix put itself on the right side of technology's evolution, betting on DVDs over videotapes and positioning itself for an age when video could be delivered electronically, with no waiting or inventory at all.

Every one of these differences was a consequence of choices about operating model and service design that created strategic options for Netflix and ways to put design tools to work to improve the business. And, as they say, we know how that movie ended.

But how did it begin?

The Rise of Design

The word *design* comes from the Latin *designare*, meaning "to mark out." The idea of design entered business with the Industrial Revolution in the eighteenth and nineteenth centuries. Before then, products were designed while they were being made, by individual craftsmen or small ateliers of masters, journeymen, and apprentices. With mass production, design and manufacture become separated as a matter of practical necessity. The specifications for a product— size, shape, appearance, materials, and production process—had to be marked out in advance, tools and parts assembled, and workers trained so that every copy made was the same as the one that came down the line before.

It wasn't long before practical necessity took on aesthetic dimensions, and designers became known by name and reputation. The curved dashboard of the 1901 Oldsmobile, designed by William Durant, served no purpose other than looking good. Today's table fan is little changed from the classic designed by Peter Behrens of Allgemeine-Elektricitäts-Gesellschaft in 1908.

Behrens took the view, revolutionary at the time, that industrial design must break with the legacy of craftsmanship and be proudly itself. "We refuse to duplicate handmade works, historical style forms, and other materials for production," he proclaimed. Great industrial designers like Walter Gropius, Raymond Loewy, and Henry Dreyfuss followed in the first half of the twentieth century; it is easy to see the line of succession between their work and that of Apple's Steve Jobs and Jonathan Ive.

The study of management and the art of design emerged in parallel. Curricula at Wharton (1881), Tuck (1900), Harvard (1908), and other business schools developed in the years when Frederick W. Taylor and Henry Ford did their pioneering work on organizing factories. Managers and business schools, it might be said, were learning to allocate resources and control business processes; designers worked to ignite customer desire and create a new aesthetic for the products that rolled off those assembly lines.

This increasingly sophisticated thinking about design and management centered almost entirely on manufacturing. (The business schools studied mining and agriculture as well.) It largely ignored services, in part because they were a less important sector of the economy. Today services account for two-thirds or more of the gross domestic product of all advanced economies. This vast sector comprises everything from barbershops to investment banks, from schools to seaports, from hospitals to hospitality; businesses that do not make anything but, instead, move things, sell things, or provide intangibles like advice, insurance, or personal services.

In the United States, four out of five people work in services—116 million, ten times more than work in all the country's factories. As economies develop, so do services; they already account for more than 40 percent of China's GDP, for example.

Serious people largely dismissed services as being somehow an inferior sort of economic activity. As late as 1990, Japan's great globalist Kenichi Ohmae felt it necessary to defend the service workforce, writing, "These are not necessarily busboys and live-in maids. Many of them are in the professional category. They are earning as much as manufacturing workers, and often more." That same year, Federal Express became the first services company to win the prestigious Malcolm Baldrige National Quality Award.

One knock against services was that goods were somehow superior because they are "tradeable," but that December, *Fortune* magazine discovered that entertainment—"Mickey Mouse, Michael Jackson, and Madonna"—had become America's second-largest export, trailing only aerospace. At a time of intense concern about

American competitiveness, services, it seemed, were a bright spot. Indeed, in 1995, when *Fortune* revamped its list of America's largest corporations to include services business, 291 of the Fortune 500 were in services, including three of the top ten.

The Services Economy and the Emergence of Service Design

The men and women running these businesses knew what experts and academics had not yet grasped: Banks, retailers, and other services are big, important businesses with unique management challenges. They cannot be understood or managed by analogy with manufacturing. While the tools, frameworks, and rules of thumb developed in a century of industrial design and management can help, you cannot just portage them over from one sector to the other and start paddling, because services differ in at least four fundamental ways:

* The customer shares in the act of production, where in manufacturing, the job is done when the product hits the loading dock. Services are like handshakes: For the act to work, both people have to participate. It follows that to design, manage, and evaluate a service business, you must consider both parties. Think of the classic mistake many call center managers make, rating employees by how many calls they field rather than by their effectiveness at solving problems.

* Most services involve many interactions between buyer and seller (and often multiple sellers). In flying from New York to Chicago, a person will book a seat, get to and through the airport and security, engage with gate agents, fly and be fed (or not), perhaps deal with baggage claim, then take a taxi, train, or car to the Loop. The service itself—the "sit back, relax, and

enjoy the flight" part—is just one touchpoint. Another kind of journey might involve just one company but a lot of back-and-forth between buyer and seller to get things right—developing an ad campaign, for example. There are exceptions, of course: The act of buying a KitKat bar from a corner store is a simple transaction, whose rewards are great.

* In services, it is hard for customers to know in advance what they are buying. Buyers can look at, test-drive, and kick the tires of a new car; they can read what *Consumer Reports* or Edmunds.com says about it. Sure, one buyer may want a red car and another a white one; a sunroof may matter to some customers and not to others. But while preferences may be subjective, even they are based on objective matters that can be qualified or quantified—color, speed, special features—and may well inform the buying decision. Services are intangible and often created while being consumed. It is difficult to get meaningful information about a doctor, stockbroker, or beautician beyond the fact that they're licensed. On Yelp, one person's cozy B&B is another's cramped hovel; you won't know your opinion till you check in. This opacity challenges both customers and providers who seek their business. And many B2B businesses won't appear in a Yelp or elsewhere on social media in a meaningful way.

* Customers do not own a service; they experience it. When someone buys a car, it is her property, her responsibility, and she can sell it when she is done. A car can be designed with an experience in mind—a minivan and a MINI Cooper suggest different activities. But a service is experience itself. She cannot blame the car for the potholes in the road or the kids squabbling in the backseat. Experiences are hard to control (the customer is in the mix, after all) and hard to devise (every customer is different). The customer cannot return them; there is no market for used experiences because *there is nothing to*

return. Your customer owns the experience and its memories and emotions, but you—the provider—own the service.

The service design revolution emerged against this background: the growing importance of services, the realization that they cannot be managed the same way manufacturing is, plus, as we will see, a critical infusion of information technology.

Ideas whose time has come seem to emerge from everywhere all at once, but service design has a pretty clear starting point: a 1984 article in *Harvard Business Review* by G. Lynn Shostack, called "Designing Services That Deliver." Shostack had long realized that the differences between goods and services had profound real-world implications. In 1977, when head of marketing for Citibank, she argued that services marketing must "break free" of the grip of ideas used to hawk products and focus on creating tangible evidence of the experience a service creates.

From there it was not a big step to realize that the very nature of service—not just its marketing but the thing itself—is the sum of all the experiences a customer has on his or her journey, and that each stage should be identified, designed, and managed. Shostack's 1984 article introduced the idea of a "service blueprint" to chart every interaction between a company and its customers, including what the customer sees and what happens behind the scenes. That blueprint—or map, as we will call it—is the foundation tool of service design.

Shostack's ideas lay semi-dormant for two decades, but thinking about services increased. The business school at Arizona State University opened a Center for Services Leadership in 1985. In 1994, a famous *Harvard Business Review* article, "Putting the Service-Profit Chain to Work," by James L. Heskett, Thomas O. Jones, Gary W. Loveman, W. Earl Sasser Jr., and Leonard A. Schlesinger, showed that investment in frontline employees could be a source of profits, not just of costs, because of the value of superior service. That year, service design appeared on the curriculum of the University of Cologne in Germany. The United States was a laggard: The Savannah College of Art and Design (SCAD) launched its first service design class in 2009; as of the writing of this book, it is the only university in the United States to offer both a BFA and an MFA in service design.

The 1990s also saw a surge of interest in measuring and managing customer loyalty, much of it focusing on restaurants, banks, and other service industries. Late in the decade, with the explosion of information technology and the fad for business process reengineering, came a rush of interest in mapping internal processes—a path that led inexorably back to Shostack's idea of blueprinting both what the company does and what the customer sees.

Technology Comes Out of the Glass House

The humble cash machine was one of the flashpoints of the service design revolution. The ATM created the first moment in banking history when a customer interacted directly with technology, with no bank employee in between. According to Tim Brown, CEO of design firm IDEO and a leading expert in design thinking, "Before that, service delivery was all people-to-people, not just in banking but almost everywhere. Technology didn't show up in the customer experience—it was in the back office." There were, of course, jukeboxes and Automats before, but now, for the first time, people in services businesses began to think of "the user interface" as something to be designed, just as industrialists a century before had recognized the need for product design. Previously, Brown says, "[w]hen people in services thought of design, they thought of architecture—someone to design the office or the branch—and they thought of graphic design. But that was it."

User interfaces started popping up all over, all needing to be designed. Many were and still are infuriating. ("Please listen closely, as our menu options have changed.") But on the electronic superhighway, Marc Andreessen's 1993 Mosaic Web browser overlaid an attractive design on an incomprehensibly geeky interface, and the Internet boomed. On the concrete superhighway, filling stations eliminated gas jockeys, deemphasized their repair shops as cars and tires became more reliable, and added convenience stores. In Great Britain, Brown worked with Shell to design a self-service gas (well, petrol) pump and to rethink the layout, flow, and very economic model of a filling station.

And then there was IBM. Big Blue had been a big player in the ATM industry in the 1970s and 1980s, working out much of the software and digital plumbing necessary to make and track payments, before ceding the business to Diebold and NCR in 1990. A bit more than a decade later, IBM forked out $3.5 billion to buy the 30,000-employee consulting business of PwC. (At the time, accounting firms were under regulatory pressure to amputate their consulting arms, following scandals that destroyed the Arthur Andersen firm and had shaken others. Among major firms, only Deloitte refused. PwC and the others have since rebuilt consulting businesses.)

In 2003, with the addition of PwC, IBM's Global Business Services accounted for nearly half (48 percent) of the company's $89 billion in sales, hardware less than a third. (Software and financing comprised the rest.)

Services' share of IBM's research budget, however, was zero; 85 percent went to hardware. For Paul Horn, then head of research for IBM, that presented a bureaucratic problem—they were afraid their budget would be cut in half—and a scientific opportunity: the chance to invent the science of services, much as IBM had largely invented computer science after World War II. With a serious commitment to research, IBM would be able to bring rigor and insights that had been missing from its own fast-growing services arm—and to understanding the science and economics of all service businesses.

Set high amid rolling foothills in Almaden, California, just outside San Jose, IBM's service science research center opened in 2004

under the leadership of Robert Morris and Jim Spohrer, in space that
had been occupied by researchers in disk drives (a business IBM had
exited). Looking for staff, IBM found practitioner and academic experts in services marketing and services operations, a few designers
(mostly in Europe, mostly working on narrow problems), but almost
no one who fit IBM's need for multidisciplinary thinking.

The combination of IBM's prestige (five of its employees have won
Nobel Prizes), money (the company made grants to scores of univer-
sities to fund service-science research), and help-wanted signs might
have been the single biggest impetus to the study of services and the
emergence of service design as a management discipline. Certainly
the company itself thinks service science is a big deal: "The Inven-
tion of Service Science" was one of one hundred "Icons of Progress"
chosen to mark its centennial in 2011.

IBM's grand vision of a "smarter planet" is a direct outgrowth of
services science; its "smarter" buildings, cities, health care systems,
etc., are examples of service design on a grand scale. But the eightfold return on investment Spohrer achieved in his six years as head
of service research in Almaden came from focusing on three things.

Service productivity: Getting more done with less is the life-
blood of every company and every economy, but it is notoriously
difficult to increase productivity in services. Barbers and lawyers
are not much more productive than they were two generations
ago; a hotel can prosper by increasing the percentage of rooms
that are occupied, but it cannot rent them more than once a night.
(There are of course hotels that rent their rooms more than once
in a 24-hour period. The services generally associated with such
hotels are not covered in this book.) It is difficult even to *measure*
productivity in many services—policing, for example. Technology
and service design, IBM found, can track and increase productivity in ways that could not have been imagined before, particularly
when automation replaces human labor (which costs more every
year) with information processing (which costs less every year).

Service quality: "Service quality is generally just lousy," Robert Morris grouses, and few would disagree. Some service quality issues can be addressed in a straightforward way. Bar-coded luggage tags and automated scanning have dramatically cut the percentage of bags airlines lose or damage. But services pose special quality challenges. A big issue for IBM was software development, which was changing from a "waterfall" to an "agile" design. The former was a model in which teams built software more or less offline, gathering specifications at the start of a project, going away to code, and delivering what they hoped was finished work, but never was.

"Agile software development" principles, first enunciated in 2001, involve continuous collaboration with customers—co-creation, even, with code delivered and adjusted incrementally as the project goes along. "You actually want the customer sitting with you," Morris says—a then-radical idea. The quality frontier is always pushing out: Today, it is in complex services like education and health care, where quality can be tricky to measure and accountability difficult to assign.

Service innovation: For all the innovation in products and technology, services themselves had not yet seen a burst of innovation. A year before Almaden opened its doors, Harvard Business School professor Stefan Thomke wrote: "We have well-tested, scientific methods for developing and refining manufactured goods—methods that date back to the industrial laboratories of Thomas Edison—but many of them do not seem applicable to the world of services. Companies looking for breakthroughs in service development tend to fall back on informal and largely haphazard efforts." Services—intangible, created in the moment, tailored to individual customers—are hard to study under laboratory conditions, and experiments are risky with live customers paying real money in real time.

Productivity, quality, and innovation are an agenda and an engine for improving services. It is possible to take each and every aspect of a service—the business itself and every step along the service journey—and subject them to the same test: Can we do this more productively? Can we do this better? Can we do this differently? The power of these questions should not be underestimated. Within three years of the opening of the services research center, IBM's pretax profit margin from services more than doubled, from 6.7 percent to 14.1 percent.

Some of the Parts and the Sum of the Parts

Businesspeople do not know it, but most of them are ontological reductionists. They take a mechanistic view of problem-solving, believing that the best approach is to break a problem into its pieces, fix them up, and reassemble them. Partly this habit of mind comes from three generations of management consulting. The foundational capability and value proposition of strategy consulting were to help companies quantify costs precisely (a surprisingly difficult task if you have never done it), which involved taking apart products and processes to find every nickel's worth of cost and overhead. It is not a coincidence that many early consultants and strategists were trained as engineers.

Unsurprisingly, the first practitioners of service designers like Lynn Shostack wrote about creating a service "blueprint," a technical drawing, to lay out all the points of contact between a company and its customers, and the links between one stage and another. Shostack's blueprints look like wiring diagrams. She wrote of "tangible service evidence"—what customers could see or experience—and activities that were beneath the "line of visibility"—what the company did that the customer could not see to produce the tangible evidence.

Design thinking takes explicit issue with this reductionist, mechanical view of business, whether it focuses on products, services, or both. The problem with focusing on the parts, design thinkers say, is that you can miss the whole. David Snowden describes the difference between *complicated* problems and *complex* ones. Complicated problems can be solved piece by piece, the way soldiers can take apart, clean, and reassemble their rifles, confident that afterward the weapon will function at least as well as before. Complicated problems tend to be sequential and linear: They have a correct order of operations, as there is in solving an algebraic equation. Cause and effect are—or can be—known in advance.

Complex problems are different. Often the search for solutions does not proceed in a linear fashion, but may go back and forth many times, as with agile software development; they may produce exponential returns, not linear ones. Cause and effect are not clear beforehand, and the relationship of a part to the whole may emerge only after trial and error. The parts of a complex system are not interchangeable: Replace John with Jane on a team, and the team will be different even if John and Jane have the same role. Ecosystems, ad campaigns, soccer games—all of these are complex problems. So are most business challenges.

Design thinking explicitly rebuts the reductionist approach for a holistic one, a mechanistic mindset for an organic one. Design thinkers speak of "human-centered" processes and "integrative" approaches to problems. Though these are buzzwords, they are meaningful: They speak of an approach that begins with deep understanding of a customer's needs and desires, that conducts experiments with only just enough prototyping to make the next experiment more interesting, and that attempts to solve multiple problems at the same time.

That is why we have discarded the metaphor of a service blueprint and replaced it with a map, where there are touchpoints, not points of contact, and where activities take place onstage or offstage—behind the scenes. (In the Appendix we will show you how to draw your own service map.) When a service is well designed and delivered, something happens: not just a haircut, but a whole new look; not just a bank loan, but a chance to grow the business; not just a trip, but a second honeymoon. Every part—every stage of the journey—matters: the atmosphere of the salon, the comprehensibility of the loan documents, the boarding process at the airport. Smart service design will examine each touchpoint and make it the best it can be. But the journey as a whole matters more. And the best service design will make sure that it is a success. *Experiences matter. Experiences are journeys. Journeys are designed.*

CHAPTER 3

Service Design and Your Strategy

I n Pixar's animated film *WALL-E*, what is left of human civilization lounges fat and stupefied in a gigantic spaceship, where every person's every whim is catered to by megacorporation Buy 'n' Large.

Good luck with that on earth. Every businessperson knows that a company cannot offer discount prices, premium service, a complete product line, cutting-edge innovation, top-of-the-charts wages, free shipping—and robust profits. To get the last, you must choose among the others. But your customers, by and large, do not care about your profits. Hence the conflict—let's call it "creative tension"—between great service and great strategy.

Strategy is a word so overused it has been nearly bled of meaning. These days you hear people talk about a "strategy" to cope with ants at a picnic. We reserve the term for the major choices companies make and the actions they take to accomplish those ends. Strategy demands that you choose what you will sell and what you won't, which customers you want and which you don't, which ground you will attack, which you will defend, and which you will cede to others. Service design, too, is about choice. It is not about offering your customers whatever they want; as we argued in Chapter 1, service design is what a company does so that customers get *the expe-*

rience the company wants them to have. It connects strategic intent to customer experience.

Service design also arms strategy against its enemies, which are legion. Many forces act to separate a business from its strategy: hot new trends, attempts to ape a successful rival, the natural desire of business unit and functional leaders to expand their offerings, and, most dangerous because most seductive, the desire to please customers. Just before the turn of the century, at the height of the dotcom boom, upstart consulting firms started raking in huge fees from companies that wanted help moving "from bricks to clicks," as the phrase went. Many of these clients had old, deep ties to traditional firms and asked them to take on the business. The then–managing partner of McKinsey told one of us that the best decision he ever made was to resist his clients' and some partners' demands to join what turned out to be a rush of lemmings: Most of those dot-com consulting firms crashed. Design—deliberate, well-defined service design—creates guiderails that keep these impulses in line.

The Strategy/Customer Experience Connection

In 2013 Cathy Calhoun was named to the newly created position of chief client officer at Weber Shandwick, the global public relations firm that is part of the Interpublic Group of Companies. Weber Shandwick, with more than $700 million in 2014 revenues, is the number-two player in the business (after Edelman). For the five previous years Calhoun presided over its biggest, most profitable business unit, North America. It's not often that someone gives up running an important P&L for a staff role, even one with a grandsounding title. But the Weber Shandwick team had an ambitious plan: to accomplish the firm's strategic aims by rethinking what it means to be "client-centric," then designing a new, better client experience.

Every professional services firm is imbued with an ethos of client service, but the Weber Shandwick team wanted to respond to big changes in its and its clients' environment and the mathematics of profitable growth in the industry. Clients (mostly big companies like Unilever, General Motors, and Verizon, but also government groups like the U.S. Postal Service and nonprofits like the United Nations Foundation) needed PR advisors to cope with a bewildering combination of globalized markets, balkanized media, technological change, and empowered customers. In communicating with customers, companies used to do most of the talking; now communication was not just a two-way street but—as customers and employees talked among themselves and over social media—an omnidirectional jumble, like a traffic circle in Rome at rush hour.

These trends affected PR firms as much as their clients. Clients needed the agencies to be 1) sense makers in a world of many, changing choices, 2) broadly strategic, to help them avoid playing a reactive game of PR Whac-A-Mole, but also 3) instantly responsive, anywhere and anyhow, and 4) skilled and foresighted about a digitized marketing-communications mix that included instantaneous news, content marketing, and social media. In client interviews, according to Calhoun, "[t]he very first thing they always said is, 'We want you to know our business, not just our communications. We want you to be in our business, not on our business.'" The second thing was to be real experts in the changing world of media and communications: "We need you to be ahead of us."

The economics of PR were evolving, too. The industry was simultaneously consolidating and spawning scores of specialist boutiques (in social media, for example). As client needs proliferated, the opportunity to provide more services grew, but so did the risk of losing out to specialists or wasting resources chasing every next big thing. For a large firm like Weber Shandwick, it was more important to maximize the value of a client than to maximize the number of clients. The value of client retention, already high, increased. The company needed to offer cutting-edge services (by itself or by coordinating with boutiques) while maintaining its classic services. And the link between clients' growth and the firm's became stronger.

Given these strategic imperatives—share of wallet, retention, innovation, and growing along with clients—the fuzzy concept of "client-centricity" started to come into focus, taking the shape of the customer experience that Weber Shandwick wanted to deliver. Clients

* had to feel understood

* had to deal with one firm, not many functions or divisions

* had to experience the firm's domain expertise

* had to have access to specialized services

* had to believe the firm was a partner, not just a pitchman

Those sound like bromides—till you try to provide evidence of performance at every touchpoint. Take the "one-firm" idea: A large, long-term client complained because invoices from different countries arrived in different formats and used different terminology, making it impossible for the client to fully understand and analyze its spending. Says Weber Shandwick executive vice president Michael Wehman, "Billers don't normally think of themselves as client service people, but now we are thinking of client experience in an end-to-end way." Mapping touchpoints—as we described in the last chapter—reveals this kind of hidden experiential glitch in strategy execution, and that it was more important than the company had supposed.

To get more than client survey insight, Calhoun and her team invited a group of fifty-two client leaders (from more than a thousand clients)—picked because the clients they represented were important, fast-growing, interested in innovation, or all three—to join a customer experience laboratory. Members know that they are part of a special group, and meet regularly. Though they feed into different Weber Shandwick profit centers, they're also tracked as a group for growth, profitability, and the like. Says Calhoun: "In this group we are incubating the CX [customer experience] work and then it's going to go across the company. One might call it a test kitchen. Some of the recipes don't work and we walk away."

The lab, where work was driven by input from clients, was crucial in helping Weber Shandwick understand a particularly vexing service design/customer experience issue: how to promote new services (which are imperative for innovation and increasing share of market) without stepping across the line that separates a strategic partner from just another vendor. This is a tricky problem in many professional services and other businesses as well. In management consulting, for example, both Deloitte and Booz & Company (the latter now part of PwC and known as Strategy&) created digital-transformation boutiques (Deloitte Digital and Booz Digital, respectively) with different websites, logos, staffs, pricing models—and sometimes contentious relationships with the traditional business.

Everybody understands in theory that putting the client first is ultimately best for the business, but in practice people have financial targets and honest enthusiasms. They can easily become—in Calhoun's vivid image—like an overeager watch salesman: "Want a watch? You don't like this watch? I've got another watch. Do you like digital or analog? Roman numerals or Arabic?" Take globalization. Asks Wehman: "If we're going to grow our relationship into another region, how do I start introducing expertise from that region in a way that is going to be additive to their business, not ours?" Likewise, specialized services (analytics, public affairs, content marketing, etc.) shouldn't hawk their wares so much as look for opportunities where they might be needed: "Don't sell more stuff. Solve more problems."

That seems to be working for them pretty well: Weber Shandwick's 2014 billings rose an estimated 14.7 percent, more than twice as much as those of the industry as a whole.

From Value Proposition to
Make-or-Break Moments

Saying "solve more problems," Weber Shandwick defined its value proposition: It is a *Solutions Provider*. Other value propositions were available to it. It could have chosen to be a *Trendsetter*, the hippest of the hip in communications and PR; it could have been a *Specialist*, focusing on just one industry (as Sard Verbinnen does in financial services and GSW in health care); it could have been a *Bargain*, offering bare-bones service cheaply, perhaps with à la carte PR services; indeed, Weber Shandwick competes with rivals of all these kinds, and more. Each of these implies a customer experience and a service design—we call them service design archetypes. (We will discuss them in Chapter 9.) Each service archetype expresses a value proposition.

Think for a second about that term. A value proposition is the face of strategy: It is what customers see directly. (They do not see your capital structure or value chain—your operations—which are also components of strategy.) A proposition: an offering. An offering designed to be valued by a segment of customers—and that you can deliver especially well. Pretty much any car will get you from here to there (Yugos excepted), but Volvo offers safety, Jaguar performance, Toyota reliability, and a T-bird fun, fun, fun. As long as these marques deliver on the main value propositions, they can afford to compromise elsewhere: Volvos and Toyotas can be boring, and who cares about the fuel economy of a Jag?

It is the same with services, from hair salons to stockbrokers. Consider the value propositions of Charles Schwab and Edward Jones, brokerage houses that target a similar "mass-affluent" income segment, but are otherwise as different as their hometowns, San Francisco and St. Louis. The ideal customer for discount broker Schwab is self-directed, price-conscious, and digital. Schwab promotes its online trading, its "wide selection of investment *products*" (our em-

phasis), and a fully automated advisory service. If you want to talk
to a person, Schwab offers personal*ized* advice (again, our emphasis) from financial planners; it reserves full person-to-person service
only for the biggest client portfolios, having retreated from an ill-
conceived attempt to get into personal wealth management in 2000.

The value proposition of Edward Jones is 180 degrees different.
While Schwab says "the industry too often gets in the way of investor success," Edward Jones believes its role is "making sense of
investing" for customers. Every Edward Jones client of whatever size
has an individual investment advisor; the firm states outright that it
seeks "conservative individual investors who delegate their financial
decisions," whom it serves face-to-face "through a national network
of one-financial-adviser offices"—nearly 20,000 of them. There's no
online trading. The firm's website includes page after page about its
advisors, how to work with them, and what to expect from them.

Neither of these value propositions is inherently better: Both are
hugely successful companies. But their different strategies have profound implications for the way they design their service—and service design and delivery have impact on their ability to execute the
strategies they have chosen. To take just one example: Both companies maintain fast, secure, and sophisticated IT systems to execute
trades and manage accounts. Schwab's customers use and experience
it themselves. But the IT system is behind the scenes for Edward
Jones's customers: They benefit from it but do not interact with it
directly, except to view statements.

Strategy also dictates that some touchpoints are more important
than others—and this, too, will vary from company to company.
Just as safety is critical to Volvo and looks not so much, so every
services company has make-or-break moments. This isn't to say that
others do not matter, but this handful of critical customer interactions delivers your value proposition. Other touchpoints might lose
you a customer—these get you one.

To understand critical customer interactions, it helps to think of
the moments at which you interact with customers in three catego-

ries. *Table stakes* are basics of doing business and apply to everybody. They may vary from place to place or industry to industry: In Manhattan, every dry cleaner will deliver; in Los Angeles, every shop has parking. There is nothing strategic—that is, differentiating—about these. However, without them you will not enter a customer's consideration set, and if you screw one of these up, an otherwise happy customer may walk (or, in Los Angeles, drive) elsewhere. The client who complained to Weber Shandwick about its bills was talking about a table stakes touchpoint.

Market segment essentials are offerings that you need to go up against your direct competitors. Segment essentials separate one class of competitor from another, but do not distinguish rivals within a class. Downtown business hotels like Marriott and Starwood all meet a certain standard for rooms, bedding, and amenities; budget lodgings for travelers like Motel 6 or Red Roof Inn do not need to match those—but they have their own set of segment essentials, such as having locations alongside interstate highways. Says Hyatt's Mark Demich, vice president of talent and organization development at Hyatt Hotels Global Operations Center, "Most guests don't say Marriott is known for this and Hyatt is known for that and Hilton is known for something else—they say, yeah, you're all kind of the same" when it comes to segment essentials.

Differentiation comes from *critical customer interactions*. These are moments of truth—when you do something special in customers' eyes—that are also part of your value proposition. Most make-or-break moments are experiential, and the experience is the customer's. They may come at emotionally charged moments; an auto insurance company's response to a claim after an accident is more critical than its process for adding a new vehicle to your policy. They should also be strategic, in that they demonstrate what you want to be known for and why you deserve our business.

Research by the A. T. Kearney consulting firm on what it calls "pivotal customer events" parallels our thinking about these opportunities to stand out. (Indeed, Kearney sees pivotal customer events

TOUCHPOINTS: A HIERARCHY

	WHAT IT IS	EXAMPLES	WHAT IT DOES
CRITICAL CUSTOMER INTERACTIONS	Make-or-break moments: Why customers choose you	Edward Jones: Investment advisor interactions Amazon: Fast search and fulfillment, reliably low-priced	Define your identity; are central to your value proposition; differ from your rivals'. No more than a handful
MARKET SEGMENT ESSENTIALS	Required to compete in the markets or for the customers you want	American, Delta, United: Comprehensive flight networks High-end restaurants: Good wine list	The price of entry to a given market. Likely to be similar across your direct competitor set
TABLE STAKES	Basics every company must provide	Accurate billing, regulatory compliance, hygiene and safety, appropriate hours of operation, etc.	Your "license to operate." May differ across industries or geography

as a chance to "design 'wow' customer experiences.") Kearney consultants had observed a common breakdown in companies' efforts to "fix" customer service or become more customer-centric. Says Robert Bustos-McNeil, a partner in Sydney, Australia: "Companies were spending a lot of money and energy, and the customers weren't feeling the love. Marketing would do something, sales would do something, and they wouldn't tie together." When projects are successful in their own right but do not make a difference overall, you have clear signal of a disconnection between activity and strategy.

Four things are needed to make them connect:

* First, find interactions that express your company's identity. Critical interactions are, remember, strategic: Yours should not be the same as a competitor's, so they should make a statement about why you are you. Here is one: The Virgin Atlantic business-class lounge. For most international airlines, business and first-class lounges are oases of peace and quiet, wine and Wi-Fi—segment essentials. For Virgin Atlantic, they are opportunities to express its cheeky but upscale charm: Called "clubhouses," they feature sleek bars staffed by mixologists and spas that offer facials, hair styling, beard trims, manicures, and hot stone massages. Over-the-top? Yes—and that is the point. There should be no more than a handful of these events, and you should try to make every one of them distinctive. On Southwest Airlines, you can count on hearing a joke (often a bad one) during the flight attendant's pre-takeoff patter, something that underscores the carrier's informal, we're-in-this-together mien.

* Second, critical customer interactions create differentiation in use. In the world of product design, differentiation often lies in the product itself—its features, functions, looks. In services, the "product" may not be all that different across a competitor set, like those business hotels with similar beds and amenities. Services companies create differentiation in use by understanding how the customer experiences what they are offering. To find these, you will need to rev up your empathy engine and journey alongside your customers. After studies of and with customers, Hyatt realized that the moment of truth came when, at the end of a flight or a day of meetings, customers picked up a room key, went up to their room, tossed a suitcase onto the bed, and exhaled. To earn that *Ahhh*, Hyatt carefully looked at every step in that process, from curbside to bedside—just five or six minutes, but such critical minutes! Differentiation in use connects individual projects to larger business opportunities. As the Kearney consultants note, an event that is a transaction

to you may be much more to a customer. You see a customer who wants a loan; she sees a financial advisor who can help her expand her business. If that is so, how would you design that interaction so that you're not just handing over a form but creating a chance to woo, wow, and win?

* Third, because they are critical, these are places to clean up strategy-execution gaps. Every company makes mistakes. But from the customer's perspective, mistakes at critical junctures look like broken promises—betrayals, even. In services, strategy-execution gaps often show up when a customer is handed off from one department to another ("let me put you on hold while I connect you . . .") or from one company to its partner (from a hospital to rehab, for example).

* Fourth, moments of truth are opportunities to understand and leverage the customer's presence. Remember, customers are in the room with you when a service is produced and delivered— they are your co-creators (a subject we will explore in more detail in Chapter 10). How should you use this fact? For example, the degree of consultation and choice a customer wants might vary from moment to moment. Someone choosing an insurance policy—a critical interaction—might want a lot of consultation and choice; the same person making a claim— another make-or-break moment—probably just wants the job done fast and hassle-free.

There is, we should add, a fourth kind of activity, after table stakes, segment necessities, and critical customer interactions: *distractions.* Truth be told, every company fields customer requests that it should not and offers services that can be done better by others. These are the tempting sirens that lure an elegantly designed service away from a profitable course and drive a thriving company onto the rocks. The decline of Radio Shack is a sad example of a company that chased more ideas than it could handle. If you are pursuing some of these temptations now, count your blessings: These are the unneeded activities you can eliminate to fund the investments you make in *Ahhh* moments.

The Strategy-Design System

Strategy without design is as useful (or more to the point, as useless) as a binder full of PowerPoint slides left on a shelf. Yet when companies implement strategy, or when they try to close a strategy-execution gap, design is seldom given a sufficiently big role. Bent on execution, companies may rethink their operating model, but usually undertake that work from the inside out, generally trying to cut costs via automation or staff cuts or reorganizations, starting by grabbing the proverbial "low-hanging fruit" and moving on to bigger things.

When strategy is examined and implemented through a service design lens, three other important choices appear, valuable options not usually considered in strategy development and often screwed up in implementation.

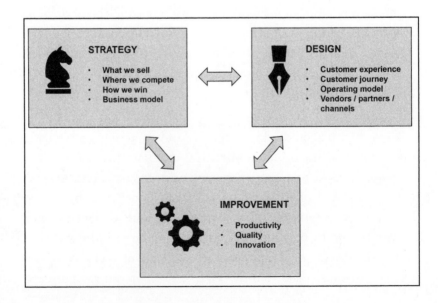

The first is the degree to which your service offering can be industrialized or customized. The second is how much authority and discretion to vest in frontline employees, those who talk directly to customers, and how much should be set by company policy. Finally, there is modularization versus comprehensiveness. These are, as we will see, strategic choices, but they are choices that are made possible (and much richer) through service design.

Industrialization versus customization. By industrialization we mean the degree to which a service must be bought as is, off the shelf. A McDonald's hamburger is an example of industrialization, which extends all the way from the limited, "have it our way" menu to the kitchens (mini-factories with strictly prescribed processes), the supply chain, and more. Two generations ago both G. Lynn Shostack and legendary Harvard Business School professor Theodore Levitt cited McDonald's as an exemplar of using industrial processes in the design and delivery of services. Though time has revealed weaknesses in his argument, Levitt proposed that the only way to improve the quality and efficiency of services was to replace "the high-cost and erratic elegance of the artisan with the low-cost, predictable munificence of the manufacturer."

Industrialization does not have to mean mass market. A first- or business-class trip on Singapore Airlines is elite, expensive—and highly industrialized. It is actually a commodity, albeit a "really, really good one," points out Andy Boynton, dean of the Carroll School of Management at Boston College. The airline does not need to know anything about you to provide a great experience. You will have a wide choice of excellent food and wines, a near-infinite selection of films and other entertainment, and superb, solicitous flight attendants who will come at your every call and address you by name. The next day, however, seat 2A will be occupied by someone else who will be offered the same choices and be coddled exactly as you were.

The other end of industrialization is customization—the burger made from scratch, the bespoke suit, the highly customized consulting project. These command high prices, usually, but the producer cannot guarantee uniformity or profit from economies of scale.

The strategic choice between industrialization and customization is not either/or, but a continuum. The urban car-sharing service car2go, owned by Daimler, is highly industrialized. It offers only one kind of car, a blue and white Smart Fortwo; the price is fixed; there is no staff present where customers (who must be members) pick up and drop off vehicles; billing (to a credit card or PayPal) is automatic. The car2go service is designed for short, in-city trips by people who live there, like taxis: You pay by the minute. Its rival Zipcar (now owned by Avis) is similar. Avis and archfoe Hertz are less industrialized, though no one would call them custom: You have a choice of vehicles at different prices, a menu of fuel and insurance options, the option to take the car across the country, attended counters and lots, and, of course, a network of airport locations, because they are chiefly designed for visitors from out of town.

Enterprise Rent-A-Car is more customized still: While it serves business travelers, its original business was providing rentals from in-town locations, and it has an immensely profitable niche renting loaners to people whose own cars are in the shop, which is why, famously, "we will pick you up" and why the company has deals with mechanics. Finally, taxis, limo companies, and services like Uber and Lyft offer pickup and drop-off rented transportation that is highly customized and priced accordingly.

These strategic choices—different value propositions, different business models, activities, assets, and capabilities—are built by (and built into) service design. They have different critical customer interactions. Airport car rental transactions must be fast. Enterprise makes a point of hiring extroverted, cheerful staff because the drive from pickup to paperwork is so crucial (and an opportunity to upsell). As one executive says, "We hire from the half of the college class that makes the upper half possible. We want athletes, fraternity types— especially fraternity presidents and social directors. People people." Unlike employees at Hertz or Avis, they can earn commissions.

Regimentation versus discretion. The second strategic choice enabled through service design is how much authority to vest in employees who have face-to-face contact with customers. This, too, is a dimmer, not an on-off switch. Making the case for top-down control, legendary marketing professor Ted Levitt wrote, "Discretion is the enemy of order, standardization, and quality." About the time he wrote those words—in 1972—both customers and employees were protesting that they were treated as if they were little more than a number. Yet he had a point. When banks get in trouble it is almost always because headquarters turns a blind eye to frontline misbehavior, and in some cases winks at it. These are "hygienic" reasons for standardization.

However, a substantial body of research shows that even in mass-market retail and convenience stores, investing in frontline employees and giving them leeway improves morale, customer experience, and profitability—provided the opportunity for the front line to add value is strategically meaningful and built into your service design.

At the other end of the spectrum, some professional services partnerships, such as law and consulting firms, offer an extreme example of decentralized decision rights. In some of these firms, partners act almost as free agents, insisting that the needs of their clients (as they perceive them) trump any firm strategy and almost any firm policy or process. Partners' compensation reflects the choice. In the world of strategy consulting, where McKinsey, Boston Consulting Group, Bain, A. T. Kearney, and a dwindling few others operate, people speak of "eat what you kill" versus "socialist" models. In the first, partners keep most of their after-overhead profits and tithe only a small amount to the partnership; in the latter, a higher percentage of the partner profit pool can be apportioned as firm management decides.

Both kinds of firms attract highly entrepreneurial people, but "eat what you kill" outfits tend to invest less in staff functions (like customer relationship management and thought leadership) and go to market emphasizing the talent of individuals and teams rather than the breadth and depth of firm resources. That pattern shows up in the client experience: Clients get passionate advocates who may, however, be less than enthusiastic about cooperating with colleagues if it means splitting the pie; a certain amount of "socialism" is necessary, also, to make long-term investments in capabilities, human capital, and resources. Similar tensions exist in law firms.

Modularization versus comprehensiveness. There is a classic choice in strategy between going narrow and going broad. With service design, you can bring an additional dimension to this choice: the question of whether to offer services that are modularized or ones that are comprehensive. Managers are often tempted by comprehensiveness—shoes to go with the bag, fries to go with the burger. Expanded offerings are easier to see, somehow, and they hold out the promise of more and possibly easy money. The alternative is breaking a service into modules and components—taking apart a comprehensive offering and selling the pieces.

Yet modularization can produce extraordinary returns. It can attract customers who are in the market for only a piece of a service (time-shares in a Caribbean resort), convert a business from one based on buying to one based on renting (software as a service; service as a subscription), or disrupt and transform entire industries and even the world economy. The shipping container has done more to change the global economy than any innovation except packet switching (the basis of the Internet)—and both are examples of modularization.

*   *   *

This, then, is the context in which service design matters: the emergence of an economy based more on services than on manufactured goods; the development of management practices and research that are grounded in services, not translated from manufacturing; the appearance of technologies that allow customers to interact with machines as surrogates for people. These changes produced an opportunity and an obligation for business leaders to:

* Bring to services the same attention to design and process they had long brought to manufacturing

* More deeply understand customers' experiences, not just their needs

* Connect strategy to experience in ways they never had to before

You, as a leader, have to understand what the company is, what its strategy is and what your customers care about, and what jobs are toughest to do for them. Then you can know what great service is and apply the design principles that will ensure that you deliver it. It is to those principles that we now turn.

PART II

The Principles of Service Design

CHAPTER 4

The First Principle:
The Customer Is Always Right—
Provided the Customer Is Right for You

America runs on Dunkin'" is more than just an advertising slogan for Dunkin' Donuts. The tagline is a salute to Dunkin' customers, "everyday folks who get things done," as described on the internal blog of Hill Holliday, the chain's long-time Boston-based advertising agency. "They're unpretentious, comfortable just being themselves, and like to order their coffee in small, medium or large, thank you very much. They're busy people who use Dunkin' to get fueled up for work or play. They do not have time to linger, because they've got things to do. But they do like to have fun. This is their brand."

In many ways Dunkin' Donuts, one of the high-visibility names owned by Dunkin' Brands (the other is ice cream store Baskin-Robbins), positions itself as the opposite of Starbucks. Dunkin' promises to get you going, small, medium, or large; Starbucks invites you to sit and stay, tall, grande, or venti. That get-up-and-go brand is the driving force behind Dunkin's service design. "I'm a firm believer that everything that touches the consumer defines your brand. The products that you offer, your store design and location;

how your crew interacts with customers," says John Costello, president of global marketing and innovation. "We have a 360-degree approach to service design."

It starts with partnering with franchisees who intimately know their markets, neighborhoods, and customers. But just as important is that Dunkin' as a company knows its customer, identifying its target market by mission and motivation: "In many ways coffee, which is our core product, and breakfast, our key day part, appeal to everyone," says Costello. But within that the Dunkin' customer is more defined by personality than by a demographic.

To keep the Dunkin' customer running, the company has been selective (as good service design demands) with new products, both in-store and online. That means choosing menu items that can be made quickly and consumed with minimum fuss—think Munchkins and hash browns in containers that fit in your car's cup holder. There are lots of competitors selling morning coffee and breakfast— from corner delis to Starbucks to McDonald's. In that crowded space, says Scott Hudler, vice president of global consumer engagement, "[s]peed is one of our brand differentiators."

Dunkin' was not the first to create a mobile app for on-the-go customers, but its features—including a store locator and a partnership with Waze, a navigation app that uses social sourcing to tell motorists how to avoid traffic delays—are directly on-brand.

Americans are clearly happy to keep running on Dunkin': When the American Customer Satisfaction Index released its restaurant report for 2015, Dunkin' saw its customer satisfaction rating jump to 78, a 4 percent increase from the 75 rating it garnered a year before.

Why the Customer Isn't Always Right . . .

"The customer is always right" isn't a strategy, but rather a comedy of manners born of shopkeeping etiquette in the first part of the twentieth century that has been played out (and overplayed) since.

The phrase is popularly ascribed to Harry Selfridge (of United Kingdom–based Selfridges stores) but may have actually originated with his former employer, Marshall Field of the Chicago department store chain. Regardless of its origin, it was a well-worn phrase by the early 1900s, and has long worn out its welcome.

A customer who does not understand your value proposition, or care what you as a company uniquely promise and deliver, is the wrong customer for you. Service design helps you define your right customer, then arrange the links of your value chain to capture and encourage the customers you want, while siphoning away customers whom you cannot serve profitably or well. Dunkin' does not want the sit-and-stay crowd working on laptops in Starbucks, and Starbucks does not do a particularly good job for the grab-and-goer in a hurry to get to her desk.

It is not only acceptable but necessary to decide which customers do not make sense for you to pursue or keep. Customers who are not right for you might still pursue you, but if they do not have the sense to look elsewhere, you must make the break, or at least serve them only in a transactional way, without investing to create an experience designed specifically for them. Within your customer base, there may be segments, of course, for which you design different experiences at different prices or in different places. But the first analysis is to determine which customers you want and can profitably win.

Up till now, we have been writing about customers as if they were all the same. That is not true, of course. Customers differ demographically. They come with different expectations. They come with different missions and motivations. Above all, they differ in how valuable they are to you—and how valuable you are to them. In this chapter, we will explore how you define your customer(s), design your offerings to suit the customers you want, and look at different types of customers and how much effort each type of customer is worth to you.

Manufacturers cope with customer heterogeneity by making products in different sizes, at different price points, sending them out into their distribution channels with appropriate marketing and advertising, and letting customers sort themselves out. This was the classic General Motors segmentation strategy, rolled out by Alfred P. Sloan in the 1930s—Chevrolets for less wealthy customers, Cadillacs at the top, and Oldsmobiles and Buicks in between.

Service providers segment, too. Whether it is a hotel company that has different brands (Marriott offers sixteen, ranging from budget-but-chic Moxy to the elegant Ritz-Carlton); a health insurer with bronze, silver, and gold coverage plans; or a cybersecurity vendor offering service as a subscription with increasingly sophisticated features, companies match price to offerings—a key strategic decision.

The key difference between goods and services is their nature. Goods are a fixed thing; customers can know exactly what they are paying for. Services are experiential; hence service providers must contend with customers who want something more or different than what they paid for: the beer drinker with champagne tastes. You must think through the different offerings you will make to different customers, and design the appropriate service experiences—that is, the ones that meet their expectations and are good for you, too. In fact, the process of segmentation should start with what's good for you (and what you're good at), with the definition of the right customer coming out of that. Service design helps keep both you and your customers in line, ensuring they feel they are being treated fairly, and that you do not give a level of service that isn't being paid for.

Making these choices is complicated by business's long tradition of living by the adage "The customer is always right." Is she? Only if she is the right customer for you, and only if you have carefully worked out the design that makes you right for each other.

In saying that you should start with yourself—with what is right for you—we are not retreating from the idea that service design starts with empathy, that is, with understanding your customers' needs from their point of view. Of course it does. But before you can empathize with your customers' needs, you need to know who is your customer—and who isn't.

Who Is Your Right Customer?

The right customer is one you are prepared to serve in every sense. It is the one you are targeting—not the other way around. You have the capability, you understand what the customer wants and needs, this is the customer around whom you have proactively designed your service offering, and a customer whose business you can realistically win—that is, win and serve profitably.

"Design is about decisions and trade-offs and therefore everything is designed. It is just that most things are often not designed well," says Jon Campbell, vice president of customer experience and innovation capability for Boston-based design firm Continuum. "Positioning is the art of sacrifice, and it goes for selecting customers as well as defining brands." Selecting customers, like so many things, is both art and science. It is easier to define the customer experience—that is, the one you want your customer to have—than it is to define the customer, because odds are you have more than one right customer.

And it is easier to define your *wrong* customer than it is your right one: By definition, the customer who you are not designed to serve profitably is wrong for you. We will look at wrong customers in more depth, and what to do about them, later in this chapter.

One way to determine your right customer is to examine your most valuable customers. Data vary about the cost of acquiring a new customer, with studies putting it at anywhere from 5 to 25 times the cost of retaining a current one. It is logical that keeping a customer would cost less: You do not have to spend time and resources hunting and capturing; you've just got to keep who you have happy. If you're not convinced that retaining customers is so valuable, consider research done by Frederick Reichheld of Bain & Company (the inventor of the Net Promoter Score) that shows that increasing customer retention rates by 5 percent increases profits by 25 percent to 95 percent.

The stats on retention are compelling; clearly, keeping customers matters. But there's a premise hidden behind those stats, and it might not be true: that all those customers are equally worth retaining. The statistics do not make distinctions between the value different customers represent. Your most valuable customers are those who not only are loyal but who spend more per transaction and from whom you have a significant share of wallet. (The customer who comes to your restaurant every day for a bowl of soup and a cup of tea may be beloved but isn't as valuable as the person who comes in once a month with a group of hungry—and thirsty—clients. That isn't to say the first customer isn't *important*; a key distinction. There is likely a lot of customer capital between the two of you, but you are not likely to extract a lot more dollar value from them.)

Peter Fader, a professor of marketing at Wharton, believes companies focus too much on customer retention rather than deriving maximum value from the *right* customers. "It is really important to understand who your valuable customers are, to find ways to enhance their value, extract it for your shareholders, and find more like them," he says. "Given that magical extra dollar, I want to spend it on acquiring great customers—premium customers—and keeping them happy. It is always tougher to change customer behavior than to find new customers similar to your existing top-buyer profiles."

Keeping nonpremium customers happy is fine as long as they remain profitable, but that is not where you should focus your efforts. There is a natural tension between staying focused on that sweet spot—the groups of customers for whom you are perfect and who are perfect for you—and the pursuit of growth. By focusing on customers with the greatest potential in terms of repeat purchases and large average transactions, marketing and customer service efforts (and costs) can be allocated where they matter most. Growth focused solely on building a larger customer base may be the wrong strategy. For a business like the *Boston Globe*, new customers and readers matter. But in many businesses, the focus should be on the quality of revenue, not the number of new accounts.

Your right customer may not just fit one neat demographic category or be easily segmented. If that is the case, you need to find a common element around which you can build an experience. The original idea behind Bonefish Grill—a casual dining restaurant that is now part of Bloomin' Brands—was to give diners a relatively up-scale experience centered on fresh fish.

Says John Cooper, former president of the Bonefish Grill restaurant chain, "In the diners who were looking for a restaurant focused on fish, we realized there would be some who wanted aggressive price value, some who wanted convenience, and some foodies who are willing to pay more. We couldn't capture everybody, but what all the customers we wanted had in common was an experience that fit into their active lifestyle." With that in mind, Bonefish Grill initially set out to cater to customers whose expectations were at a higher end of the dining experience, with the idea that if they could delight those more selective customers, those with lower expectations would naturally be satisfied as well. "However you define a miss, if you miss meeting expectations, everyone is going to be unhappy, from your lower-level-tier customer to your higher one," says Cooper.

Online clothing subscription and styling service Stitch Fix's goal is to serve as broad a range of women as possible—from the edgier client in Manhattan to moms in Montana. "We feel like no other company is as well-equipped to be as many things to as many people as we are," says founder Katrina Lake, who styles at least five "fixes" a week herself. "I have a client who is a nineteen-year-old college student and one who is sixty-five, and they see very different inventory, but we work for both of them." And as wide a range of customers as Stitch Fix is aiming for, Lake knows there are customers for whom Stitch Fix isn't right: "An eighteen-year-old who loves shopping and goes to Forever 21 and H&M every week isn't for us," she says.

Your Right Customer Isn't Only Yours

Just as you have more than one "right" customer, you very well may not be your customer's only answer. Price, convenience, desperation, necessity, your inability to meet all of your customer's needs (or their unwillingness to rely on only one service provider, which is often good business practice) means you not only have competition for their business but you are being compared, perhaps unfairly, to other service providers.

Consider the following examples: Upscale Restoration Hardware and DIY fave IKEA are both well-known furniture retailers, but the similarity pretty much ends there. IKEA is known as much for its low prices and warehouse-like stores (complete with Swedish meatballs and child care in most locations) as it is for the often-challenging assembly instructions that accompany its spare but stylish furniture.

Restoration Hardware, on the other hand, has transformed itself from a seller of primarily high-end home accessories (vintage-inspired doorknobs, light fixtures, and the like) to a brand that sells a lifestyle as much as it does furniture. Enormous "galleries"—stores as large as 60,000 square feet—have carefully curated rooms that contain everything for the "Buenos Aires Villa" or the "Antwerp Canal House." Attractive salespeople hover nearby with iPads, ready to assist with everything from information about wood origin to arranging decorating services.

Two very different services designs, two very different customer experiences, but not necessarily two different people. The customer for each may be the same person, but with vastly different expectations from each retailer.

The examples are numerous: Think about Costco versus Wegmans. Both enjoy almost cultlike status among fans. Costco sells huge quantities of day-to-day basics: 64-ounce jars of oregano, 48-roll toilet paper packages, five-pound sacks of chicken breasts. (And its fair share of upscale food products: lobster tail, anyone?) People must bring their own bags or boxes (or grab some old boxes on the way out, or buy the supersized, superstrong bags Costco sells) and pack their purchases themselves. The stores are clean, and there are food samples and savings aplenty, but if Costco does not have the brand of razor that you favor, or the paper towels where you can pick the sheet size, tough luck. Nevertheless, bargain hunters at all income levels shop there.

Wegmans is a supermarket chain based in upstate New York that appeals to an upscale clientele with its carefully laid-out stores, soothing lighting, and preternaturally cheerful help. Thanks to multiple small food stations, you can snack your way around the store—just like you can at Costco. The Wegmans shopper isn't looking for bulk or particularly low prices, but a level of quality, variety, and knowledge that he or she won't get at Costco. And don't even dream about packing your own groceries!

These dual-personality customers create two potential problems for you. One is making a mistake about who your competitor is. There may be more overlap in the customer set—and hence more competition—between IKEA and Restoration Hardware than there is between IKEA and a discount furniture company like Value City Furniture.

The second and graver danger: working too hard to accede to the wishes of a customer who is unprofitable or otherwise wrong for you. There is something worse than losing a customer, and that is bending over backward to keep one who loses you money. Any service design needs a degree of flexibility—after all, each perfect customer is different. But once you start doing things that conflict with your brand, your strategy, and what you are designed to deliver, your attempt to not disappoint customers will inevitably mean you will disappoint yourself.

The Not So Subtle Art of Saying No

There are customers you have to say no to. Let's start with the ones you do not want: customers or clients who want what you are not prepared to deliver. Not what you *cannot*; what you *won't*. This is not about the heroics we advise you against in the Second Principle. Cannot is about capability; won't is about strategy.

In most cases, saying no to a potential customer is easier than saying goodbye to a current one, because a current customer was, at some point, your right one. The former is often a matter of paying attention to the red flags that are waving so fast and furious they cannot be ignored. And wave they do. You'll get a clueless potential client who makes ludicrous requests that show not only that they do not get your value proposition, but that they do not get it, period. "Sometimes people are dumber than they appear in the rearview mirror," one CEO told us. "You just know they are going to be trouble."

One company we interviewed saw the red flag in the form of abusive behavior on the potential client's part to internal staff, another in the demand from a member of the potential client's team that he insert himself in the service provider's business in a role that would have blurred the boundaries between the respective teams.

"It was tempting because they dangled the prospect of more business if this engagement went well, which could have been extremely lucrative in the long run," the partner recalls of the latter example. "But the process would have been disruptive, confusing to the rest of the staff, and sent mixed signals to external stakeholders. Would this be a one-off? Were we changing how we engage with clients going forward? In the end, the answer was a no-regrets 'Not for us.'"

Deciding to part ways with a current client is about acknowledging that something has changed: their needs, your strategy, the chemistry of the parties involved. The more personal the nature of the service or the more direct the interaction is between you and the customers, the harder it is, because, well, it feels—and is—personal.

When you are thinking about saying no, look at why:

* Are you saying no because it is something you haven't done or do not want to?

* If you haven't done it, why not? Is it resistance to change or genuinely a question of strategy?

* Is it something you do not do well enough, but could with training, practice, or judicious addition of capabilities or staff?

When Your "Wrong" Customer Is Right

Sometimes clients will ask you to do things you do not have the capability for but perhaps should. If you get enough requests for a service or it is something most of your competitors provide, maybe you should take the hint. Nordstrom offers in-house tailoring (only some of it complimentary but regardless a convenience); Macy's, after long leaving most customers to fend for themselves with clothes that needed altering, has partnered with zTailors to save customers the hassle of finding someone to provide the service.

One of us worked with a strategic communications firm that barely dipped its toe in the social media waters despite increasingly frequent requests from clients, given social media's growth and the increasing importance of social media as a way to reinforce brand. This firm saw business—both from long-standing and potential clients—walk out the door. Even though the firm eventually added social and content capabilities to its offering, it had a reputation for being "old-fashioned," "stuck in its ways," and, worst of all, "out of touch."

You will outgrow clients and they will outgrow you. One midsize manufacturer we know broke with a local bank that had serviced it well for decades because the bank could not support the manu-facturer's growing international business. Once you can no longer profitably meet your client's needs, they have become wrong for you—or you're wrong for them. Ideally you will recognize it first, because that will save you from trying to contort your design to fit their needs.

There must be alignment between companies and customers. If a customer wants what you are not promising, prepared, or designed to deliver, you need to go your separate ways. In a market economy, customers and companies can find their match. Service design helps you increase the odds that customers who find you readily will be the ones you want. Once you know who your right customers are, you can design experiences that predictably and profitably meet expectations for those customers/segments while they encourage customers to become more deeply (and profitably) tied to you.

B2B Versus B2C

In most of this book, we make few distinctions between practices among B2B and B2C because the principles of service design and delivery hold true in both worlds, and across industries. But in defining and understanding your customer, there are some distinctions worth noting. Relationships in the B2B sphere tend to be more ongoing, intricate, and intimate than in the B2C world. In some ways, that makes segmentation simpler. You have lots of information about your B2B customers, you have proportionately fewer of them than you would have in the B2C world, and there are likely people assigned to service your B2B accounts. In B2B, you're going after larger targets, one great white rather than a school of small fish.

In B2B businesses, customers create two special challenges to the service designer. First, the fact that they are big and complex may blind you to the importance of creating experiences and capabilities that are common across your customer set. You may become so focused on each customer as a set-of-one that you lose sight of your identity and miss the chance for economies of scale. Second, losing one major customer can make a huge difference to the bottom line, tempting you to do anything to make that customer happy.

In the B2C world, you need lots of fish in your net—but again, they have to be the fish you want. The temptation can be to chase volume rather than value. And the frustration is in not knowing what drives customers. Customers are increasingly comfortable answering questions about themselves—but their answers are meaningful only if the questions are the right ones. It is one thing to know that a business traveler spends ten nights a month away from home;

it is another to know how many of those 120 nights a year your chain is getting and why.

That is why we think it is helpful to think about your customers as falling into different types, an exercise that can reveal what motivates them, why they are or are not doing more business with you, and how you can get them to be more frequent or higher-spending customers. This information may not always be apparent, which is why you should consider rethinking your customer surveys and how you mine customer data. To hark back to an example we used in the beginning, a customer satisfaction survey usually asks how well your people performed their job. They usually are not designed to get to the heart of the customer's experience, their motivations/expectations, and how good the match was.

A Customer Bestiary

THE LOYALIST/E-VANGELIST

This is the customer who loves what you do and is happy to tell the tale—ideally to potential customers, and with a robust social media presence (hence the E- in *E-vangelist*). There is an emotional bond at least on the customer's part. It is worth trying to understand why your customer has such strong feelings. Did a parent do business with the firm? Is there an employee about whom they feel special? Did you perform marvelously at a critical moment? Do you embody their aspirations?

This customer will forgive more than others, but the flip side of that is he or she will expect—and perhaps even feel entitled to—love in return. If you take them for granted, they will feel it. They might also tempt you to do something that does not make sense for you, "just this once." Recognize these for what they are—requests for heroic action and, possibly, the end of, if not a beautiful friendship, a profitable relationship.

Effort-worthiness: high, but within the bounds of your offering.

THE CAPTIVE

A customer who does business with you repeatedly may not be genuinely loyal or satisfied. The Captive customer may be forced to use your health care services or get their prescriptions filled at your chain because of limits imposed by their health insurance plan; a corporate travel department may demand that customers stay at your hotel or fly your airline; loyalty programs, with discounts and rewards, may be the motivation to keep customers coming back, grudgingly, always kicking themselves—until the time they kick you to the curb and leave.

While contracts for providers of things like cell service and broadband are more liberal than they used to be, companies are relying more on discounting to lock customers in. The Captive does not feel like pleasing them is a high priority for you, which may or may not be a fair characterization. Captivity is risky, because locks get opened. You may be lucky enough to have Captive customers—many utilities do, for example—but the landscape is littered with busted jails. For example, cable companies, under threat from increasing competition, are now promising on-time service calls, narrowing the window of time, and calling when they are on their way.

Effort-worthiness: medium. This customer may someday have a choice, and why not try to really earn their business?

THE BUTTERFLY

This customer isn't necessarily difficult to please or dissatisfied so much as he or she is one whose motives may be hard to discern and who exhibits little if any loyalty. In contrast to the Loyalist, the Butterfly won't seek you out or make the effort to stop in.

In the B2C world, variety and a wealth of choices could be what keeps him or her happy. A B2B relationship is more likely to be governed by a contract, but the Butterfly won't feel bad about leaving you or hesitate to go elsewhere if they perceive a "better" alternative.

Effort-worthiness: medium. It is not that they're necessarily difficult to please; they are difficult to understand and to keep.

THE BARGAIN HUNTER

The price-driven customer may have unrealistic expectations about what he or she can get for what they are willing to pay. This customer does not always have a clear sense of the relationship of price to value, unfairly comparing you to others. "Anyone with a valid prescription and $95 isn't necessarily the right customer for us," says Neil Blumenthal, cofounder and co-CEO of Warby Parker. "The customer segment that is price-conscious above everything else isn't brand loyal. They switch brands a lot, which means they can leave as easily as they return. They are just less valuable customers."

Effort-worthiness: usually low. Serving Bargain Hunters can be a viable, profitable strategy—as Walmart and Costco show. But it is not a game for amateurs. If being the lowest-price provider isn't genuinely part of your value proposition, this isn't a customer you should try to please.

THE SNIPER

The Sniper wants one thing, and one thing only from you. It could be because of the service they get from a particular employee; it could be that you really are that much better at one particular thing that matters to this customer more than anything else ("So and so has the best"—fill in the blank). The trick with Snipers is knowing why they come to you, and where else they are spending their money. It is worth examining not just their individual data but also the data around categories of goods or services. If you're seeing a cluster of demand, you need to either look at expanding your ability to meet that demand or figure out what is lacking in the quality of what else you are offering.

Effort-worthiness: medium to high. You might be able to convert them into more broad-based customers.

THE ASPIRANT

Think of Aspirants as kids looking in the window of the candy store. They like what they see; they just cannot have it—or at least not very often, or in great quantity. It is the Macy's customer who wants to shop at Barneys; the Holiday Inn customer who wishes he or she could stay at the Ritz; the Southwest flyer who yearns for the luxury of flying upper class on Virgin Air.

Their profile or credit card information tells you how often they use your service, not how often they want to. It might be hard to tell the Aspirant from the Butterfly, because you very likely do not see them, interact with them, or know them well enough to know what their motivation is. If you treat them too casually you could lose a potential customer down the road.

Effort-worthiness: high: For the most part, the service environment is such that you do not run the risk of over-servicing them. It is usually a defined type of interaction.

In some service environments, segmentation matters less than in others. Ellis O'Connor, asset manager, MSD Hospitality, and general manager of Santa Monica, California's Fairmont Miramar Hotel & Bungalows, knows the hotel and its award-winning restaurant, the Fig, have countless regulars—and knows many of them. But he feels the same level of obligation to offer an outstanding experience to the customer for whom a stay or a meal is a rare or even once-in-a-lifetime treat as he does to the Miramar's countless regulars. "The young couple celebrating a first anniversary deserves to be treated as specially as any of our longtime customers," he says fervently. "For the time they are in our care, it is our obligation to give them the level of service that we are known for, regardless of whether they are known to us."

Two lessons: First, the customer should be assumed right for you until proven otherwise. The proof may come quickly; the "rightness" will depend in part on the service environment. Make the decision based on what they show you, not what they tell you. Second, you are in control. For the time the customer is in your hands—whether during a hotel stay, a meal, a flight, trying on clothes in your store, on your website, talking with a customer service rep—you have the ability to say yes or no, to help this person decide if you two are indeed a match, or may be in the future.

Even when you're recognized as the very best in your field—a sure sign that you are doing not just something right, but many things—you can still be the wrong choice for some customers. In August 2002, Charles McDiarmid, owner of the Wickaninnish Inn—"the Wick"—got the delightful surprise that his hotel had been named the number-one hotel property in North America and the number-three property in the world. No small accomplishment for a hotel on Canada's remote Vancouver Island.

The hotel became a destination for people who wanted bragging rights about having stayed at the top properties in the world—not knowing anything about its less-than-urban location. "I had people asking, 'Where is the Gucci store?'" remembers McDiarmid. "We just couldn't make these people happy and some of them checked out early," he says. "My lesson: We are not for everyone. But those we are for, we really are for."

Just as there are customers you should get rid of, as McDiarmid reluctantly realized, there are customers you want to have a more than casual but less than exclusive relationship with, and those with whom you want a privileged, special relationship. This isn't just about giving the latter group perks or access (think high-end credit card customers, high-net-worth individuals, high-spending B2B customers); it's also about them giving *you* access to their wants, needs, thoughts, both directly and indirectly, because of a level of trust and comfort that has developed. This is part of what makes them right for you.

This profitable, delightful exchange allows you and your customer to develop the kind of relationship that leads to co-creation of services and their delivery, and to generate customer capital, two concepts we will explore in the next chapter.

The Second Principle: Don't Surprise and Delight Your Customers—Just Delight Them

Orphan drugmaker NPS Pharmaceuticals (now owned by Shire) got Food and Drug Administration approval in 2012 for GATTEX, a drug for short-bowel syndrome—a chronic disease that affects at most 5,000 people in the United States. But the pharmaceutical company realized that its work in helping patients had just begun. NPS specialized in commercializing orphan drugs—those that treat complex and rare diseases. Such drugs are costly to develop because there is a small patient population with which to conduct research and from which to recoup costs.

The cost of GATTEX would be about $300,000 a year per patient—a figure in keeping with the economics of "orphan drugs," according to former NPS Pharmaceuticals CEO Francois Nader. In both the United States and Europe, legislation has granted such drugs special status. Among other things, orphan drug designation allows the drug's maker not only to deal with physicians and insurance companies but to work directly with patients as well, something not normally allowed.

FDA approval does not automatically translate into insurance coverage. Insurers have to be educated and persuaded that paying for a drug this pricey is a sound decision. "We made the decision that no patient would pay more than $10 a month out of pocket for our drug," says Nader. To make that happen, physicians and insurance companies would have to be convinced not merely of the effectiveness of the drug but its ability to alter patients' lives. And of course, effectiveness could only be demonstrated if people were taking it.

There were multiple obstacles: the cost of the drug, the lack of knowledge about it among patients and the medical community, and the condition of the patients themselves—extremely sick people who usually could not hold jobs. NPS's solution was to design a multipronged program that educated doctors, insurance companies, and patients, and also included a concierge service to help patients with every aspect of introducing the drug into their lives.

"Once we made the decision around payment, it meant we as a company would have to manage the whole process," says Nader. "These patients were in no way equipped to deal with insurance companies." The solution was a designed service that started when a patient was first prescribed the drug and ended only when the patient felt comfortable enough to handle things without extra help. As soon as a patient got a prescription, he or she was assigned a care coordinator to collaborate on every aspect of incorporating the injectable drug into their lives—including dealing with insurers.

This was a far cry from the traditional model of service for drug companies. It involved looking at every aspect of the patient experience and making sure no part was untouched. Care coordinators held training sessions for patients at home so they learned how to use the drug, what to expect from side effects, and how to handle reimbursement. Coordinators were available by phone 24/7 to patients. Given that this was a new approach for the company, it rolled out the program one patient at a time. And yes, NPS underwrote the entire cost of the care coordinator program.

"Our goal was to delight patients because they had been waiting for us forever," says Nader. "We were not an answer; we were *the* answer." Insurers saw it the same way. Every payer in the country ended up paying for the drug, according to Nader. "We were able to demonstrate value for our patients who were now leading very different, healthier lives, which ultimately saved the [health care] market money."

While all stakeholders benefited, NPS's success was rooted in *empathy*, looking at the situation from the patient's perspective, and making sure every patient had the resources to navigate effectively and reliably among doctors, the insurance companies, pharmacies, and NPS itself. It was equally grounded in *engineering*—the efficacy of GATTEX itself—and in the company's determination to design a patient journey that met the *economic* needs of all concerned: the company (to be paid), the patient (to have an affordable price), and the insurance company (to be shown the cost was worth it). Above all, however, the service designed for GATTEX was built to set, manage, and deliver a program that patients, physicians, and insurers could count on.

Defining Delight

"Surprise and delight" has become a mantra for customer experience. We think that is wrong. Forget about surprising customers: Just delight them. We know that is counterintuitive. Indeed, Wikipedia's definition of customer delight is "surprising a customer by exceeding his or her expectations and thus creating a positive emotional reaction." But why, we ask, should doing a good job be a surprise?

Delight might seem like an odd word when thinking about something as ordinary as delivering a good cup of coffee quickly, or as life-changing as helping critically sick people figure out how to integrate a much-needed drug into their daily existence. In the former case *delight* seems overblown, in the second inadequate. Yet comparison is not really the point: A company's job is to design and deliver delight on its own terms, by fully meeting the expectations of customers, just as *Harry Potter and the Philosopher's Stone* is delightful and *Hamlet* is, too.

Designing your services and their delivery to delight customers enables you to woo them, wow them, and win them predictably, scalably, reliably, and economically. You deliver every time. That is tough enough. It is the foundation on which delight must rest. If a surprise comes as well—a chocolate mint on the pillow—that is fine. But the heart of delight is getting it right.

Service design allows you to figure out where your opportunities for delight are and are not, and to create the conditions that enable you to make the most of them. Complex services like auditing financial statements generally involve many more touchpoints than simpler transactions; many more things can go right or go wrong; they usually occur over a more extended time frame—weeks, months, even years, compared to minutes or hours for, say, a restaurant meal. Though the circumstances differ, the principle remains the same: Do not surprise: Delight.

Delight is the product of the *experience* the customer has and the *excellence* you provide, each of which is a function of the elements of service design excellence we showed you in Chapter 1.

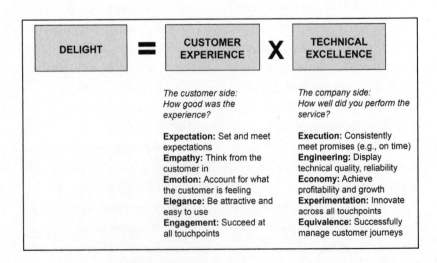

DELIGHT	**=**	**CUSTOMER EXPERIENCE**	**X**	**TECHNICAL EXCELLENCE**

The customer side: How good was the experience?

Expectation: Set and meet expectations
Empathy: Think from the customer in
Emotion: Account for what the customer is feeling
Elegance: Be attractive and easy to use
Engagement: Succeed at all touchpoints

The company side: How well did you perform the service?

Execution: Consistently meet promises (e.g., on time)
Engineering: Display technical quality, reliability
Economy: Achieve profitability and growth
Experimentation: Innovate across all touchpoints
Equivalence: Successfully manage customer journeys

Both excellence and experience are opportunities for differentiation, and while both are important aspects of your service offering, they are not necessarily equal. In a crisis, most people would put up with a rude, overbearing physician if, like TV's fictional Dr. House, he was also a genius. But if you were choosing long-term care for an aged parent, you might put more weight on the quality of the experience, provided there was enough technical competence (and access to Dr. House if Mom needed him). "A good experience needs to set the right expectations for customers as they transition from one step in their journey to another, and from one touchpoint to another," says Jon Campbell of Continuum. "Good design makes every next step feel inevitable."

The Element of Surprise

Surprise is a trap: It increases the likelihood that you will lose focus. When you do things that are not part of your value proposition or go beyond the expectations you have established for your service, you confuse customers, reset expectations, blur boundaries for employees, and alter your ability to be consistent. Removing the element of surprise isn't about making the customer's experience dull or lacking in the touches—the lagniappe—that endear you, such as doing pro bono work for an important client's favorite charity. But the ability to offer an extra must be built into both your service model and your economic one, and the extras must make sense given the context in which they are offered.

While customers may be surprised at the beginning of your relationship, particularly if you are delivering service that is superior to what they got elsewhere, the element of surprise should fade quickly, replaced by the reliability and predictability you have designed in. Continuity and consistency keep you on-brand and on-message. "You earn people's loyalty by being consistent," says Michelle Shotts, executive director of business analytics for Edmunds.com, the online automotive resource.

Trying to surprise can be a distraction. "I don't care about a free snack box when I fly. I want to board on time," says "the Wick's" managing director, Charles McDiarmid. The key to the success of his super-luxury hotel: Get the basics right, and build delight from the ground up. "There is a pyramid, and the foundation of it is delivering the basics every single time. Only after you do that do you have the opportunity to think about surprising them in a good way."

The opposite of delight is disappointment, which, you will note from your own experience, almost always comes when you fail to keep a promise you made, or when a customer did not know what to expect. Both are failures of service design.

What happens when you disappoint customers?

* 96 percent of unhappy customers do not complain; however, 91 percent of those will simply leave and never come back.

* A dissatisfied customer tells between 9 and 15 people about the experience. Around 13 percent of dissatisfied customers tell more than 20 people.

* It takes 12 positive experiences to make up for one unresolved negative experience.

Why Delight Matters

It is obvious that delighting customers should be a good thing, but the subtleties are revealing. Delight matters because it taps into four benefits for you.

Delight creates goodwill between you and your customer. We call this Customer Capital (and will look at it in more detail in Chapter 10). "When service design is done well, it strengthens and nurtures the relationship between the customer and the entity in question, ideally altering how the customer feels beyond the moment of transaction," according to Victor Ermoli from the Savannah College of Art and Design.

Delight improves retention and customer value. In a bank McKinsey studied, after a positive experience more than 85 percent of customers increased their value to the bank by purchasing more products or investing more of their assets.

Delight generates good word of mouth. Delighted customers are an unpaid army of advocates, selling your service at no cost to you. Word of mouth has proved to be the primary driver of growth for online stylist Stitch Fix (see Chapter 10), according to founder Katrina Lake. "For the first two years we had a waitlist that was entirely developed through word of mouth," says Lake. "I'm not sure we could have grown any other way. Even today the vast majority of our customers find out about us through friends."

Delight buys you a break. Delight as we've defined it—the regular drumbeat of reliably delivered expectations—earns you a second chance if you screw up or some time as you work to refine your service design. That benefit is unquantifiable, but no less critical. "When you've earned people's trust, there is a forgiveness factor," says Erik Olsson, CEO of storage company Mobile Mini. "One area where we were doing a terrible job was in leaving inventory at customer locations. It was incredibly selfish on our part to leave it there until we had a place to move it to when the next customer wanted it. People liked us and our product enough that I do not think this cost us business, but it was a bad approach."

Designing for Delight

The ability to delight begins with the customer-experience side of the equation on page 86. You cannot delight customers unless you know what is important to them—not what you think is important to them. That means understanding what their challenges are, the problems they need solved, and what they are trying to accomplish.

Empathy and experience, then, are the first steps toward designing delight. Your goal is to understand what purpose your customer has and then design an experience that fits the need. Scott Cook, founder of Intuit, and Harvard Business School professor Clayton M. Christensen have made famous the story of a fast-food company whose efforts to improve milk shake sales had come to naught, despite enormous investments studying taste preferences, price points, and the like. It turned out people were buying milk shakes not for the taste but for the ease of having something long-lasting and satisfying to get them through long car commutes. Armed with that insight, the company redesigned how shakes were sold (to make buying them faster) and reformulated the contents (to make consuming them slower)—and sales skyrocketed.

Field research—actually watching customers in action, not listening to focus groups from behind the mirror—is the key to empathy. It is a powerful antidote to the natural tendency of executives to believe that new features and functions pave the path to greater sales. As Christensen and Cook say, "Making it easier and cheaper for customers to do things that they are not trying to do rarely leads to success."

A team from Continuum demonstrated the power of field research working with a home security company. As they and the client visited with customers, recalls Toby Bottorf, a principal at the firm, they learned that the company was heading down the wrong path with one of its core products. "We found out what people wanted out of the system, which was life simplification—not something superpowerful and complicated," recalls Bottorf. That is, the company had been pursuing technical excellence at the expense of the experience customers really wanted. Continuum's research led to a redesign of not just the functionality of the system, but of its looks and user interface—a dramatically different path than the company would have followed had customers wanted lots of features, functions, and options.

Empathy is a powerful tool in figuring out what matters to your client. Be your customer. Try navigating your website; try getting through to the right person in customer service; try ordering products; booking a flight—and flying coach; finding a casita without a map; shopping in your store. While walking in your customer's shoes, however, it is important to resist substituting your own instincts for what direct observation reveals about customers. Says Surf Air's Jeff Potter: "I suspect that a lot of things that we think are important to most of the members actually are not."

Case in point: in-flight Wi-Fi. To Potter, it seemed essential, yet he was surprised to find out that members were just about evenly split on whether it was something they wanted. Indeed, studies show that personal empathy can actually blind you to what is really going on in customers' minds. (See box, "The Empathy Experiment.") Similarly, traditional market research can confirm the insights you get from observation but is no substitute for it. Says HBS professor Len Schlesinger, "You do market research, you do focus groups, and too often all you learn is what customers want you to hear. But they do not tend to behave the way that they talk." Data are part of the answer, but never forget anthropological observation. You ask, you pay attention to social media, you see what your successful competitors and peers are doing and what is being said about them, and you find out what customers actually do.

THE EMPATHY EXPERIMENT

In service design, empathy is not a matter of personal psychology. Ironically, highly empathetic people cannot always distinguish between their emotions and the feelings of others, according to research done by Imperial College London's Johannes Hattula and co-researchers Walter Herzog, Darren Dahl, and Sven Reinecke. They interviewed marketing managers about their own preferences for a selected product or service. Then the researchers encouraged some of the managers to describe a typical customer's thoughts and reactions.

"All managers were asked to predict customers' desires and took a survey assessing empathy levels. The more empathetic managers were, the more 'egocentric' they became; that is, the more likely they were to say that the customers' preferences were the same as their own," Hattula told *Harvard Business Review*. "The more empathetic managers were, the more they used their personal preferences to predict what customers would want. Another key finding that should get people's attention is that the more empathetic the managers were, the more they ignored the market research on customers that we provided them."

Empathy helps you focus on designing the experience that customers want—but it can do more than that: It will help you understand the needs and purposes they themselves do not know or cannot express. Empathy can sometimes put you one step ahead of your customer, says McDiarmid. "If I can delight you with something that you haven't even thought about yourself, if it is right you'll think, 'Ahhh. That is perfect. How did you know?'"

Such was the case with Virgin Atlantic's decision to put a bar in the upper-class cabin, according to Simon Glynn, senior partner at marketing and advertising agency Lippincott. "[Virgin Atlantic] built the bar because the company had made the effort to build a great cabin crew, and realized that customers didn't get a chance to talk to them," he wrote in online publication *Marketing Daily*.

Beyond Your Control

Though reliability is the key to delight, there will be circumstances that even the most meticulous service design cannot anticipate—

where events are beyond your control or where customers bring powerful emotions when they come to you.

A Dunkin' Donuts customer might be annoyed if burst pipes put their regular store out of service for a day or two, but even the most loyal Dunkin' customer would lose patience if the company were to offer complicated-to-make products that slow up the line in the morning. That need for simplicity and speed has influenced the way Dunkin' has designed its stores, its menus, and its equipment. McDonald's, which makes a similar get-out-quick promise, has annoyed both customers and store owners by reengineering its menu to include items that take too long to make, take it away from its core offerings, and require reconfiguration of stores.

Emotion: The state a customer is in when he or she receives your service can affect the way it is perceived—even if you are consistent in your quality and delivery. While you cannot control the emotion customers bring to the situation, you can often make good guesses about what it might be and design your service accordingly, from guiding your employees' actions to providing an appropriate physical and visual environment. A funeral home can safely assume its clientele feels shock and grief—no modern art on the walls or slickly dressed staff here.

Nor do you need to be at the mercy of customers' emotions. The Schopf & Weiss law firm in Chicago, a litigation boutique, has modern, loftlike offices, but in a corner near a room where depositions are taken is a clutch of upholstered couches and chairs, a place to relax before or decompress after what might be a trying experience.

When a customer's emotions are intense, the very least you can do is not make things worse. A frictionless payment process at the doctor's office will do little to assuage the anxiety of a mother dealing with a sick child—but a cumbersome one may send her over the edge. You may not be able to wow a customer in such cases, but the absence of reliability and predictability makes for *Ow* experiences. (For more about how to acknowledge customers' emotions in your service design, see "Improve How You Manage Customer Emotions" in the Appendix.) Providing solutions should also involve a level of proactivity, not just reactivity, says Glenn Goldman of Credibly, an online lender to small businesses.

"Delighting your customers in ways they haven't thought of isn't about surprising them but it is about looking ahead and sometimes to the sides," he says. An example: Credibly recognized that while only approximately 20 percent of small businesses need capital at any given time, nearly all small businesses are constantly looking for help in managing and growing their businesses. With that in mind, Credibly established InCredibly, a daily blog featuring original content written by small business owners and experts. Since the launch of InCredibly, Credibly's Net Promoter Score has doubled, the company's rate of revenue growth has soared into the triple digits, and repeat customers for Credibly's loans are at an all-time high.

Solving a problem in a new way, or pointing out a problem and providing an immediate solution, is an opportunity for you to delight your customer. Case in point: Every hotel probably has one or two rooms full of mattresses or other inventory on hand to replace things as needed—bureaus, chairs, whatever. Every night those rooms are not rented, they're losing revenue. Says Rob Loy, marketing director of Mobile Mini, "We suggest to them they put that stuff in a container in their parking lot. They pay $125 a month versus losing $125 every night the room isn't rented."

Delight's Front Line

Customer-facing employees, regardless of pay grade, title, or level of responsibility, may be your greatest resource in your efforts to delight customers. They are the ones who meet customers (whether virtually, by phone, or in person) at a critical juncture in the service process, so they will have a huge impact on your experience score. Even if customer delight is everyone's responsibility (in both the front and back of the house) and you consider yourself a customer-centric organization, the actions of whoever the customer deals with will have a big influence on the customer's perceptions of your service.

Frontline employees are critical not only because of what they do, but for what they know. They hear the *Ahhh*; they hear about the *Ow*. They see what customers actually do.

That is why we're big believers in empowering frontline employees as much as possible. Companies that excel in service design not only do so, but do it with clear understanding of expectations and boundaries. "Whatever your job description, everyone understands that it is their responsibility to fix customers' problems. You do what you have to do, and ask forgiveness later," says Kenneth J. Worzel, executive vice president of strategy and development at Nordstrom Inc.

At McDiarmid's hotel, employees go through a rigorous training program every two years. Its title: "You Are the Experience." It is not a rulebook drill. "We have standards; we do not have policies around what employees can do for guests," says McDiarmid. "A big aspect of that is there are no limits. If you hire a private jet for a customer, you damn well better have a good reason. In hindsight, we might realize there was a better decision to be made, but we are never going to chastise or discipline you for being proactive about taking care of a guest," he says. His rationale: "If a guest leaves unhappy, by the time the situation reaches my desk, it is going to take ten times more effort to resolve it."

Giving frontline employees discretion is a key part of empowering them. "You have to give them space to use their judgment," says Continuum's Jon Campbell.

"Organizations cannot anticipate every possible situation they will encounter, and therefore you cannot make a rigid and defined process for everything. Otherwise, there is a risk of service failure when something goes off-script." And something will go off-script because, as we have emphasized, the very nature of services is that the customer is an active, and quite possibly idiosyncratic, participant in the creation of value.

It seems paradoxical, but automation can be a great way to increase frontline autonomy. Handheld computers at Nordstrom Rack improve the productivity of shop floor personnel and make lines move faster for customers. At Restoration Hardware, their use reinforces the upscale furniture retailer's at-your-side, walk-you-through-the-process value proposition.

Is It Working?

So far, we have been talking about the "experience" side of the equation. Now let's switch over to the other side—technical excellence. All the empathy and expectation setting in the world will not make a difference if you are unable to keep the promises you make.

Just as there are multiple ways to find out what customers want and need, there are multiple ways to find out whether you're satisfying those wants and meeting their needs. Customers who feel invested in your brand will be more inclined to give you constructive and useful feedback. Dunkin' Donuts has what John Costello, president of global marketing and innovation at Dunkin' Brands Inc., describes as a "very sophisticated guest satisfaction program" that produces more than a million customer feedback data points a year. The company also uses ongoing consumer tracking to measure how well it is delivering against its brand promise.

"The questions that we ask our clients all ladder back to what the mandatories were that they told us make for a great experience," says Weber Shandwick's Cathy Calhoun. "We do not want to only get feedback on clients once a year. We want to be getting feedback from them all the time, but we want to have one time a year where we have a systematic way to get it."

McDiarmid points out the need to find out what's subjective versus what is a genuine trend. He recalls that when the Wickaninnish Inn underwent a complete renovation in 2012, new bed frames were built that had a sharp angle. The frames made their debut in one building, and when the staff got the first one or two complaints about people banging their legs against them, they didn't think much of it. "After four or five, we realized that we had a problem—it wasn't that our guests were clumsy or careless." The result: All the bed frames that had been built were redone, and a new design was used for the remaining buildings. "Follow a trend to the logical conclusion and you will know what you need to do," he says. (For more about building strong feedback loops, see Chapter 10.)

An organization can measure the results of good service design not only by using traditional methods—increased revenues and customer loyalty—but also through the transformation of customers into heroes, those who under self-initiative will generate a positive remark about the entity to others, points out SCAD's Victor Ermoli. "Service designers designing the system for developing the relationship between an entity and those it serves," he says. "You know when you have succeeded when people will talk about your company in a way that they want to be associated with it."

Armed with real knowledge about whether you in fact understand and are meeting customer needs, you can move quickly to address all the elements of the "technical excellence" side of the equation. Execution problems—failure to keep delivery promises, lost or incomplete orders, inaccurate invoicing—usually can be addressed with standard operation excellence tools like Total Quality Management, lean, and Six Sigma; the critical point is that you are using your customer data to define and prioritize your list of actions.

Some customer problems point to failures in engineering; those can be challenging if it turns out that you have fallen behind technically. Randall Stephenson, the CEO of AT&T, made that discovery in 2012 when he invited technologist Sebastian Thrun to talk about online learning and found that his company's own network was not sophisticated or fast enough to run the demo—prompting AT&T to accelerate a multibillion-dollar technical upgrade. You may find that solving one element of the equation helps you solve another one. For example, you'll discover that almost every time a customer complains that you have wasted his time or inconvenienced him, something is wrong with your processes, and putting it right will make you more efficient.

Not a Static Thing

Delight is not a onetime, unchanging thing. Customers' needs will change, as will their expectations about what great service is. Your capabilities and economics will change. Your rivals will improve and technology will force changes on you both. (We will return to the topic of innovation in Chapter 8.) The fact that you're never done is both a blessing and a burden. The blessing is that even though we believe excellence in service design and delivery should be built into your offerings from the beginning, the truth is it is never too late. Because excellence is a moving target, you have the chance to move with it and either catch up with or surpass your competitors.

Says Olsson of Mobile Mini, "We were fortunate that our competition was no better than we were [in the areas where we were really disappointing customers], so service became an area of opportunity and differentiation for us." Where it can seem like a burden is in the idea that "you're running laps in a race yet no one is ever drawing the finish line so you can never reach it," says Surf Air CEO Jeff Potter.

It is also not static because the customer is part of the process in service—which is another reason to lead and empower your front line, rather than try to control it. "Robots make poor people, but people make terrible robots," asserts Continuum's Bottorf. It is equally true of those trying to deliver the service and of those who receive it: "Consistency in philosophy and intent will guide you in practice and process. Be rigid with your standards, not your behavior."

In the next chapter, we will look at how to design your service in such a way that neither your employees nor your customers are required to go to extremes to ensure a delightful experience.

The Third Principle: Great Service Must Not Require Heroic Efforts on the Part of the Provider or the Customer

Nothing is more satisfying than a company that really knows its stuff. Both customer and company win when the job gets done well: one call, logical user interface, a single point of contact, flawless execution. Efficient and reliable every time. Kitchen chaos that sets the staff aflutter but nevertheless results in a sumptuous, gracious meal may provide comic relief on *Downton Abbey*, but relying on behind-the-scenes heroics is an untenable operating model for a business. Service—whether in a great house or a great business—must be designed so that it is scalable—and the delightful nonsurprise to your customer we described in the previous chapter.

Think of the apparent ease with which a great pianist plays a complicated sonata. You should be delivering your service with the same mastery and confidence, based on practice and preparation—and design. To deliver service in that way, your organization must be skilled, agile, and conditioned. The customer should never see you sweat, because you're not sweating.

Well-designed and delivered services do not waste time or money—yours or your customers'. This is our Third Principle of excellence in service design and delivery: Great service must not require heroic efforts on the part of the provider or the customer. It is a combination of efficiency and elegance—nothing is left out, nothing is superfluous. The two elements—efficiency and elegance—should be mutually reinforcing. Often, however, they are not; sometimes they are at war.

Consider what happens when companies manage to deliver great service without great service design—that is, when they place the burden of customer experience solely on the backs of employees, without providing the structure and tools they need. Across the business world, companies celebrate "customer service heroes" who go out of their way to deliver that order, fix that problem, or get that document out in time. Every heroic effort is an indication of an opportunity to redesign work so that you do not need superpowers to deliver superior service. As HBS professor Frances Frei and Anne Morriss, authors of *Uncommon Service*, say, reliance on heroics "by its very definition means we're going to have *episodic* [emphasis ours] excellence."

For decades, top law and consulting firms, as well as investment banks, have run junior associates ragged—in a few cases literally killing them with exhaustion—always decking the practice in the holy vestments of client-centricity. Only recently have some firms started to question the practice of keeping teams away from home at client sites four days a week and begun to invest in videoconference and secure cloud technologies that make it possible to deliver equal service with less abuse of the staff.

In health care, the combination of inefficient processes and nettlesome regulations makes life miserable for thousands of workers. Sometimes the misery is more than mental: Remarkably, hospital orderlies and nursing assistants suffer on-the-job injury rates as high as firefighters do, often from being asked to lift heavy patients without proper equipment or enough help. The amount of waste in the U.S. health care industry is estimated to be a staggering $750 billion a year, equal to about 80 percent of the profits of the Fortune 500. "The number-one waste in health care is waiting. The number two is defects," says Dr. John Toussaint, M.D., director of the ThedaCare Center for Healthcare Value. "Every 79 seconds, we kill someone in the U.S. due to medical error."

Or consider the flip side: instances where customer experience is sacrificed on the altar of efficiency. Operations teams—which rarely deal directly with customers—usually are asked to meet specific cost targets, while being vaguely reminded that they should do no harm to customer experience. We know how that works out. Costs are easily measured and reliably attributable to specific activities, and savings are quickly booked. The value of improved customer experience is harder to quantify or trace to a particular initiative—it usually comes from a combination of actions performed by different groups—and won't necessarily help you make budget this year. If you save time and money backstage by making your customers work harder, you may win this quarter, but you will lose the game.

Then think about what happens when superior efficiency and superior experience come together. Hospitals in America today confront that opportunity. We say "confront" because it is being imposed on them by the federal government's Centers for Medicare & Medicaid Services, which wants to see improvements in both the process of medical care (that is, evidence-based standards of excellence) and in patient satisfaction—and may withhold up to 2 percent of Medicare reimbursements for hospitals that fail to improve in both dimensions. That is a multimillion-dollar stick for a typical hospital.

Improving patient experience, it turns out, is not a matter of sprucing up the décor and ordering sheets with a higher thread count. It requires redesigning how and how often nurses and doctors (especially doctors) communicate with patients during their stay and at the time of discharge, according to Aravind Chandrasekaran of the Fisher College of Business at The Ohio State University. Research by Chandrasekaran and Claire Senot of Tulane's Freeman

School of Business demonstrates that improving communications and process-of-care simultaneously can cut hospital readmission rates by as much as five percentage points—which would amount to about a quarter of all readmissions of elderly patients.

The Chief Officer of Pain Points

Mobile Mini is the world's largest provider of portable storage, with a fleet of more than 200,000 metal storage containers that the company leases to customers in the United States and United Kingdom. Sales of the Tempe, Arizona–based company were $530.1 million in 2015—a healthy increase of more than 15 percent from the year before. About half of that came from builders, who use containers to store equipment and materials during construction and for on-site offices. But the company's customers also include retailers, who might put a container in the parking lot to serve as a mini-warehouse or to make room in the store for seasonal goods, and schools and universities, which use containers to store band uniforms and instruments and off-season gear like football tackling dummies. (Mobile Mini also leases specialty containers for secure storage of petroleum and industrial products, but the bulk of its business is renting out big steel boxes.)

It is a gritty business, and Mobile Mini wants to be the class of the field, "the Mercedes of storage," says CEO Erik Olsson. At Mobile Mini that translates into providing superior containers—the right size, clean, not banged up or rusted, with differentiators like a door that can be opened with one hand and a patented, tri-cam lock—via processes that make the company easy to do business with. Mobile Mini is one of many disciples of the Net Promoter Score. This is a customer loyalty measurement developed by Fred Reichheld and described in his December 2003 *Harvard Business Review* article, "The One Number You Need to Grow." It is calculated from responses to a single question, "How likely is it that you would recommend

[Company X] to a friend or colleague?" scored on a 0–10 scale. The "net" part is derived by subtracting the percentage of detractors from the percentage of promoters.

Mobile Mini has gone beyond NPS and added another number: a Customer Effort Score. It is a simple measure, adapted from work done by the Corporate Executive Board, which asks customers, "On a scale from 1 to 5, how easy are we to do business with?"

CES numbers provide plenty of insights for Olsson's chief operating officer, Kelly Williams, who calls himself "Chief Officer of Pain Points." These range from managing availability to removing a container immediately when the customer is done with it; as Williams says, "Our value proposition is that we're easy to do business with. Most of that is driven through logistics."

But not all. "Two things really upset customers," Olsson says. "You have bad product—a container with a rusted roof or something like that. And the second is delivery and pickup: You say you are going to pick it up today and then you do not." Late pickup—leaving containers on customers' sites till they could be moved to another customer—was endemic when Olsson became CEO in 2013. It was such common industry practice that, apparently, no one even knew how much it irked customers.

Information management and hands-on customer service help eliminate pain points. A big service design challenge has been to strike the balance between centralization and decentralization. As the biggest player in the industry, Mobile Mini has scale advantages, but runs the risk of imposing one-size-fits-all ways of working on a heterogeneous customer mix. For example, the decision to set up a national call center in 2009 turned out badly. True, big customers like Walmart and Target wanted national account management and centralized ordering and invoicing—which Mobile Mini provides, now along with individual Web portals so these companies can manage some of their business directly.

But the bulk of the business is nothing if not local, even with major accounts. Williams says: "We are looking to transition back so all the touchpoints become local. So if the customer calls and asks for Suzy and Bill answers, he can say, 'Yeah, she's right beside me, Frank, hang on one second. As a matter of fact, Jim—you know Jim, our driver—he'll be there in five minutes.' The customer loves that. And we lost it when we brought in a call center."

Mobile Mini's service design seeks to combine sophisticated back-office services, logistics, and fleet management with highly local sales, service, and delivery, with the aim of providing a better product with less hassle for customers. As a result, Mobile Mini gets a premium price—20 percent higher than what rivals charge, Olsson says. The customer's time, in other words, can be your money.

Lean Production + Lean Consumption

The idea that your customer's time and money matter to you as much as your own derives from what James Womack and Daniel Jones call "lean consumption," which is the demand-side analogue to lean production. In the words of Womack and Jones, "Lean consumption isn't about reducing the amount customers buy or the business they bring. Rather, it is about providing the full value that consumers desire from their goods and services, with the greatest efficiency and least pain."

Why is it, cranky Tom wonders, that Orbitz insists on offering him a hotel, a car, and flight insurance on *three separate screens* before letting him pay for his flight and get on with his life? Why is it, Womack and Jones write, that one out of five customers looking for a pair of shoes will not find what they want in stock—while the industry has to remainder 40 percent of what is on the shelves because it is inventory no one bought? You can fix that with a special order (heroics on your part) or abandon the customer to look elsewhere (heroics on hers).

Time is money—and customers value their time as much as companies value theirs. There's a reason Amazon patented (with no small amount of difficulty) its One-Click ordering process. Viewing your customer's resources as equal in importance to your own is critical for the co-creating partnership we talk about in Chapter 10. Indeed, if you design service to save customers' time, you may earn the right to receive some of the value you've created. Consider the case of Progressive Insurance, which in 1994 decided to reduce customers' need to hassle over auto accident claims by settling them immediately— writing a check on the spot if possible, even at an accident scene. A quick, simple process—and a check right now—turned out to be a good deal all around: Customers were delighted and Progressive found that overall claims costs went down because customers disputed fewer settlement amounts, a process that cost plenty.

Moreover, Progressive acted like a friend, easing customers through what is almost always an emotionally charged event. (They'd just had a crash, perhaps someone was hurt, their car was damaged, their plans were disrupted . . .) Did the company open itself to the possibility of paying too much, or paying a claim that after investigation might have been denied? Sure. But that risk turned out to be minuscule compared to the value gained.

By contrast, United Airlines managed to create work for its customers while trying to make up for inconvenience it caused. In May 2015, one of us had a hellish trip after a United plane had to turn back in midflight due to mechanical problems. By way of recompense, United immediately sent an email to passengers directing them to a website to claim a discount coupon or extra frequent-flyer miles: so far, so good. But once at the website, passengers had to go through a complicated process of proving their identity before they could claim their compensation—even though the United system, which had generated an email to direct them to the site, already knew who they were. (The website's name: united.com/appreciation [*sic*].) Progressive's service design saves its customers time and makes them feel taken care of. United's design wastes customers' time and says it mistrusts them.

The Doctor Will See You *Now*?

Every fortnight, a hundred or so physicians, nurses, and medical administrators come to Appleton, Wisconsin, a city of 75,000 located thirty miles up the Fox River from Green Bay. They come—roughly 2,700 executives from 500 health care organizations each year—to attend workshops at the ThedaCare Center for Healthcare Value, an educational offshoot of ThedaCare, which operates seven hospitals and thirty-five clinics in northern Wisconsin. They come because ThedaCare has transformed itself into one of the best health care systems in the country—it is the highest-quality, lowest-cost Accountable Care Organization in the United States and comes in consistently high in other rankings—by applying the lean management principles developed by Toyota and others.

That journey started in 2003, when John Toussaint, M.D., became CEO and continues under his successor, Dr. Dean Gruner. ThedaCare was among the first to apply the principles and practice of lean manufacturing and the Toyota Production System (which are well known and need no exposition here) to health care, along with Virginia Mason and Seattle Children's hospitals in Seattle. Unlike patients, cars on assembly lines *are not* unique, do not talk, and do not have families, but the core tenets of TPS apply in this most complex of service environments: Standardize what you can, eliminate waste and defects, improve continuously, and manage the whole system, not just its parts.

ThedaCare's transformation has been driven by the simultaneous search for efficiency and elegance—that is, steadily improving operations to reduce waste and error, while putting the customer at the center of service design.

ThedaCare gave the customer a name and a face—she is Lori—and prefers not to call her a patient, on the grounds that "patient" implies that the customer is a passive recipient of care, not an active partner in the system.

Arraying hospital services so the patient is actually at the center has led to significant changes in service design at ThedaCare. In ThedaCare's Collaborative Care model, patients are served by a team that includes a doctor, nurse, pharmacist, and case manager, plus needed specialists or therapists. The entire team gathers at least once a day at the patient's bedside. Consequently, information is passed from one to another—and to Lori or the family—directly. Questions are answered—on the spot.

The hospital also changed the layout of patient rooms to put more supplies and electronic record-keeping systems for real-time documentation near the patient's bedside. Documentation time has been halved; time nurses spend with patients has increased 70 percent. A whiteboard in each room lists the names of all the care team members, describes the plan of care, and posts the estimated discharge date. Patient satisfaction has increased from 68 to 85 percent.

The search for ways to save staff and patient time is unending. In most hospitals, surgeons have their own, often idiosyncratic, ways to lay out tools in the operating room. Not at ThedaCare, where the setup is standard, based on careful time-and-motion studies that showed how to reduce unnecessary steps and get patients out of surgery faster. Some surgeons balked; they work elsewhere now.

The image of the heroic surgeon is as deeply embedded in health care lore as that of the kindly pediatrician, but ThedaCare looks for something else: top-notch medical care delivered by a well-organized team that configures itself around patient needs and respects customers' time as much as it does providers'. "The point is to eliminate firefighting. You get firefighting because processes are broken or because you're asking people to do too many things," says Toussaint. "If you want to be a hero, go someplace else."

Three Ways to Design Service to Save Time for Both You and Your Customer

Service design offers the best way to search out, find, and eliminate occasions when you and your customers put forth heroic efforts.

Initiatives to fix these problems are inherently cross-functional, so you need an approach that links departments, especially those offstage and those onstage. Second, it is important to track both your workload and the customer's along the full length of the customer journey. If you are simply pushing work downstream or from one department to another—or offloading work from you to your customer—you have accomplished nothing. Here are three ways to look for improvements in efficiency and elegance simultaneously.

Eliminate touchpoints. The biggest gains in efficiency and elegance may come from service redesign that entirely cuts out complicated or annoying stages in the customer's journey. The worst part of air travel is rarely the flight itself: It is the airport. Surf Air has almost entirely eliminated it, as we saw in Chapter 1.

Not every company can redesign so radically, but almost any company can eliminate or streamline a touchpoint here or there. Other airlines have tried to shield at least their elite customers from airports by means of curtained-off check-in bays, special lounges, including some that cosset passengers until they board the plane from the lounge, and the like. Waiting in line to pay for merchandise is a classic example of a touchpoint from which neither buyer nor seller receives value in most circumstances; retailers ranging from the upscale Apple Store to discounter Nordstrom Rack have eliminated or alleviated it by giving salesclerks iPhones or other handheld devices so customers can be checked out on the spot or in shorter lines.

Enable parallel processing by reordering operations. The need to hurry up and wait—which frustrates both buyers and sellers—can sometimes be eliminated by doing things in a different order. ThedaCare's Physician Services Division runs primary care clinics that handle about 450,000 patient visits each year. Usually patients coming for an exam need a blood test or other lab work. ThedaCare rearranged the steps in a patient's journey to draw blood as soon as the patient was in a room and before the doctor arrived, with the aim of getting results back before the end of the visit.

Jenny Redman-Schell, chief operating officer for Physician Services, explains: "We want lab work turned around so that as the doctor is talking with the patient, they can discuss the lab results, what changes need to be made in terms of medication, dosage, specialists, all that stuff." That produces a better doctor-patient visit and increases the likelihood that patients will follow instructions; it also reduces waste for both clinic and patient on the back end, eliminating phone calls and missed connections when trying to reach a patient later with test results. Because ThedaCare owns its labs, it was able to do this without increasing patients' wait time—indeed, the net effect of clinical care service redesign has been to shorten the duration of a visit.

Modularize and aggregate. Unnecessary complexity wastes resources for service providers and customers alike. Consider the efficient elegance of the U.S. Postal Service's Flat Rate package shipping. Customers know how much they are spending so there's no sticker shock; more important, since packages are not weighed and the need for customers to fill out labels is eliminated, effort and time are reduced for both customers and postal employees.

The Fourth Principle: Service Design Must Deliver a Coherent Experience Across All Channels and Touchpoints

Wherever and however you choose to play, you must play well. A retailer that provides a fabulous in-store experience needs a website that is just as good. A hotel that coddles a customer during a stay needs to be equally solicitous if that customer leaves something behind in the room. An advertising agency whose digital and print teams do not synch with each other has failed. A company that prides itself on no-frills efficiency shouldn't force its customers to navigate a tortuous phone menu while a recorded voice assures them, "Your call is very important to us." Upmarket brands like American Express adopted this principle long ago, but it is applicable to all businesses. In a well-designed company, customers should never experience cognitive dissonance—yet it happens all the time.

Warby Parker's Progressive Lenses

A good example of a company that has become channel-agnostic is Warby Parker, the hot seller of prescription eyeglasses and sunglasses. Warby Parker, conceived by four students at the Wharton School at the University of Pennsylvania and born in 2010, achieved "unicorn" status—a valuation greater than $1 billion—in 2015. It began as an online seller of prescription glasses that pulled off a customer experience hat trick: a nerdy-hip fashionable brand that is a darling of urban millennials; a disruptive, low-price business model (at $95 a pair, Warby Parker glasses cost less than half as much as people pay elsewhere); and social purpose (for every pair sold, the company distributes a pair to someone in need through its Buy a Pair, Give a Pair program).

The founders' intent was to start and stay digital. Co-CEO Neil Blumenthal says: "We were trying to sell a brand that no one had heard of, over the Internet where no one had bought glasses, at a fraction of the price of what people are used to paying, so it naturally invited skepticism." Warby Parker fought doubt in every possible way: with necessary licenses, of course, but also with elegant design, easy user interfaces, free shipping and returns—and an offer to send five sample frames to customers to try on, at company expense.

Warby Parker might have stayed digital but for a fluke: It caught on so quickly that it ran out of inventory and had a waitlist of more than 20,000 customers for its Home Try-On program, so the founders started inviting nearby customers to stop by their apartment to try on glasses. When Warby Parker moved into a real office, some space was dedicated to a showroom. Customers could visit, try on glasses, and then place an order on the Web using an iMac in the showroom. "It was crazy the sheer volume of people that were coming to our office," Blumenthal recalls. "So we opened a pop-up shop. Then we bought an old yellow school bus, turned it into a mobile store and went to fifteen different cities." As of May 2016, Warby Parker operates 30 retail locations in 23 cities.

How does a person buy specs from Warby Parker? Let us count the ways. Say someone reads about the company in a magazine article. (There have been dozens.) Says co-CEO Dave Gilboa, "They immediately pull up our website on their phone, they browse a couple frames, and then when they're back at their desk at work they spend some more time on the site reading about us. Then they walk into the store and try on a few frames. They want to get their husband or wife's opinion so one of our retail advisors will take photos of them wearing the frames they're looking at, and generate an email for them. Then they go home and consult with people that they trust"—often including Facebook and Instagram friends—"and then they're ready to check out." That, says Gilboa, is typical. The vast majority of customers have multiple touchpoints.

The heart of Warby Parker, the founders came to realize, was the direct-to-consumer model, not online selling. With no middleman to pay, Warby Parker could provide high quality at half the price of rivals—and those economics work for bricks and clicks alike. "Our customers don't think of engaging with us through separate channels. They think of engaging with Warby Parker, not whether they do it on our website, on their phone with our mobile experience, or in retail," says Gilboa.

The happy by-product of all that channel hopping is extraordinary word of mouth: On average Warby Parker customers ask five other people how they look in the glasses they're considering. Also, because it's a technology-enabled brand, Warby Parker built strength and flexibility into its IT systems from the start. The company has found many clever—and brand-appropriate—ways to reinforce its image. When the company started opening retail stores, it added photo booths, encouraging people to take and send pictures of themselves as they tried on glasses. Though nearly all their customers can just pull out their smartphones, a photo booth reinforces the company's idea that glasses—and shopping for them—can be fun. (You wouldn't expect to see a photo booth in Brooks Brothers.)

The model carries serious obligations, too. One is after-sales service: Phone calls are answered within six seconds by a live person in New York or Nashville who has the authority to act. Says Blumenthal: "Too many companies think of customer service as a cost center that should be outsourced and minimized." Warby Parker designed customer service as a core part of its brand strategy, a way to build long-lasting relationships, and even as a way to acquire new customers.

What It Takes: Harmony, Integration, and End-to-End Excellence

To deliver a coherent experience across all channels and touchpoints, service design must meet three requirements:

* **Harmony:** Wherever you engage with customers—in a conference room, on the phone, via an app, through advertising and branding—they should sense they are in your hands. It should feel the same to them. It should feel like *you*.

* **Integration:** All parts of your organization should play well together for the customer's benefit, making it possible for customers to hopscotch from one channel to another and back again.

* **End-to-end excellence:** You must deliver consistently high-quality work from the beginning of the customer experience to the end and at every point in between.

In this chapter, we will look at why it is important to engage customers in this holistic way and how companies use service design to meet these three requirements. We will also examine two corollaries to this principle. One is that a strong part of the organization cannot make up for a weak link: Free checking won't get you off the hook if your branches are shabby and tellers are crabby. The second corollary is that the most carefully designed service can be enhanced or ruined by partners over whom you have little control. To take an obvious example, a customer's satisfaction with a flight is influenced by airport management, the FAA and TSA, ground transportation, and of course the weather—and the smart service designer does as much as possible to manage the company's ecosystem.

Why a Coherent Experience?

The case for consistency seems open-and-shut, but is worth examining because the details yield insights about how to do it right.

The first point of the case is that your customers engage with you in many places, sometimes in many places at once. They browse on the Web, then buy in a store. They visit bank branches, ATMs, websites, and apps; in the fourth quarter of 2015, 15 percent of all Bank of America deposits were made using mobile devices. They have questions about their credit card bill at 11 p.m. Friday. Students take courses in classrooms, labs, and online. Every consulting engagement is a multiplatform experience, combining hours spent face-to-face in windowless team rooms with email, WebEx meetings, and conference calls. You do not have Web customers and mobile customers and store customers. You have customers.

Second, platform-crossing customers tend to be especially valuable. According to technology and research firm International Data Corporation, "omnichannel consumers" have a 30 percent higher lifetime value than single-channel purchasers. In the last quarter of 2014, Merrill Lynch brought in $1.3 billion in new assets to manage thanks to cross-platform relationships within Bank of America, which owns Merrill. And that is a drop in the bucket: Bank of America estimates that its customers have $18 trillion in assets with other financial institutions. At SunTrust bank, typical customers use the mobile app ten or twenty times more than they visit a branch.

Third, you get dinged when you fail. Platform-hopping increases the number of potential *Ow* moments in your relationship: You can aggravate customers on each platform, and also during the handoffs from one to another. (Just try exchanging a gift by mail to Blooming-dale's that was purchased in a store.) You can also learn things from different platforms you could never have picked up from just one. We know of one health insurance company that studied telephone transcripts from its call center—and used them to improve the clar-ity of its written communications.

Fourth, consistency is valuable across time as well as across space, because customers change during their journey with you. Consider a commercial bank serving a family business. When the business is young, the bank might provide little more than a checking account. As it grows, it will need more: merchant services like payment pro-cessing for credit cards; financial, investment, retirement, or eco-nomic advisory or planning services; investment banking, securities brokerage, dealing, and underwriting services; treasury services like payments and receipts management; international banking services; and more.

The family's private banking needs will grow, too, including wealth management and fiduciary, trust, and estate management services. The bank needs to coordinate those; more important, the family and management need to know they are coordinated. When the founder/CEO, who started out dealing with a platform officer at a branch, walks onto the executive offices on the thirty-second floor of headquarters, the receptionist had better offer to take her coat.

Consistent, coherent service depends on having a unified view *of* the customer and presenting a single face *to* the customer. A unified view means fully understanding how customers interact with you at all points and how they would interact if you'd let them. The second, the unified face to the customer, involves identifying and removing internal obstacles to effective collaboration across departments and business units.

Changing from one channel to another should be easy for cus-tomers, like throwing a switch on a model railroad and sending the train down another track. Time was (and not long ago) it was all but impossible. Before digitization, customer records were in someone's file or ledger, difficult to share with a colleague down the hall, let alone in another division. It took decades before banks' computer systems were integrated enough to allow them to see if a checking account customer also had a mortgage. The problem is still thorny: Everyone who has ever phoned a credit card company quickly tires of reciting his or her account number several times during the same call.

Solving the *information* problem does not mean you have solved the *behavior* problem: If divisions of a company spitball each other, customers get hit. Hence cross-platform excellence is more than optimizing each channel and the links among them; it starts with experience, and works back to channels. Similarly, customers should not feel a difference when they are passed from sales to service.

The goal is for channels and departments to be something customers do not need to think about. That does not mean *you* can afford to not think about them—on the contrary, coherence demands your closest attention. But channels are a means to the end, and when you achieve coherence, customers will recall the experience, not how they get there. This is beyond the omnichannel world; call it the nonchannel world. It is one where both companies and customers put customer experience first, with the choice of channel being completely irrelevant.

Letting the Customer Drive

Companies used to have much greater ability to march their customers through a process they devised. Like the organizers of guided tours ("if it is Tuesday, this must be Belgium . . ."), companies moved customers through the marketing funnel, into the actual delivery of service, and then into an aftermarket of post-sales service and a new selling cycle, with some confidence that they were in control.

The marketing funnel (the origins of which date back to 1898 and a Philadelphia adman named E. St. Elmo Lewis) showed companies how to cajole prospects from awareness to consideration to purchase; it is schematic, but it resembled reality well enough to be useful. A company might advertise in national media about the beauty and benefits of its offering to create awareness of its product; then in local outlets, emphasizing price and availability, to bring interested customers closer to a purchase; then it would seal the deal when the customer came by. Word of mouth was important—everyone knew that—but it was mostly friends telling friends, and happened mostly out of sellers' reach.

Nowadays a classic marketing funnel can trip you up as much as it can help you out. Customers are more in control. You put your ad on TV—they DVR around it; they google you, go to your website, check you out on Glassdoor or Pinterest. You may offer an introductory price; they pull out their phones to comparison shop while your commercial is still running.

These changes affect advertising agencies directly, says Karen Kaplan, CEO of Boston-based Hill Holliday. "Advertising or communications used to be about things that people see—on television, on a billboard, in a magazine," she says. "Now you have to design not just things to see but ways for people to be able to act on what they see. The ad itself has to be valuable, or people will choose not to engage with it—something they had little choice about before, other than getting up to grab a snack or a beer at a commercial break." In other words, marketing that used to play only at the top of the funnel—generating awareness—must now act everywhere else, too, down to the "buy" button. In the business-to-business world, Forrester Research found, potential customers or clients engage with three or more pieces of content about a vendor for every one they see from the vendor itself.

It can therefore be as important to develop influencers as it is to attract customers. Both buyers and influencers go to events, talk to salespeople, consult with peers, read bios on LinkedIn, and, all in all, design an idiosyncratic journey that doesn't look anything like a funnel. Instead, with its twists and turns and multiplicity of paths to a purchase, it appears to be the handiwork of a demented designer of brass instruments. These changes affect every aspect of service design and value creation, not just marketing. Customers have the ability, desire, and incentive to be more active participants in creating their experience. For an advertiser, this means making it easy and attractive to move from desire to delivery. For other service providers, it is about rethinking touchpoints: Do they serve the customer's ability to have the experience he wants?

How to Make Harmony Happen

The principle of harmony includes two elements: harmony among the various touchpoints of a customer's journey and harmony among the different brands or services a company offers. In the first instance, harmony matters because customers interact with you in more than one place, as we have discussed. Harmonization across touchpoints helped TD Bank Group, the second-largest bank in Canada and one of the ten largest banks in the United States, roll out an aggressive invasion of the States under then CEO Ed Clark, who retired in 2014. The expansion was fueled by acquisitions, but its success was enabled by relentless focus on customer service, notably in changing branch hours to be more convenient. That brought people inside—past the ATM—where they could interact with staff. (This was a strategy that Clark first employed as CEO of Canada Trust, which was purchased by TD in 2000; he became CEO of TD in 2002.)

Clark's overall goal was to have the customer walk away saying, "Wow, that was a different experience!" he told CBC News in 2014. One of his tools was a TD Bank Checking Experience Index, a detailed survey of retail customers, which included deep dives for each of four cities and another to understand the experience of Hispanic customers. Remarkably, the bank made the results fully public.

Harmony among different parts of a brand is important, too, but different, because there is segmentation of services that goes with price. Why else would someone pay $95 for an American Express green card, $195 a year for gold, or $450 for platinum? At Hyatt's Andaz hotels, designed to appeal to well-off, trendy customers, lobbies are often dim, the look is expensive and minimal, and guests are checked in by someone carrying an iPad; at the chain's luxurious Grand Hyatts, lobbies tend to be gilded and front desks are just that: handsome fixtures behind which stands someone ready to help; and at lower-cost, casual Hyatt Place hotels, the front desk is a kiosk in the middle of the lobby, with a display case that holds snacks and drinks.

Each sub-brand needs to be consistent across its own platforms— the Hyatt Place website harmonizes with its physical environment and appeals to road warriors; Andaz's site matches its look and appeals to prosperous people at play. But certain experiences need to be shared. What are these? Mostly accountability. Customers understand that Amex has designed fancy concierge services for platinum cardholders that are not available to the hoi polloi. But fraud protection and redress? These and similar services and features cannot vary.

The Challenge of Channel Integration

Getting integration right—which can be something as simple as transferring a bar tab to the table—is partly a question of backstage capabilities and information systems. The lack of information technology that can talk across departments and platforms is a problem that persists in many companies, but as legacy systems are replaced and as new companies supplant old ones, it is (all-too) slowly disappearing.

But even when technology is right, people and processes get in the way. "We use the term 'your back-of-house is showing,' when processes or systems fail," says Jon Campbell of Continuum. A classic example: sending many salespeople, each one representing a different P&L, to call on the same customer. The back of the house appears because, while you try to develop the single view and present the single face, you are also managing the economics of the relationship, trying to encourage customers to behave in the ways most profitable for you, and keeping score internally.

Scorekeeping becomes a battlefield because, first, it affects budgets and goals and bonuses and, second, because assigning profitability to one unit or another is not a simple matter of objective fact: "If I can control how costs and overhead are allocated, I can make profitability appear to be anything I want," a dean of Harvard Business School once said. Though customers care nothing about your bonus, it is no wonder that at companies like IBM internal disputes over who gets how much credit for sales to a cross-platform customer have long been a stumbling block to integration.

Cross-platform integration therefore depends on the gritty work of redesigning internal accounting so that you are not wasting your customer's time (see Chapter 6). Even more challenging, it means changing incentives so they link up to the customer's experience rather than individual departmental or service line budgets. That in turn depends on overcoming the zero-sum mindset that says that customer revenue is a pie to be divided rather than a field to be cultivated.

Most of what we know about cross-platform sales is that they are accretive, not cannibalistic; that is, the total value of a customer grows when he or she engages with you across multiple platforms. According to Marvin Ellison, CEO of JCPenney, an omnichannel customer shops two and a half times more often than one who shops in stores alone, and Ellison says Penney is late to the game. Nordstrom gets three to four times more money from multichannel customers than it does from those who engage just one way—and its low-price Rack stores have added one million new people to its customer rolls, with no evidence that they have siphoned sales from the flagship, full-price Nordstrom department stores.

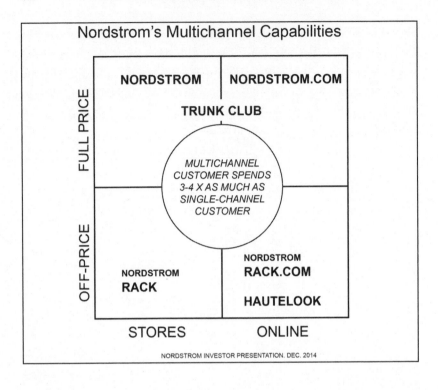

It is not all gravy, of course. Retailers, media companies, and others have endured terrible pain as customers have moved their business from the mall to the cloud. "Retail's Hottest Spring Trend? Store Closures," read a headline in a trade publication in February 2016. Newspapers and magazines have seen advertising revenue plunge as "print dollars become digital dimes" and as major advertisers use the Web to appeal directly to consumers without a media intermediary.

Service design can no more halt a megatrend in its tracks than King Canute could hold back the tide. But it can do three things. First, it can change the conversation from internal strife to customer experience, which you can control. Second, it can help you devise and manage a disengagement strategy—or, third, mount a defense. Paywalls at the *New York Times* and *Wall Street Journal* have given both newspapers value propositions to offer consumers (digital-only or print-digital combos), new kinds of stories (video, virtual reality) that have created new ways to engage, and new kinds of services (wine clubs, newsletters). The *Boston Globe* has shown how regional papers can do the same. Partly as a result they have weathered the media storm better than others, as have magazine publishers that did not abandon print subscription revenue in fool's-errand pursuit of digital eyeballs that could never be monetized.

End-to-End Excellence

We began this discussion with marketing; let's conclude it by looking at what happens after the sale. Continuing our focus on retail, let's consider the problem of returns. Every retailer gets them. Every retailer takes them. Most have very similar rules about what returns to accept. But two, in our experience, have turned returns into selling points: L.L.Bean and Nordstrom.

A return means something went wrong. For an online order, there might have been customer or company error, or disappointment that the item in the box wasn't as nice as the picture in the catalogue. A gift for a grandson, bought in a store and mailed across the country, might be the wrong size, or just plain wrong. A return is also complicated. The grandson might not want his grandmother to know. The customer might want to take something bought on the Web back to a store—or at least get an easy-to-use store credit. There may or may not be receipts. There are numerous permutations, but one is almost certain: The customer has had an *Ow* and wants help.

"People give us a lot of credit for our return policy," says Nordstrom's Ken Worzel, "but we do not have a return policy. We have a philosophy, to empower frontline employees." It begins by recognizing the emotional state of customers—some level of anxiety—and has a simple underpinning: If you know you're going to take the return, make it a delightful experience. If you know how the conversation is going to end, why make the customer sweat if she does not have the receipt? "We want a relationship," Worzel emphasizes.

Given that, what process would you design? Nordstrom makes online returns easy (and usually free) but prefers customers to return items to the store, even (or especially) items bought online. Why? Because it fosters a relationship between the store and the customer; if a customer is anxious or angry, says Worzel, "the salesperson will disarm them with niceness." Today, more than 60 percent of Nordstrom.com returns end up at Nordstrom stores; for the company's low-price Nordstrom Rack brands, more than 70 percent of returns go to stores.

L.L.Bean's approach is similar: Get the customer in front of a person. The website explains: "When you contact us by phone, chat or email, you'll be connected with a friendly representative right here in Maine. Why? Because to us, Maine is more than just an address—it's a part of who we are. It's tough winters, Yankee ingenuity and a unique character you just won't find elsewhere." ("Wayahs like ihon," the nice lady told Tom when he asked about a shirt—"Wears like iron.")

These are service design choices based on maximizing value in and across channels. Why do they work? First, because company insiders—the person on the phone or at the counter—can navigate company systems better than customers can. They will have saved the customer time, and probably are more efficient than customers would be acting on their own. Second, because staffers allow you to put a relationship right by actively helping a customer with a problem, rather than compounding the *Ow* by letting him flounder. Third, because these are opportunities to make a relationship grow with an exchange or with a new sale. Excellence at one end feeds forward, and begets excellence at the other.

For the *Globe*, a New World

For Mike Sheehan, CEO of the *Boston Globe*, the journey to designing success in an omnichannel world has come in parallel with an opportunity to redefine the paper's mission. "My mission for the *Globe* is to take it from a pillar of old Boston, which means it was a pillar of the community and reported on what was going on, to be a catalyst for the community," says Sheehan.

To serve readers in an omnichannel way, the *Globe* must manage, first, the product itself (what stories, what cadence), and second, how the news is delivered, online, on the newsstand, at your doorstep. The *Globe* has struggled with the latter (see Chapter 12) but has conquered the former. One aspect: recognizing that its community may be geographically dispersed but is still local at heart. The *Globe* expanded distribution of a locally printed paper from Southwest Florida to Florida's east coast in the winter of 2016.

The snowbird edition (the exact same product that's on sale in Boston, minus circulars for local advertisers) is printed in Fort Myers and shipped across the state and is now a profitable initiative. "In addition to turning a profit, it helps us retain subscribers," says Sheehan. "Instead of canceling and restarting—maybe—when you return to the area, your subscription follows you to Florida and then back again in the spring."

Serving snowbirds with a print product isn't about simply classifying readers. "It isn't as cliché or stereotypical as 'old people read print,'" he says. He describes many of their readers as "portfolio readers," who may read print at home, view the eReplica on their tablet, and check the news on the Web from their desktop throughout the day. To meet the needs of those readers, the *Globe* updates the paper's website more regularly than it used to.

"It is not just about recognizing that readers do not fit into neat categories," Sheehan says. "For readers, no two days are alike, so you have to take that into account and provide information in a way that is just easily accessible to people."

Viewing new channels as presenting an opportunity rather than representing a threat is part of the *Globe*'s secret for success. In addition to a paywall, the organization has its free site, Boston.com, which serves as an entry point for many eventual subscribers. Video is a big part of the new *Globe* experience, as are commerce sites, including a new real estate site that is advertiser supported. Says Sheehan, "Because we have the traffic we can own verticals."

And traffic they have. As of May 2016, the *Globe's* number of digital-only subscribers is behind those of only the *New York Times* and the *Washington Post.* "We have more digital subscribers than the entire Tribune organization," he says with a quiet pride. "It's because we started earlier with a hard paywall and we're constantly perfecting the offering, from the number of free views to the introductory offer. We continually come up with better digital products, which is all about creativity. We are adept at aggregating our content in certain areas and selling adjacent advertisements, sponsored content, and sponsorships."

The Ecosystem

Sophisticated service designers take an ecosystem-wide view of customer experience. That is why a company should do everything in its power to select and manage the partners—OEMs, distributors, agents—whose actions it depends on, and do its best to influence what it cannot control. There are four types of partners: those you rely on for *adjacencies*, those that provide *access* to your service, those you rely on to deliver *essentials* of your service, and those who inhabit the same *ecosystem* but do not necessarily work directly with you.

* **Adjacencies:** Department store Macy's has a partnership with zTailors, an on-call tailor that will go to a customer's home or office to make alterations. Like all good adjacencies, it provides something Macy's prefers not to, operates at a similar price point, and provides a compatible experience.

* **Access:** Dealers who register on Edmunds.com (see Chapter 8) get the chance to put their names and inventory in front of millions of active car shoppers. (And vice versa: For shoppers,

Edmunds becomes a yellow pages of dealerships.) It is important for access partners to hold each other to similar high standards, just as you would expect your physician to refer you only to a reputable specialist.

* **Essentials:** Hundreds of thousands of companies rely on partners for capabilities like shipping, insurance, and call center support. A company called Invaluable operates platforms that enable real-time online bidding for thousands of auction houses across the globe. This allows smaller auctioneers to compete with giants like Christie's and Sotheby's in ways they could never afford on their own—and gives aficionados the world over the chance to participate in auctions. (With this side of its service, Invaluable is providing access.) Often these are outsourcing partners; they save you from having to build noncore capabilities.

Sometimes, however, bringing these functions in-house makes sense. Restoration Hardware in-sourced delivery when management realized that the company it used was not brand appropriate and was preventing the company from offering end-to-end excellence. The company had completely redesigned its shopping experience, building 60,000-square-foot galleries to showcase its wares, offering in-store design services, investing in new IT infrastructure. But then, says Harvard Business School professor Len Schlesinger, an RH board member, "The final result was two scruffy guys who didn't care about what you bought dumping it at your house."

* **Ecosystem:** Visitors to Orlando might stop at Disney World, Sea World, Universal Studios, or Legoland. They will also use the airport or the highways, stay in a hotel, and eat. The various service providers coexist and co-create even if they do not interact—and the actions of one can help or harm all the others. From a vacationer's perspective, the overall experience is the trip. Consequently, ecosystem partners have an interest in finding ways to improve that experience together.

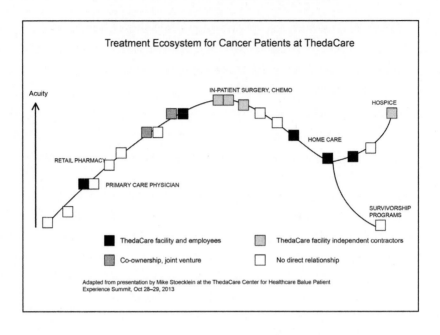

In all these cases, your partners' execution abilities are part of the service delivery you cannot control. You should do whatever you can to bring them up to your standard, or insulate yourself from them if you cannot. Consider the map of the journey of a cancer patient in a ThedaCare hospital. During the course of her care, Lori and her family will engage as many as two dozen different unconnected providers, only a few of which will be under the hospital's hierarchical control. Nurses and orderlies will generally be on staff. Some oncologists will not be on staff but will have hospital privileges—a different relationship. Pharmacists, counselors, clergy, physical and occupational therapists—even local gyms—may be part of the patient's care.

Designing service partnerships is important among and between all companies that serve a common customer: for example, airlines, airports, and resorts; online retailers and delivery services; physicians and pharmacies. A system-wide view of the customer journey is trebly valuable. First, it allows you to identify and close execution gaps that are not of your making but that affect your customers as much as foul-ups that are yours alone—in freight forwarding and customs handling, for example. Service designers pick suppliers, distributors, and other partners carefully; co-design handoffs; write service-level agreements that incorporate the customer experience specifications.

They also identify ways in which they and their commercial partners and rivals can win together—the second benefit of an ecosystem-wide view. It creates opportunities for you and your partners to increase the total value of what you do for customers. For cities like Orlando and Las Vegas, effective chorography across industries and firms can be the difference between winning business and losing it.

Third, opportunistically, this is a great way to look up and down the value chain for places where you can capture revenue other companies are getting now—or to outsource activities that you cannot do well or profitably. Sometimes, as we will see in Chapter 11, that chance comes to manufacturers who provide services for their product; but it can come to services that add other services. A familiar example: rent-a-car companies that make extra money by selling insurance, gasoline, navigation systems, and the like. These opportunities can be subtle. Working with Holiday Inn, Continuum created a plan to redesign both the look and services of the lobby to encourage business travelers to spend more time (and money) there—buying food or drink while talking or working on laptops—after they noticed how many people were bringing in pizza or asking the front desk to direct them to nearby fast-casual restaurants like Panera.

....

CHAPTER 8

The Fifth Principle: You're Never Done

ITERATE, CREATE, ANTICIPATE, AND INNOVATE— AND REPEAT ALL STEPS AS NEEDED

W alk into any Victoria's Secret store and you can be sure of one thing, says Les Wexner, the seventy-nine-year-old genius who leads L Brands: "In ten years that store will be worn out and whatever design intention we had will be obsolete. As sure as hell this location might be at risk, the design's going to be wrong, and probably the fixturing was designed to match an assortment which we know is going to be wrong."

Speaking to his annual investor meeting in 2015, Wexner went on: "If you walk down a mall and you say, here's a store design and a mix that hasn't changed in a decade, it is probably dead on its ass." Wexner knows of what he speaks: His L Brands has created more value for shareholders than any other retail store operator in this century.

It is no surprise that businesses need to renew themselves continuously, which is why it is startling that many companies in the services sector have no systematic way to think about innovation, whether in new offerings, new processes, new forms of customer experience, or new business models. To be fair, goods-producing industries had a head start. The first business R&D facility, Thomas Edison's Menlo Park, New Jersey, laboratory, opened in 1876. In 2004—128 years later—IBM established the first-ever center to study services science. When it comes to research, experimentation, and science-based progress, services have a lot of catching up to do.

Even the *idea* of experimentation and innovation in services, let alone the development of a solid, effective process for doing so, is new to many service companies. They think of themselves as the downstream recipients and beneficiaries of manufacturers' R&D. The CEO of a multimillion-dollar truck dealership in Ohio, a family business more than a half-century old, told us: "You'd think innovation is for a manufacturer, but I've come to realize that it is important for our dealership, too—we can innovate things, we can plan better ideas of how to take care of our customers."

Consider the explosion of service innovation in this young century, ignited in large part by ever-faster, ever-cheaper, ever-more-flexible information technology. The financial services industry has been upended by innovation, from simple transactions (the number of bank tellers has fallen more than 13 percent since 2000, as consumers do more banking at ATMs and online) to the most complex (dangerously so, some argue) financial derivatives. While derivatives date back to pre-Roman times, innovation in these new "products" has contributed to a sevenfold growth in derivatives markets just in this century. Bank branches today look as different from their turn-of-the-century ancestors as, well, Victoria's Secret stores do.

Take communications: Today's fifty-year-olds entered a workplace where people communicated by mail, phone, and fax, and left messages on voicemail. Americans make three billion phone calls daily, but send five times as many text messages and nearly 200 billion emails. The volume of first-class mail has fallen nearly 40 percent from its 2001 peak; the stand-alone fax machine is now an integrated copier and scanner, as likely to send a document to an email address as to a phone number, and a growing number of companies,

JPMorgan Chase among them, have eliminated voicemail except for employees who deal directly with customers.

That said (and much more that could be), individual companies' capacity to design and invent new service offerings is underdeveloped. Services lag in part because of what the truck dealer said: People think of innovation chiefly in terms of new products and do not recognize the opportunity to innovate and improve along the length of the value chain—or, as we would say, at every touchpoint, onstage and off. L Brands, for example, typically earns a return greater than 16 percent from remodeling investments. In 2015 it was getting upwards of 25 percent from test redesigns of its Bath & Body Works stores—an astonishing payback from the core, in-store business that, Wexner told investors, is "way bigger than the Internet. . . . Gigantically bigger."

Wexner's emphasis on the physical design and redesign of stores points to three profound insights. First, in services, the distinction between "new" and "improved" may be misleading if not meaningless. Modifications in customer experience can create just as much value as new-to-the-world services do. (For the most part in this chapter we will use the term *innovation* to cover both.) Second, innovation in services is rarely about just one thing; at L Brands, it is about merchandise mix, location, fixtures and lighting, and channels—it is about experience, and experience touches all the senses all at once. Third, design is the key to unlocking service innovation and renewal. It is not necessary to import and translate methodologies developed for goods producers into a services environment. It may not even be desirable.

Edmunds.com: Empathy and Analytics

"We want to be the ones who continually come up with new ideas, new tools. It is a survival issue. If you do not do it, someone else will. You are never, ever done," says Avi Steinlauf, CEO of Edmunds.com. The company was founded in 1966 as a newsstand paperback quarterly that published information about used car values and prices. Today it is a multiplatform online information-services provider—the Bloomberg of the auto industry, Steinlauf says.

Edmunds reviews and values new and used cars, publishes research about quality and technology and industry trends, and connects shoppers with local dealers who have what they're looking for. The paperback is long gone. Now more than 19 million people visit the Edmunds site monthly, six out of ten Americans consult it at some point in their search for a car, and about four out of ten U.S. new-car franchised dealers pay to list on the site. A family business, Edmunds does not release financials but Steinlauf says revenue is "well into nine figures." More than a data and information provider—but emphatically still that—it has become a guide, mentor, and matchmaker.

Edmunds has grown by extending its role in the customer journey. When the business moved from paper to online, Edmunds added directories of dealerships, enabled communication between sellers and potential buyers, and offered a wealth of data that would have been impossible before, steadily moving closer to the moment when customers actually purchase a car and increasing the timeliness and frequency with which it engages with customers.

Now Edmunds is actively facilitating deals between buyers and sellers. With Price Promise, a program launched in 2013, customers can search the Edmunds site for a car they like, compare offers from various dealers, and lock in a price—eliminating hassle for everyone. "We are all about saving time," Steinlauf says. "To the extent that we can be the grease that lubricates the system and helps to reduce friction and reduce time, that benefits all the parties—shoppers and dealers."

Edmunds explicitly uses design thinking to turbocharge both improvement and new service development. With its emphasis on empathy, design thinking helps staffers build better products by understanding what their customers know and do not know.

The art of putting oneself in the other guy's shoes also matters because automobiles are freighted with emotions—for buyers, anticipation and perhaps anxiety, given that a car is the second-most-costly item that most people buy; for owners, pleasure and pride in the vehicle they drive. By definition Edmunds customers come because they want to do research, but that means different things for different shoppers. A guide for first-time new car buyers (introduced in 2011) is one way Edmunds responded to the realization that some customers want hand-holding as much as they do data; that same year, Edmunds Live, a multichannel advice line, came into being, too.

Empathy ignites employee engagement and a passion to improve products without waiting till managers ask. For innovation to become everyone's job, a company needs a culture of sharing, which Edmunds encourages through design, too. An enormous open staircase, a place for serendipitous encounters, connects the floors in Edmunds's Santa Monica, California, headquarters, home to most of its 600 employees. (The office was designed by Studios Architecture, whose projects include, among others, a "kid-friendly" headquarters for the Nickelodeon television network.) Every Friday the staff gathers in a large space alongside a sixty-foot-long coffee bar for an all-company update.

If empathy is the heart of Edmunds, analytics is its brain. "We have a customer-journey data center," says Chief Technology Officer Paddy Hannon, who oversees the analytics department. "There is movement that happens between wanting a car and buying one. We need to understand the different paths that people take or why they stop." With upwards of 19 million visitors and a quarter of a billion page views a month, there is a lot to analyze. "We can experiment. Do we move more cars if we give them a gas card or $500 off? When people browse a SUV, they fall off here—why?" Empathy inspired Edmunds to develop Price Promise; analytics taught the team that customers responded better when they saw three options rather than just one—or five.

Now Edmunds is adding another tool to its approach to innovation: open innovation events it calls "Hackomotives." These started off as internal competitions to solve problems or invent cool things that might end up coming to market. They were so successful that in 2014 the company took the next step—a Hackomotive open to outsiders, with a $20,000 prize for the best idea. The winning team got a payoff bigger than anyone expected. Edmunds liked their idea—an app called CarCode that helps dealers manage text messages from customers—so much that it bought the company that developed it. It was Edmunds's first-ever acquisition, and a ringing affirmation of the value of openness in service design.

Redesigning Renewal

Innovation value is created in three arenas: ideation—coming up with a goodly number of ideas of high quality; selection—the art and science of picking the best ideas; and execution—bringing the selected ideas into being and to the market. As we will see, in service design the lines between them blur, but it is useful to look at each by itself.

Because organizations tend to be inward-looking and bureaucratic, they drive innovation around what they think should matter, often based on a superficial understanding of the customer. "To be able to build value, you've got to understand the lives of your customers, whether it is B2B or B2C," says Andy Boynton, dean of Boston College's Carroll School of Management. To do this, you need to design a way to bring the customer into each innovation arena.

Ideation. Ideation is not the same as creativity; confusing the two is why brainstorming sessions, while fun, often lead nowhere. The service journey map, as described in detail in the Appendix, is a powerful tool to increase both the quantity and quality of ideation. The map is a reminder that valuable ideas can emerge at any touchpoint, anywhere along the value chain. Your map becomes a checklist: What can we do new or better at *this* stage of the journey? What new technologies could change what we are doing *there*? You add quality because it helps you to identify opportunities to sharpen or extend your value proposition. What new things can we do to create an *Ahhh*? How can we strengthen a critical customer interaction? Where do we make mistakes, force our customers to work too hard, or cause *Ow* moments?

In addition, the service journey map invites you to look outside the edges of the map as it exists. In other words, you can ask not just about the *Ahhh* and the *Ow* you know, but about what might be. A hotel chain approached Victor Ermoli, head of the service design faculty at the Savannah College of Art and Design, about redesigning its lobbies. "But where does the lobby begin?" Ermoli asks—a nonrhetorical question. "The CEO says, 'When you open the door.' The VP of service says, 'When the doorman greets you.' Someone else says, 'When the valet opens the door of the cab.' Or perhaps it begins a block away when I first see the sign?"

In the late 1990s, Amtrak asked the IDEO firm to design seats for its soon-to-be-launched high-speed Acela service. At the time the firm was known mostly for product design, but the assignment got them thinking. IDEO CEO Tim Brown recalls, "We realized—and we said to them—'Yes, we can design the seats, but what you're really selling is a journey.'" The IDEO team mapped out a nine-step journey from awareness to disembarkation, and designed it all.

Selection. Service design vastly improves idea selection, because design thinking starts with empathy—putting yourself in customers' shoes to understand their wants and needs, especially those they cannot articulate. "It is not the consumer's job to know what he wants," Steve Jobs famously said, but he also said, "You've got to start with the customer experience and work backwards to the technology." A decade's research by Strategy& has borne him out: Innovators that seek out unmet customer needs and act to be the first to address them outperform companies driven primarily by new technology or by following trends.

These "need seekers," according to the firm, "encourage openness to new ideas from customers, suppliers, competitors, and other industries, and they prioritize directly generated consumer/customer insights and enterprise-wide launch capabilities." You do not have to go whole-hog into open innovation to get many of these benefits. In the middle market, companies that constrict the flow of new ideas by limiting innovation to a close-in, dedicated team do significantly less well than companies that encourage broad in-house participation and input from marketing and customers.

Execution. Commercializing innovative ideas is different in service companies. This is because service innovation can occur anywhere on the value chain; new tools for salespeople and new portals on the World Wide Web can be as powerful as new service offerings. When it comes to managing innovation projects, familiar stage-gate processes may not be relevant. Financial tests that work well in manufacturing (ROI, real-options value, etc.) may be meaningless when there is little capital cost (no factory needs to be retooled) and next to no production cost beyond writing, testing, and uploading new code, though of course some service redesign is highly capital intensive.

Often service design improvements can be as simple as changing the prompts on an automated phone system. That is the good news; the bad news is that every functional head and every business unit might be rushing to innovate, making a coherent approach both more important and more elusive.

All In, All at Once

Ideation, selection, and execution bleed into one another via service design. A great example is Bank of America's clever "Keep the Change" product—a program that helps customers save by automatically rounding purchases up to the nearest dollar and depositing the difference in a savings account. Developed with help from design firm IDEO, Keep the Change has produced more than 12 million new customers and generated more than $3.1 billion in deposits—savings for customers, assets for the bank.

Whenever possible, service changes should be tested "in the wild"—with real customers making real choices to spend real money. Fifteen years ago Bank of America began a formal program of experimentation, using selected branches in Atlanta as its "laboratory." (Best Buy did something similar with a group of stores.) Harvard Business School professor Stefan Thomke went to study the bank and explained the rationale for the living lab: "Because a service is intangible, often existing only in the moment of its delivery to a customer, it is difficult to isolate in a traditional laboratory. And since many services are tailored to individual buyers at the point of purchase, they cannot be tested through large samples. As a result, experiments with new services are most useful when they are conducted live—with real customers engaged in real transactions."

Using service design tools, high-powered analytics, and in-the-wild techniques, advanced companies are fundamentally altering the innovation process. This happens when the three stages of innovation—ideation, selection, and execution—conflate. "Services are not milled in prototype. The thing that is unique to service design is that a prototype is performative—you enact it. You do not sit around and look at it," says Toby Bottorf of Continuum. Instead, service design starts with a simultaneous process of visioning and observing—watching customers while imagining what could be—then moves directly to live experimentation. The result is innovation with a much higher metabolic rate.

To measure the heartbeat of service design innovation, consider Intuit, the provider of Quicken, TurboTax, Mint, and other financial software and services. About a decade ago, its growth slowing, Intuit turned to design thinking as a way to engage the whole company in innovation, not just a handful of researchers, and to increase its ability to execute new ideas. Intuit's "Design for Delight" process (inevitably, now D4D) begins with field research to uncover customer pain points, then uses rapid prototyping and experimentation to shorten the cycle between ideation and execution. Roger Martin, the design-thinking evangelist who is former dean of the Rotman School at the University of Toronto (and an adviser to Intuit), reports that the TurboTax team went from running just one live-customer experiment in 2006 to 600 in 2010. During the 2012 income tax season alone, Intuit ran experiments in weekly batches, with each week's results feeding into the next week's experiments, for a total of 140 different tests.

One reason rapid-fire innovation works is that research in the wild offers a high degree of validation compared with small pilot projects or studies done only in controlled conditions; this makes the decision to scale easier. Says Boston College's Andy Boynton: "You want to avoid big bets. You're better off testing a lot of things and seeing what works for real rather than making a few big bets hoping they're going to work." According to Intuit CEO Brad Smith, many of his company's experiments are aimed at finding ways to save customers time, for example by copying data that does not often change (address, number of dependents, etc.) from one year's return to the next, or by highlighting what's new this year, which saves time when the tax-preparing spouse shows the ready-to-file return to the other.

How well do the lessons of IT service design apply to other industries? Software is unique, or nearly unique, in that almost all its costs occur up front—in conceiving, writing, and testing the stuff; its "manufacturing" and distribution costs are near zero. Yet four design-led principles apply across the spectrum of services:

* Assume you are never done. We love the software industry convention of numbering successive releases (1.0, 1.1, 1.2 . . . 2.0 . . .) because of its implicit promise that features and functions will be added, and mistakes corrected. As Continuum's Bottorf says, "Always be in beta."

* Set and keep a cadence. Establishing a rhythm of new and improved offerings is especially valuable internally, since nothing concentrates the mind like deliverables and a deadline. Doing

so ensures that you have a platform, process, culture, and triggers for innovation. Even better, punctuate the rhythm with special events—hackathons, customer events and trade shows, limited-time offerings, and the like.

* Work in the wild. Sure, there may be reasons to keep things confidential or to fail in private before you fail in public (however, fewer of them than your lawyers think), but remember: Service is a handshake and you cannot shake hands with the air.

* Build renewal into your business model—measure both the value customers receive from it and the contributions they make to it. That way you create a virtuous circle: The experience of customers propels forward your work to improve the experience of customers—customer feedback becomes customer feed-forward—and you are measuring both the input and the output.

Consider how these tenets have been applied in the fast-food industry—about as far away from software as you can get. These restaurants need to balance two conflicting imperatives: familiarity (for when you have a Big Mac attack) and novelty (to refresh an aging brand; stimulate a jaded appetite; attract newcomers). Dave Thomas, the late founder of Wendy's, described how, instead of paying a research firm to test-market a taco salad, the company simply bought three ladles and three weeks' worth of taco chips and set up a station to let customers tell headquarters if they liked it. (Customers did.)

These days, "limited-time offers" are living labs for the industry. Wendy's has used them to test the upper limits of pricing (with burgers on a pretzel bun designed to appeal to devotees of fast-casual restaurants) and the lower limits (igniting a price war with a "4 for $4" promotion). Noodles & Company, the Broomfield, Colorado–based chain, carefully plans and sequences new menu offerings in six-month cycles: one round in development, another in test, and a third coming to market. "We do not want to be too far out in front of trends. Instead, we want to be on trend," executive chef Nick Graff told Gretchen Goffe for the National Center for the Middle Market.

Innovation plays different roles depending on where an industry—or a company or an offering—finds itself on the service equivalent of the product life cycle. This is the theory that products (and industries) pass through four stages—market development, growth, maturity, and decline—each of which creates different opportunities and imposes new demands. In mature industries like fast food, companies are not breaking new ground but coaxing new crops out of oft-tilled fields. Translating from products to services, paraphrasing Theodore Levitt, companies in the maturity stage should innovate:

* To promote more *frequent* purchase of the service among current users

* To develop more *varied* purchases among current users

* To create *new purchasers* by expanding the market

* To find *new uses* for the basic service

But notice this: The same goals apply in the growth and market development stages of the life cycle—only in reverse order. In young industries, focus your innovation agenda on finding new uses and new customers.

A Platform for Design-Led Innovation

For service companies, innovation needs to become a firm-wide, design-based capability—a platform. That is true for three reasons. First, as we have discussed, it can and should happen at any and every point on the value chain; making innovation the responsibility of a handful of people in a lab is a mistake. You want an end-to-end view of the service journey; the ability to map what's new (or what could become new) at every point on the map; and the ability, then, to see and measure how changes at one touchpoint can create problems or opportunities upstream or down. According to Matthew May, consultant and author of *The Laws of Subtraction*, "The mindset around innovation being tied to a physical product can actually get in the way of what you're trying to achieve, which is everyone coming into work every day looking for a way to do things better— how do I do it better than I did yesterday."

Second, rolling out a service innovation often requires behavior change by the staff. That is sometimes true of new products, particularly knowledge-intensive ones: Sales reps and doctors need to be trained in how to use a new medical device, for example; electronics salespeople must learn to demonstrate a new gadget. But rarely does their behavior have to change. More often than not, new services require much more internal change and training, particularly on the front line; indeed, the innovation may *be* behavior change.

For example, California medical group Kaiser Permanente cut nursing staff shift change time from 40 minutes to 12 by involving nurses and practitioners in a design thinking exercise and live tests of prototypes. Having extensively studied service innovation, two European scholars concluded, "Those who are responsible for sales and service delivery [who may be highly trained accounting professionals, minimum-wage restaurant workers, or everything in between] usually play an essential role in embodying a new service, in differentiating it from competitive services, and in helping clients to make the switching decision."

Third, while some changes in service design can be protected by patent, copyright, or trademark, many cannot. In other words, training and cultural change are an essential part of raising barriers to keep copycats out. The emphasis on the in-store experience at L Brands, for example, requires store employees who actively *sell* to customers—chatting them up, making suggestions—and that in turn has motivated the company to raise their pay, increase training, change incentives, and decrease its use of part-timers.

With a platform for innovation, you can use rapid prototyping to create high-fidelity front-end experiences for customers without big back-end investments. You can test to see what works and does not work, including testing changes in information flow and logistics; and you can lay out the systems and rewards you need to make the human side of innovation work. And, to a remarkable extent, you can do all that on an experimental basis, without committing the full resources of your company until you are confident of the outcome.

PART III

Service Design in Action

CHAPTER 9

Service Design Archetypes

Every industry has at least one important player that competes on the basis of price. Walmart in retail, Spirit in air transportation—these companies built a whole business model and service design to maintain low costs and deliver low prices. Similarly, just about every industry has a trendsetter, a company with a gift for finding the next big thing and an operating model built to exploit that gift. Most industries have luxury players. And there are somewhat old-fashioned, middle-of-the-road companies—not trendy, not cheap, just solid.

We call these different approaches "service design archetypes." They are ways of going to market that share common characteristics regardless of industry. We count nine of them—nine generic ways to play the game that embody different value propositions and suggest different approaches to SD^2: the Aggregator, the Bargain, the Classic, the Old Shoe, the Safe Choice, the Solution, the Specialist, the Trendsetter, and the Utility. Each of them is present in most industries. (An exception: the Utility, which is generally but not always a highly regulated business.) Each can be highly successful. And they are as different as chalk and cheese. The critical, differentiating customer interactions for passengers on Singapore Airlines (a Classic) are not the same as those for Ryanair (a Bargain). Macy's (a Safe Choice) shouldn't try to out-Amazon Amazon (an Aggregator).

Service design archetypes can be valuable in two ways. First, they can help you evaluate the choices you have about what offerings to make, what expectations to set, and what experiences you wish customers to have—and what offerings, expectations, and experiences are just "not you." Understanding archetypes will help you see how to embody your strategy at every point of interaction with customers, and backstage, in a coherent way. "We're a Specialist," you might say. "How do we make sure we're the best in our specialty? How do we avoid getting distracted? How do we help customers who need services we do not provide—and make sure they come back when they want something in our field?" The essence of strategy is not to beat the other guy. It is to become the best possible you, so that you win where you want to.

The second use of archetypes is to provide fresh sources of inspiration. Many of the most valuable insights in SD^2 come not from your direct competitors, but from companies of your type in entirely different industries. The Genius Bar at the Apple Store was modeled on the concierge desk at the Four Seasons hotel chain. Surf Air offers a fly-all-you-want subscription for air transportation inspired in part by Netflix's watch-all-you-want model for video rentals. Mark Holthoff, senior manager of community for Edmunds, told us: "I do not look at my competitors as the benchmark. My big product is consumer-generated content. I look at Yelp, Trip Advisor, Amazon, and try to apply those things to the automotive experience." In the discussion below, we have offered names of companies that represent each of the archetypes; you can add your own examples. Studying their service design choices can trigger ideas—quite possibly, ideas that no one else in your industry has tried.

Archetypes are not straitjackets. Very few companies will fit an archetype precisely. Most are mongrels. Do not use these as a pattern by which you must cut your cloth. But use them.

* **Recognize** that one of these is the essence of your value proposition.

* **Focus** there. Make sure you express that essence at every touchpoint and whenever you set expectations for customers.

* **Complement** that essence where you can; pare away anything that conflicts with or contradicts it.

* **Discuss** this identity across the executive team; make sure it is shared and understood by everyone who has a budget to propose and manage; school frontline employees in what it means for how they interact with customers. An organization aligned to an archetype makes better decisions at all levels.

* **And** have fun with it.

* * *

The Aggregator

* We're the place to go for all your needs.
* We've got everything under one roof.
* If we haven't got it, it does not exist.
* "We're the Amazon of ____."

"One Stop Shop . . . Have it all done in one place. Save your time—Save your money." So read a 1930 ad taken out by the John Bracelen Company, an auto mechanic in Lincoln, Nebraska. It is one of the first recorded uses of the phrase "one-stop shop," but far from the last example of the service design archetype we call the Aggregator. As the name implies, Aggregators attract customers by

bringing a vast array of products or services together. "Under one roof" may be
a dated phrase: better to say that aggregators pull many suppliers together to one
common experience, since the Aggregator
is a service design particularly suited to e-
commerce. Indeed, the Internet spawned
aggregators almost from the start, ranging
(in the automobile industry alone) from
an Indiana company that had a comprehensive catalogue of hubcaps to a Japanese
website that hosted online auctions for
used car sellers throughout the archipel-
ago, to, of course, Edmunds in the United
States.

| Alibaba |
| Amazon |
| Axial |
| Bloomberg |
| Craigslist |
| eBay |
| Edmunds |
| Farmers' markets |
| Invaluable |
| iTunes |
| Kayak |
| McKesson |
| New York Stock Exchange |
| Open Table |
| The Range |
| Seamless |
| W. W. Grainger |

Aggregators create powerful competition for traditional sellers. Shopping
malls—operated by Aggregators like
Simon Property Group and General
Growth Properties—devastated shops that congregated on Main
Streets. Online, companies like Craigslist, Monster.com, and Edmunds have cut the heart out of newspapers' classified advertising.
Kayak, Expedia, and others have decimated the ranks of travel
agents. (The U.S. Bureau of Labor Statistics predicts a 12 percent
decline in the next decade.) Amazon thinned the ranks of small
booksellers and killed or weakened big chains. But Aggregators have
also opened markets for local and specialized sellers that would have
been out of reach without an Aggregator's platform. Used booksellers, for example, have thrived since Amazon gave them a national
market; thanks to eBay and Etsy, every collector and craft maker
can set up a shop; and China's Alibaba has enabled businesses everywhere to find suppliers and other partners.

HOW THE AGGREGATOR CREATES AND CAPTURES VALUE

"Save time—Save money." Those four words are the essence of the Aggregator's value proposition. Unlike a Solution provider, which carefully selects and assembles components into a complete package that may well be customized, Aggregators put items on the shelf—virtual or literally—and let customers choose and assemble what they want.

That is not to say Aggregators are passive vessels for others' goods and services. The "common experience" they provide includes assurances based on the Aggregator's brand; Aggregators also provide platforms, rules, and processes to make commerce efficient. Thus the New York Stock Exchange sets standards that companies must meet to be listed and rules that traders must obey. Amazon, eBay, and others post customer reviews and ratings so that the market is self-policing, which is good for sellers and buyers alike.

The sheer reach and range of an Aggregator's offerings is a source of value: Customers come like ants drawn to a picnic, confident they will find something they want. Suppliers come, because customers are there. The power to draw a crowd gives Aggregators tremendous purchasing power: Business history is replete with examples—from the original Sears, Roebuck catalogue to today's Amazon—of aggregators that have squeezed sellers' profit margins.

Size matters: In general, aggregators create value by assembling as comprehensive a set of offerings as possible. Notice how the arrow in Amazon's logo goes from A to Z. Ads for the Range, a British home furnishings retailer, have boasted, "If we do not sell it, you won't need it" (though surely the Range is neither the first nor the last company to use that slogan). But there are "specialist Aggregators"—a business model that can be hugely successful, oxymoron be damned. In these cases, the Aggregator adds value through comprehensive collection of a specific product—if you have feet, Zappos has shoes—or by bringing a unique audience together, like the dating site ChristianMingle. Other specialist Aggregators include McKesson, the world's largest pharmaceutical distributor, and Axial.net, an online capital market that connects 20,000 private-company CEOs with investors, lenders, and finance advisors.

SERVICE DESIGN AND THE AGGREGATOR

Successful Aggregators provide not just a place to gather but a set of shared services for both sellers and buyers. Some of these are onstage, some off. The user interface of eBay is a common onstage experience; so is the parking lot of a shopping mall. Backstage, Aggregators may bring in financial services such as PayPal and credit cards that provide convenience and protection, connections to intermediaries such as shippers and distributors, or real estate services and their digital equivalent, Web hosting. From the standpoint of service design, Aggregators must consider which of these matters, how much choice to offer, and how to provide and pay for them.

Navigation—the ability to search, browse, and compare—is a critical aspect of Aggregator service design. Tourists may enjoy getting lost in the Grand Bazaar, but shoppers want to find what they need. A busy, cluttered design may actually serve an Aggregator well, as long as it is easy to use: Contrast the cluttered Amazon home page with the spare elegance used by Warby Parker (a Trendsetter).

TRAPS AND PITFALLS

Aggregation isn't easy. It demands lean and powerful back-office capabilities. Aggregators combine the widest possible choice with the most efficient possible service—but there is an inherent tension between the two. A number of academic studies show that the more products (or product categories) an online retailer offers the harder it is for the customer to find what she wants and the more likely it is that something will go wrong.

Most Aggregators operate in "two-sided markets"—that is, they provide and capture value from both buyers and sellers. (Other examples of two-sided markets—which do not always involve

Aggregators—include newspapers and magazines, which sell to both readers and advertisers; banks, which take money from depositors and loan it to borrowers; and credit cards, which connect shoppers and merchants.) Aggregators provide an arena where the interests of buyers and sellers may conflict, and Aggregators need to decide if they serve sellers foremost or buyers. Most choose buyers. Edmunds, for example, puts the interest of the car buyer ahead of that of the dealer; Amazon is perfectly willing to let price wars erupt among companies whose products it offers.

Aggregators may be tempted to become Solutions. Some pull it off. W. W. Grainger, for example, is a full-service supplier of office and industrial equipment, whose catalogue includes everything from staplers to test instruments. Customers can shop at Grainger, the Aggregator, or they can outsource the management of their supply closet to Grainger, the Solution. But it is not an easy marriage— Aggregators maximize choice, Solutions make choices for you; Aggregators generally work to cut prices on individual products or services, Solutions generally work to maximize value on the purchase of a bundle of products or services.

You therefore need a tiebreaker. Says Jeff Bezos: "Whenever we're facing one of those too-hard problems, where we get into an infinity loop and cannot decide what to do, we try to convert it into a straightforward problem by saying, 'Well, what's better for the consumer?'" That is his tiebreaker. We imagine another choice might be possible, but hate to think what it might be.

The Bargain

* If price is your problem, we're the solution.

* We will not be undersold.

* Do not come here for anything fancy.

* "We're the Walmart of ____."

Every industry has bargain players—those that combine low prices with a resolute determination to be the lowest-cost producer. Price is the main reason they attract customers. They are often low on amenities and ambience, and careful with their own money, just as they are with their customers' money. Rivals might occasionally use lower prices or special deals to attract new customers. The Bargain offers (as the Walmart tagline says) everyday low prices.

Tax preparer H&R Block is a good example of a Bargain. You won't find its

Costco
Dollar General
H&R Block
IKEA
Minute clinics
Payless ShoeSource
Red Roof Inn
Ryanair
T.J.Maxx
T-Mobile
Trader Joe's Wine
Value City Furniture
Walmart

offices high in a big-city skyscraper or nestled among luxury merchants in a tony mall. You're more likely to find them in a storefront, in a strip mall, or online. H&R Block promises efficiency, accuracy, to go through your previous years' returns, and to get you through an audit. You can file your taxes without ever actually speaking to an accountant. You can even get your tax refund "in advance," through a preloaded money card.

Bargain services are usually mass-produced, offering little or no personalization. Choice may be limited: Costco offers everything from toilet paper to spices to tube socks in enormous quantities at great savings, but you won't find as many choices as you would at a giant supermarket, nor can you buy small quantities as you can from a corner grocer. You take what you get. You get what you pay for. And you do not pay much.

HOW THE BARGAIN CREATES AND CAPTURES VALUE

The Bargain creates value with low prices, and captures it with low costs. You cannot have the one without the other. That said, the Bargain cannot be *only* about low prices: It must offer enough quality and enough convenience to keep cost externalities manageable.

Oscar Wilde's definition of a cynic—someone who knows the price of everything and the value of nothing—should be hung as a warning in the boardroom of every Bargain.

Sometimes a new entrant in an industry can redefine low cost and create enormous value. Think of Walmart, which exploited two new technologies—the superhighway and the supercomputer—to bust apart the large-retailer model in which Sears and department stores had thrived for decades. It is estimated that, while the Walton family picked up some $150 billion in shareholder value from the success of Walmart, American consumers pocketed some $250 billion *a year* in the form of lower prices. Now, using the information superhighway, Amazon has done to Walmart what Walmart did to Sears.

Bare-bones lenders and insurers have similarly tried to commoditize all or part of the offerings of established competitors, just as storefront minute clinics have with basic medical care. In many cases, upstart Bargains create value by bringing new customers into an industry: Studies show that 58 percent of visits to minute clinics are "new utilization"—people seeking care for ailments they would have left untreated before.

SERVICE DESIGN AND THE BARGAIN

Successful Bargains set clear customer expectations and stick to them. An airline like Spirit makes no bones about being bare-bones: The fare pays for a seat and just a seat; everything else—even water and a paper boarding pass—costs extra. Bargains can create distinctive brands if they design expectations creatively. IKEA's combination of stylish furniture and do-it-yourself assembly ("you do a little, we do a little, and together we save a lot") works because customers know what to expect. Indeed, the right customer finds getting out the Allen wrench fun, to the consternation of IKEA's rivals, one of whom told us, "I don't know why their customers put up with having to do the work."

Complexity is the enemy of clear expectations; thus a Bargain generally has simplified pricing and offers relatively few bells and whistles. For example T-Mobile calls its cell phone deal a "Simple Choice Plan" and offers fewer options than Verizon (which is an example of a Classic service design archetype).

The same is true backstage. Complexity behind the scenes is not just a luxury but a danger, because it increases the possibility of error. Returns, rework, repairs—these are the bane of a low-cost model.

There are customers for whom those ancillary services are important, however much they distract from the lean service design that defines a Bargain. In those cases, the Bargain's best bet is to bring in a partner. IKEA customers who are klutzy or rushed can pay for delivery and assembly, but the service is provided by a third party. Note the contrast between IKEA's contracting out the service and Restoration Hardware's decision to bring delivery in-house (see Chapter 7).

Industry standards are a boon to the Bargain. The more standardized a service or product is, the greater the benefit from being the low-cost producer.

TRAPS AND PITFALLS

Being the Bargain is a powerful position, but it is not easy to maintain, because the very design and delivery elements that make a Bargain succeed can turn against it. The first trap it may lay for itself: rigidity. Many investments needed to keep costs low involve automation, industrialization, and scale—buying in bulk, creating assembly-line-like processes, and rolling them out to very large markets. By their nature, these reduce flexibility. Yet there is more than one way to be a Bargain: offering something à la carte that others provide only in a bundle (like a prepaid cell phone versus a subscription); selling direct to consumer when others go through middlemen (as Dell did with computers); giving customers DIY options (as IKEA does). All these are ways in which Bargains can design flexibility into their business model and avoid the rigidity trap.

A Bargain may mismanage innovation. It may skimp on investments in new service offerings and go stale. Almost by definition, Bargains do not exist at the bleeding edge of new science or technology—they are more likely to be followers who exploit innovations others make. Consequently they may underestimate or misread technological change. Yet, as we saw in Chapter 8, Bargains often need novelty to attract new customers and keep old ones engaged. It is often possible for a Bargain to use the constraints of its business model to stimulate innovation; for example, restaurant chain Applebee's regularly reconceives its menu to give customers new choices while keeping their check at a prescribed price point (for example, $20 for two entrees and an appetizer).

But the biggest danger for a Bargain is to think nothing matters except price. As Abraham Maslow said, in what is known as the Law of the Instrument, "It is tempting, if the only tool you have is a hammer, to treat everything as if it were a nail." (This comment is one of many often misattributed to Mark Twain, who was by then dead.) A low price does not exempt the Bargain from the need to provide table stakes and market segment essentials. And the most successful companies of this type add something distinctive: stylish Swedish furniture and tasty Swedish meatballs at IKEA; for H&R Block, a national footprint that allows customers to stay with the firm wherever they move; on Southwest Airlines, flight attendants who crack jokes.

*   *   *

The Classic

* We're top of the line. Not the hippest, probably not cutting-edge—just the best.

* We're not only excellent, we're reliably excellent.

* We're expensive. We're worth it.

* We're the Mercedes of _____.

Walk into Bobby Van's Steakhouse on West Fiftieth Street in Manhattan. To your right you see a staffed coat check; in front of you is the podium where the maître d'hotel greets you and checks you in. A bar stretches out behind the podium; dining tables are off to your left, spaced well apart. All the wood is rich and dark—walnut?—and from the high ceilings hang big chandeliers whose lights glow golden, not silver. There's a masculine feel to the place, though you notice that a fair number of the clientele are women. If you had come in blindfolded, and even if you had not been alerted by the aroma, you would have immediately known where you were once the blindfold was removed: a high-end steakhouse.

The best address in town
Brooks Brothers
Cravath, Swaine & Moore
Four Seasons Hotels
Mayo Clinic
McKinsey & Company
Mobile Mini
Ralph Lauren
Singapore Airlines
Smith & Wollensky
"21" Club
Verizon Wireless
Yale University

Every American city has something like it, standing alone or part of a chain—Ruth's Chris, Fleming's, Hyde Park, the Palm, Morton's, Smith & Wollensky, the Capital Grille. While each has its fine points of distinction they're all, actually, rather alike. And why not? Who would mess around with a classic?

The Classic mode of service design is, well, classic—even stereotypical. Blue-chip companies hire white-shoe law firms like Cravath, Swaine & Moore, which are run by partners who went to Yale, wear suits from Brooks Brothers, live on Manhattan's Upper East Side or in suburban Chappaqua, dine at "21," and stay at the Four Seasons.

HOW THE CLASSIC CREATES AND CAPTURES VALUE

A company that aspires to be Classic is both top-of-the-line and reliable. It is not exciting (for sex appeal, go to Specialists or Trendsetters) but it is prestigious and perhaps powerful, and it confers prestige and power to its customers. It is beyond reproach, and so is the customer who chooses it: "When E. F. Hutton talks, people listen," went the tagline of a celebrated series of 1970s–80s television commercials for the old-line brokerage house.

Above all, the Classic offers consistent excellence, whether in the form of a room service breakfast delivered under a silver dome or a tax audit the CFO and CEO can trust implicitly. We're the best, the Classic says: end of discussion. As Verizon has said in its advertising, "There's simply no comparison."

SERVICE DESIGN AND THE CLASSIC

Classics declare themselves in every aspect of design and at every touchpoint of service. Their brand is strong, consistent, unmuddied: The Ritz-Carlton hotel chain is owned by Marriott, but few outside the hotel industry know that. They are located in traditional, up-scale parts of town—on LaSalle Street, Wall Street, and Wilshire Boulevard, not in Wicker Park, Williamsburg, or Silver Lake. This is not to say Classics are stuffy, though they might be. Classics give the impression they have been around forever. Many have. But this is a club that admits newcomers if they dress the part: Ralph Lauren created a Classic brand from scratch, cleverly using the Polo logo to give it a WASPy aura.

What makes a Classic feel like *your* Classic is the attention each customer gets. That onstage personal touch requires, backstage, a superbly chosen and trained workforce (full-timers and long-timers), careful job design and adequate staffing, and meticulous record keeping: The staff at the Ritz-Carlton in San Francisco knows you want the *Wall Street Journal* in the morning because Ritz staff in Atlanta added it to your profile when you stayed there. Because personal service is part of the value proposition, Classics never require self-service from customers, though they may offer it. (European private banks have begun to wrestle with the fact that their younger customers sometimes prefer interacting with a website rather than with a banker.) Because any misstep at any touchpoint can destroy a Classic's aura, these companies work only with top suppliers and distributors.

TRAPS AND PITFALLS

Classics must not chase fads. There is no quinoa on the menu at Bobby Van's. They must navigate between the twin perils of trendiness and obsolescence, for Classics must also not fall behind the times. There is no quinoa on the menu at Bobby Van's *at this writing*. More subtly, Classics risk becoming stale. The fact that you cannot improve on a Classic does not mean a Classic can stop improving. A Classic by definition attracts picky customers. Classic status must continually be earned.

Classics must project the brand at all moments and protect it at all costs, because they attract and keep customers in part because of their reputation. Good governance is a customer-facing activity for Classics. They can survive ethical lapses, as McKinsey and others have, but not a pattern of them. (RIP, Arthur Andersen.)

It is dangerous for classics to pursue growth by going down-market or to seek greater profitability by cutting corners. Classics may be better off selectively entering adjacencies—selling more services to the same kind of client or customers—than seeking a broader audience. Cost savings should never dilute the richness of the customer experience. People who pay top dollar expect top service.

*   *   *

The Old Shoe

* You know us and we know you.

* Good place, good service, and a good price

* We're your local; you're our regular. Would you like your usual?

* "We're the Cheers of _____."

Globalization, schmobalization: When a dollar bill changes hands in the United States, chances are better than fifty-fifty that it will have traveled less than seven miles. More than two-thirds of money spent with a local business stays in the local economy in the form of wages, rent, and other items. Community banks, though their market share has dipped, account for a quarter of U.S. credit market debt and hold a whopping 95 percent of deposits. Two enormous industries—health care and education—are fundamentally local.

> Credit unions
>
> Family lawyer
>
> Local bookstore, toy store, diner, coffee shop, housewares store . . .
>
> North Country Public Radio
>
> Poconos
>
> Rotary clubs
>
> Wrigley Field, Fenway Park
>
> *but also . . .*
>
> Cracker Barrel
>
> The Ivy
>
> Shake Shack

There are few market positions more powerful than being a familiar, comfortable, hometown business—whose archetypal form is what we call the Old Shoe. This is the corporate equivalent of comfort food, an organization that actively creates and projects warmth and intimacy, cultivates a first-name relationship with customers, and designs the business and service around it. Old Shoes might not be tops in quality, but if the waitress calls you "Hon" and knows you take your coffee with milk, two sugars, you don't care if the brew itself is second-rate.

Most Old Shoes are unpretentious and modest, but not all. And while the Old Shoe is classically local, national companies have successfully exploited the Old Shoe archetype, usually by appealing to nostalgia. The Cracker Barrel restaurant chain decks itself up like a country store and sells nearly as much gimcrack as it does food; the very name of the Shake Shack burger chain evokes flattops and ponytails, belying the fact that it was founded by three-star restaurateur Danny Meyer in 2004. The CEO says Shake Shack's strategy is to be "the anti-chain chain." Though it is a product, not a service, Campbell's tomato soup is emphatically Old Shoe.

We have named a lot of eateries, but Old Shoes can be found in any field, from banking to barbering. Many are family businesses—and promote that fact as part of their Old Shoe bona fides.

HOW THE OLD SHOE CREATES AND CAPTURES VALUE

You do not study them in business school or see the CEO on the cover of *Fortune*, but Old Shoes are resilient, tough competitors, able to hold their own against larger and richer companies. They command intense loyalty. It is not *brand loyalty*, exactly, since the brand may not be known beyond the borders of a neighborhood: It is *experience loyalty*. The value an Old Shoe creates comes from the connection it forges with customers through familiarity, warmth, and force of habit. In this sense, it differs from the Safe Choice. The Safe Choice is a rational, considered, deliberate decision. The Old Shoe is a reflex.

Businesses like these anchor and strengthen local economies, whose benefits are steadfastly documented by the Institute for Local Self-Reliance. Old Shoes cannot afford to go up against national chains and brands in advertising, so they link arms with each other and local institutions like the NPR station, the gas company, the Coldwell Banker realty franchise: Each one's customer is the others' lead. American Express's annual "small business Saturday" promotion decks itself out with nostalgic images of Main Street shops, implying that the value created there is more important than the low price found out at the mall.

SERVICE DESIGN AND THE OLD SHOE

The Old Shoe is first and foremost a place where everybody knows your name. Much of the Old Shoe's value comes from personal relationships, so the customer-facing elements of service design—empathy, the experience itself, emotion, elegance (not fancy elegance, but no-nonsense elegance), and engagement—have to be right. They start with the owner, who needs to be a visible presence to customers and who needs similar first-name, informal relationships with the staff. Frontline employees must be chosen carefully, trained well, and—if possible—kept around a long time.

Style matters. The place should feel as familiar as its owner's face looks. The American South is peppered with investment banks—for example, Cassel Salpeter and SunTrust Robinson Humphrey—that win business in part because their down-home manner engenders trust that Wall Street bankers do not. "When my clients see a banker wearing cuff links, they turn off," one of them told us.

TRAPS AND PITFALLS

Every action has an equal and opposite reaction. The intense loyalty—love, actually—that an Old Shoe inspires can spark equally intense feelings of betrayal if things change or go wrong. Shake Shack deeply offended customers by replacing its signature crinkly french fries with hand-cut ones—superior in freshness and quality, but just not the same. (The chain eventually retreated—see Chapter 11.) In this sense, the Old Shoe and the Classic have a similar ambivalent stance toward change: You do not want the Naugahyde on the banquette to become torn, but you do not want to remodel the place, either. Renewal is especially tricky if it gets caught up in the dynamics of family businesses.

Old Shoes make a strategic mistake if they fall into winner-takes-all opposition to big national competitors. They lack the resources to counterattack, and a defense with no offense will eventually lose. The corner bookstore is not the opposite of Amazon—it is something different. By the same token, an Old Shoe is a risky acquisition. These companies often base their appeal on authenticity and local roots. Human capital is the asset that walks out the door at the end of the day, and if it does not come back, the customers might not, either.

It can be smart for Old Shoes to create partnerships with bigger companies, the way a general practitioner does with specialists. For many years Los Angeles–based East West Bank, founded in 1973 as a savings-and-loan for Chinese immigrants, maintained a relationship with Bank of America for clients who needed more sophisticated financial services than the bank could then offer. (It has since become a full-fledged commercial bank.)

*   *   *

The Safe Choice

* You cannot go wrong with us.

* We're solid.

* You won't be shocked and you won't be sorry. Bring your in-laws.

* "We're the CBS of ____."

Though you cannot please everyone all of the time, the Safe Choice comes close: The Safe Choice is a company for all of us some of the time. Safe Choices are frequently old brands, like traditional banks and department stores; but even technology companies can fit this mold if they design themselves to be, or if they are so stereotyped. In years past, "Nobody ever got fired for buying IBM" was a mantra of IT directors who valued reliability above all, who wanted solid technology plus the assurance that their provider would always be around. (IBM has since, in our estimation, migrated from Safe Choice to Solution.) Today Microsoft occupies a similar position in the world of software—often chosen by companies because everyone else uses it, too.

> Allstate Insurance
>
> Bonefish Grill
>
> Dillard's
>
> Disney
>
> Hilton
>
> L Brands
>
> *Chicago*
>
> M&T Bank
>
> Microsoft
>
> Prime-time network TV
>
> PwC

The Safe Choice is frequently a fallback; the default choice, because of its ability to do the job and the unlikelihood that it will offend or displease. "I'm sure the Hilton will be fine," you might say when recommending a hotel to a friend from out of town, "Bonefish Grill is always good," when going out to dinner with the family.

It is even possible for a Safe Choice to be racy: With its sexy catalogue and over-the-top, not quite R-rated fashion shows, Victoria's Secret at first glance seems like a Trendsetter, but it is not, really. The Columbus, Ohio–based chain—a division of Les Wexner's L Brands—is as middle-of-the-road as its midwestern home would suggest. For every chemise in the "Very Sexy" collection, there are cozy pajamas and nightshirts; it is just as easy to shop for a daughter going to college as it is for a blushing bride. Indeed, when Wexner acquired the brand from a founder who set out to design a shop where a man could buy slinky lingerie for the woman in his life, Wexner toned town the tarty-boudoir look of the Victoria's Secret shops to make them more appealing—that is, "safer"—for female shoppers.

HOW THE SAFE CHOICE CREATES AND CAPTURES VALUE
Companies of this sort operate in the broad middle of taste, price, and service. They create value in three ways: They offer value for money; they are predictable; they are uncontroversial. If your Safe Choice is a restaurant, the salmon is always good; if it is a store, you go there confident it has what you are looking for; if it is a brokerage, it will recommend an age-appropriate mix of stocks, bonds, and cash.

The Safe Choice is often a well-known or even a household name; with these companies, familiarity breeds contentment, not contempt. They tend to be financially conservative: M&T Bank, of Buffalo, New York, was one of the few banks that did not need to cut dividends during the 2008–10 financial crisis.

The Safe Choice shares some traits of the Classic; both appeal to customers by virtue of their solidity and neither aspires to avant-garde taste. The Classic, however, is a premium brand—a choice for people for who can afford, want, and are willing to pay for nothing but the best; the Safe Choice is unabashedly democratic. Many a Safe Choice customer will feel uncomfortable dealing with a Classic, just as some folks would rather own a Ford than a Mercedes. For other customers, the Safe Choice may be a treat—Bonefish Grill rather than Red Lobster.

To the word *solid*, then, add *fair* as another way in which Safe Choices deliver value. The Safe Choice charges a fair price; its people treat customers fairly and listen earnestly to complaints. They can be inflexible or rule-bound, but they will never cheat you.

SERVICE DESIGN AND THE SAFE CHOICE

Start with safety, obviously. For a place like Disney, what could be worse than an accident on a ride, an abducted child, or a preventable incident at one of its parks? In December 2015, all of Disney's theme parks started using metal detectors at the front gates (as did fellow Orlando resorts Universal Studios and Sea World); Disney also stopped the sale of toy guns and no longer allows them on the premises. And in June 2016, Disney found itself dealing with the fallout from the death of a two-year-old who had been drowned by an alligator at one of its hotels, amid numerous claims about inadequate warnings.

Beyond physical and financial safety, however, the Safe Choice displays reliability and quality that are a clear cut above what customers get from a Bargain or even an Old Shoe. It is better for a Safe Choice to do a few things reliably well than to try to offer a multiplicity of choices at the cost of consistency.

The Safe Choice needs a sure sense of its middlebrow, middle-class customer and expresses that understanding in every aspect of service design, from physical space (nothing fancy, nothing tacky) to employee behavior (always friendly, never pushy). Marketing and positioning are key elements of service design for a Safe Choice: There's an art to setting expectations not too high, not too low; to appearing interesting while not pushing boundaries; to creating brand loyalty despite being a fallback choice; and to persuading customers (particularly in professional services) that you deliver top-quality work even if you are not considered at the cutting edge of thought or practice in the field.

TRAPS AND PITFALLS

Ironically, in seeking a broad market the Safe Choice must navigate a narrow, sometimes treacherous path. Three hazards stand out. First—broadly—is the fact that the middle ground is no longer the safe ground it was. The middle class is shrinking or stressed in most Western economies. At the same time, middlebrow culture is under assault from a proliferation of consumer choices and social media influences; in a 500-channel world that offers something for every niche, broadcast television networks' share of the audience has been falling for two decades. The Safe Choice's traditional market is being chipped away by Specialists and Bargains, and by Trendsetters whose innovations become the norm.

Second, the urge to grow is especially tricky for Safe Choices. Michael Porter once wrote that this desire "has perhaps the most perverse effect on strategy"; he pointed out that executives too easily succumb to the temptation to pursue revenue while crossing the lines that demark a company's position. When a company's position is to be in the middle— with something for everyone—it is especially easy to ignore the distracting effect of going after small, new customer segments and to take the core for granted. Conversely, and third, Safe Choices may be so devoted to their core that they underinvest in renewal and become stale, viewing that almost as part of their value proposition.

Restaurant chain Bonefish Grill, part of Bloomin' Brands, saw same-store sales drop more than 5.4 percent in 2015, as the company hit a trifecta of problems stemming from service and strategy blunders. It complicated its menus, expanded too fast, and in its attempt to appeal to younger customers, apparently left more mature "regulars" feeling ignored, unwelcome, or alienated.

*   *   *

The Solution

* We put things together or orchestrate the work of others.

* When your needs are complex, when your problems have many moving parts, when you need something specially designed for you, come to us.

* We're not just a vendor; we're a partner.

* "We're the IBM of ____."

In 2007, UPS—United Parcel Service, as it was called when founded a hundred years earlier—changed its advertising tagline from "We run the tightest ship in the shipping business" to "What can Brown do for you?" That reflected, as the company said, "a shift in emphasis away from industrial efficiency to knowledge-based innovation," and a fundamental reorientation in strategy and service design, from Bargain to Solution. The company had developed enormous expertise in fleet management, pickup-and-delivery, and more, which it used to drive relentless operational efficiency. Its routing software (including a ban on drivers' making left turns) saves the company more than 20 million miles driven annually.

ADP

Cisco Systems

Deloitte

IBM

Lockheed Martin

Oracle

Professional employer organizations

Rackspace

Stitch Fix

UPS

Weber Shandwick

W. W. Grainger

Lean UPS could deliver packages as cheaply and reliably as the U.S. Postal Service—and deliver a profit to shareholders. But its business model meant that the company would grow with the economy, not faster. Looking to do better, UPS management realized that the capabilities used to run its businesses could be redesigned and redeployed to help customers run theirs. Brown could become not just a shipper (a cost to be squeezed) but a logistics service that manages the flow of its customers' goods (an ally to be strengthened).

Many a company claims to sell solutions, often to dress up a strategy of trying to bundle what it sells. But a bank, say, is not a solutions provider simply because it offers a discount to customers that use its treasury, credit, and wealth management services. A true Solution plays a role in *managing* a piece of its customer's business. Bob Stoffel, former senior vice president of supply chain, strategy, engineering, and sustainability, cited Zappos as a good example, pointing out how the online retailer built its entire logistics strategy around UPS's capabilities, even locating its fulfillment operation ten minutes away from UPS's Louisville, Kentucky, logistics center.

Most Solutions are B2B companies. They are common in technology services, logistics, certain HR functions, and generally among technical contractor/outsourcing/consulting firms that offer systems integration. Though they are primarily manufacturers, defense contractors like Lockheed Martin also fit this archetype. But Solutions exist in business-to-consumer fields as well. Stitch Fix, the women's online clothing company, is one (see Chapter 5), as are some home security companies like Vivint, which "gives" customers products like burglar alarms as part of a subscription to its home security services. Indeed, the UPS Store retail business—a franchise operation that took off after UPS bought Mail Boxes Etc. in 2001—will not only ship boxes but sell them, help you pack them, and track them: a solution to all your shipping needs.

HOW THE SOLUTION CREATES AND CAPTURES VALUE

Solutions providers compete with each other and also with a customer's option to buy à la carte, just as home repair can be a DIY project or a job for a contractor. To buy a Solution, the customer must believe that the whole is worth more than the sum of its parts, even though in a competitive-bidding process, the parts could be bought more cheaply. This is an example of transaction-cost economics, discovered by Ronald Coase in his famous 1937 paper, "The

Nature of the Firm," and elaborated by Nobel Prize winner Oliver Williamson.

The value the Solution provides includes 1) possessing expertise that would be costly for customers to acquire and that they do not need for their core business (why should a shoemaker know the finer points of logistics?), 2) keeping up with technical advances in those fields, 3) maintaining a bank of specialists and subcontractors, thus saving search time, 4) coordinating work on a project or ongoing basis, and 5) assuming responsibility for cleaning up the mishaps inevitable in any complex project or process.

SERVICE DESIGN AND THE SOLUTION

Broadly speaking, solutions providers seek deep, valuable relationships with relatively few customers. Their proof point—the *Ahhh* they want to elicit—is demonstrated effectiveness. Solutions try not to compete on price. Indeed, most Solutions do not set a price; they negotiate contracts, each one different. Efficiency is not a selling point; it is a way to make more profit from a deal. As Geoffrey Moore says, "Complex-systems types [which most solutions providers are] focus on creating dramatically differentiated offerings that they then make as cost-effective as they can. Volume-operations strategists [that is, companies, usually B2C, that seek a mass market] do the opposite: They focus on creating dramatically cost-effective offerings that they then make as differentiated as they can."

To manage these relationships, Solutions create multiple points of contact with customers and may "embed" employees who "walk the halls" of a client to put out fires and find opportunities before less connected rivals do. The multiplicity of contacts must be coordinated. If effectiveness is the *Ahhh*, confusion is the *Ow*, because coordination is what a Solution promises. For important customers (and every customer is important for a Solution) a powerful relationship manager needs to be in place—even at Stitch Fix, each customer has her own stylist (see Chapter 10). Trust and hardwired safeguards are critical to Solutions' service design, because they are often privy to deeply confidential customer information.

For good or for ill, every employee of a Solution embodies its brand. They have to be good; they have to understand their customers' entire value chain, not just the parts they sell to, and need to be deft collaborators. The same is true of the company as a whole, not just because it partners with customers but also because it operates in an ecosystem of "frenemies." A company that may bid against you for one project may hire you for another; an à la carte rival might be exactly the specialist you need to fill out an offering.

TRAPS AND PITFALLS

Like certain caterpillars, the line between selling solutions and selling discrete services or products is fuzzy and dangerous. Companies trying to "move up" to become solution sellers often stumble because service design needs complete reconfiguration at almost every touchpoint: There is no shopping cart on the website of a Solution. On the other hand, every Solution will sometimes sell only part of what it has to offer: For example, Deloitte consults for companies it does not audit, and vice versa. A Solution must therefore be both modular—to sell the pieces—and holistic—to create true synergies across lines of business. At the high end of these industries, the opportunity to "productize" service offerings is both an opportunity and a danger, for it carries the risk of destroying the magic, the "secret sauce" that makes a Solution special.

Those synergies must include the Solution's own costs. Many solution sellers, particularly in professional services, face a new "adversary"—the procurement department of a customer where sales used to be done executive-to-executive. Pricing is now much more at issue in solution selling, which in turn has forced these firms to be more rigorous about internal efficiency. The purchasers have a point: Much of the grunt work of professional services is now semi-automated and commoditized—for example, legal research that had been done by first-year associates in libraries.

Managing competition and collaboration across service lines is therefore crucial and tricky, especially for big companies where several divisions, each with a P&L and set of goals, serve the same client, as IBM's former CEO Sam Palmisano colorfully described in an interview with the *Harvard Business Review*. Ironically, sometimes the Solution needs to create a solution for itself.

*   *   *

The Specialist

* We're the rifle to others' shotguns. No one is better at what we do.

* When your needs are demanding, when you need the highest level of expertise, come to us.

* We price accordingly.

* "We're the Goldman Sachs of ____."

For decades the advertising industry was dominated by boutique companies, usually named for their founders—Leo Burnett, Young & Rubicam, Ogilvy & Mather, Wells Rich Greene. Starting about 1980, the industry steadily consolidated to the point where now just five holding companies—WPP, Omnicom, Publicis Groupe, Interpublic, and Dentsu—control more than 70 percent of the market. A conspicuous exception to the trend: GSW, a Columbus, Ohio–based agency founded in 1977 that specializes in advertising and communications for pharmaceutical and other health care compa-

> East West Bank
> Global Marine insurance
> Gloria Allred, Esq.
> GSW ad agency
> La Maison du Chocolat
> Manhattan Eye, Ear, and Throat Hospital
> Palo Alto Networks
> Surf Air
> USAA

nies. GSW is part of inVentiv Health, which derives about 60 percent of its revenue from clinical services for health care companies (such as managing trials for new drugs) and the balance from commercialization services—advertising, public relations, patient education, etc. When a pharmaceutical or medical device company issues a request for a proposal for an advertising agency, little GSW is almost always in the running. A few forays into other markets—for example, financial services—confirmed the wisdom of serving the pharmaceutical industry's unique marketing needs. GSW is a specialist—a company designed to go deep rather than wide.

You can find specialists like GSW in almost every industry. Some are focused on particular kinds of service. Every year the *National Law Journal* publishes a "hot list" of litigation boutiques where, the periodical says, "it is all about skill, not size." The health care industry includes specialist hospitals like MD Anderson and Memorial Sloan Kettering (cancer care); Manhattan Eye, Ear, and Throat; and Shouldice Hospital, just outside Toronto, a "focused factory" that repairs more than 7,000 hernias a year and is the subject of one of the most famous Harvard Business School cases.

Other companies specialize in a customer segment. The financial services company USAA is an example: While it offers a full range of financial products, it sells them only to U.S. military personnel and their families. Some specialize in both service and segment, like Swiss private banker Lombard Odier, which offers a suite of wealth management services tailored to the needs of a limited group of rich clients. Palo Alto Networks is a specialist firm focused on enterprise cybersecurity services.

HOW THE SPECIALIST ADDS VALUE

It should go without saying that specialization works only when there are legitimate reasons for it: There is no point in a specialist filling station, but there is a reason for a mechanic devoted to repairing classic cars. GSW possesses deep knowledge of medical regulations, industry events and trade shows, and media that a giant firm would have to learn. USAA understands the circumstances of military families, not the least of which is the fact that the bread-winner might be in harm's way, and so it is able to develop offerings specifically for them. Specialists are often expensive—by definition, they have few competitors and no equals—but not always. Because Shouldice Hospital captures economies of scale, a hernia operation there typically costs about half as much as the same operation at other hospitals; with a middle-income customer base, USAA could not thrive if it cost more than non-Specialist competitors.

SERVICE DESIGN AND THE SPECIALIST

Certain elements of service design are characteristic of almost all Specialists. Compared to others, they "overinvest" in technical ex-cellence, and make that excellence visible to customers. Often they develop and publish white papers and other research, host customer conferences, make experts available to the media, and do other things to put their expertise on display. GSW established an iQ Innovation Lab, a dedicated team of engineers, designers, and strategists who develop new marketing ideas and tools, such as a digital sales tool for pharma sales reps. "We bring ideas to them first," says the president and CEO, Joe Daley. Specialists that emphasize a niche audience, like USAA, overinvest in gaining deep customer knowledge, too. They may blur the line between onstage and offstage activities, ac-tively engaging customers in workshops, educational sessions, and codevelopment events.

Specialists often have a low-key style. Their offices are not flashy—but they have the latest equipment. Their approach to sales is usually consultative; especially in professional services, they may offer a free diagnostic session before starting the meter. They prefer to market by reputation and word of mouth.

Specialists must be good ecosystem players. They compete with larger, generalist companies, but depend on them for referrals. They also depend on other Specialists to complement or complete their work. Sometimes Specialists cluster to create market power. In big

cities whole buildings are filled with dentists, orthodontists, perio-
dontists, and oral surgeons who hand patients off to one another.
Antique stores line the Connecticut shore from Mystic to Stoning-
ton, bringing more customers than any one shop could attract on its
own—like the fireflies that flash synchronously in the Great Smoky
Mountains and in Southeast Asia, creating a brighter light to attract
more mates than they could individually.

TRAPS AND PITFALLS
Specialists must be careful about ecosystem partners, who may also
be rivals. Aggregators (see page 149) are likely to be good allies for
them; Solutions providers (page 168) may be competitors—but also
could become joint-venture partners or even acquirers. These companies also need to strike their own correct balance between empathy and expertise. Arrogance is a temptation. So is overconfidence.
If focus is a Specialist's great strength, the lure of attractive adjacencies (particularly mass-market versions of current offerings) is a great
temptation.

* * *

The Trendsetter

* We're sleek and hip.

* Because you're our customer, you're hip, too.

* We give you a dazzling experience.

* "We're the Apple of ____."

When Boston Consulting Group emerged from the Management
Consulting Division of the Boston Safe Deposit and Trust Company
in the early 1960s, there was effectively no such thing as strategy
consulting. A few advisory firms—among them McKinsey, A. T.

Kearney (a McKinsey breakaway), Arthur D. Little, and Booz Allen & Hamilton—counseled clients about issues they confronted, but the term *strategy* had itself only recently come into use in business. The idea that outsiders would help clients decide or change where and how to compete was novel.

But to Bruce Henderson, a former Westinghouse executive, it was an idea whose time had come. Indeed, ideas were the building blocks of the firm, put forth in brief pamphlets called "Perspectives" that fit into the pocket of a suit jacket—an early instance of what we now call thought leadership and content marketing.

Asia de Cuba
Barcelona
Bard College
Barneys
Boston Consulting Group
Hill Holliday
Morgans Hotel Group
Uber
Virgin Atlantic
Warby Parker
Zara

BCG was and remains a Trendsetter, a company that lives on the leading edge of its industry, whether that edge is defined by ideas, fashion, science and technology, style, execution, or a combination of these. Some Trendsetters are trendy, but not all: The archetype is defined by a company that develops new practices, opens new markets, or creates new offerings—and is seen as a pioneer by its customers and peers. BCG showcases its restless pursuit of new ideas not just in client work and white papers but in a "Strategy Gallery" on the Web "designed to foster an exploration of strategic thinking from new, sometimes unusual perspectives." In the 1980s, American Airlines was the Trendsetter in its industry.

It introduced dynamic pricing, and the other airlines followed; it rolled out a frequent-flyer program that became the model for the industry. Apple is a Trendsetter in design, in creating new product categories, and in much else—but also pioneered building strong encryption into its software and devices, starting a trend that others in the industry are following.

HOW THE TRENDSETTER CREATES AND CAPTURES VALUE

Trendsetters turn the quest for first-mover advantage into a business model, leveraging their Pied Piper appeal to define the terms of competition in their industry and forcing others to play their game. Unsurprisingly, Trendsetters attract customers who want to be Trendsetters themselves—gilt by association.

Because they have a shiny aura of newness, Trendsetters almost always price high: The average price point for an item of clothing at Zara is more than double the average at H&M, for example, and a burger, fries, and a soda cost a bit more than twice as much at Shake Shack as they do at McDonald's. Higher prices do not necessarily mean fatter profits, because Trendsetters assume more risk and spend more on innovation and marketing than companies that follow their footsteps. Successful Trendsetters maintain a consistent rhythm of new offerings to avoid the boom-to-bust, fad-to-fatigue fate of companies less gifted in innovation and exploitation.

Trendsetters create value for themselves, but also can be of immense value to businesses that sell into their industry or market, because they often reveal where the rest of a supplier's customer base will follow.

SERVICE DESIGN AND THE TRENDSETTER

Trendsetters show their spots in every aspect of design, starting with the physical. Their websites are spare and sleek; their logos are elegant; their minimalist offices are lit in indiscernible ways; their receptionists are good-looking, tattooed, or both; and unless and until neckties come back, no one will wear one. Walk into an Andaz hotel and there is a feeling of being au courant that you do not sense in other brands in the Hyatt chain, even high-end, premium properties. You won't find a formal, white tablecloth dining room, but a farm-to-table restaurant.

Trendsetters walk a fine line when it comes to brand management. They are cool, but they want to foster engagement, not distance. Part of the archetype's appeal is that its customers believe they are cool, too. Employees embody the message. Frontline employees treat customers in ways that are subtly but sharply different from how employees of a Classic would. The Andaz employee who checks you in with an iPad sends a much different message—a message that you are part of the club—from what is conveyed by the more deferential employee behind the imposing front desk of the Grand Hyatt. Those playing catch-up can rarely match the magic of the Trendsetter; by the time everyone else has mastered the moves, the Trendsetter is on to a new dance.

Trendsetters need superb tools and well-developed instincts for understanding customers. Studying and working with "lead users," an established practice for new product development, is equally applicable to services—perhaps even more valuable because service innovation happens directly with customers. Consider how Weber Shandwick uses its "club" of fifty-two client leads—and clients—as a test kitchen for new ideas (see Chapter 2). Trendsetters are likely to be lead users themselves, which makes them excellent potential partners for joint innovation and co-creation (see Chapter 10).

Great customer listening will not help if you cannot act on what you hear, so it is important for Trendsetters to construct flexible, responsive systems for development and execution. Zara's supply chain is legendary in this respect, so nimble that the company does not need to overcommit to inventory on any given item and can rapidly ramp up production to keep a hit in stock.

TRAPS AND PITFALLS

Perhaps the biggest danger for a Trendsetter is losing the beat, sticking stubbornly to a design that doesn't work anymore. Abercrombie & Fitch suffered that fate. A suddenly uncool Trendsetter may have a difficult time getting back its mojo, because its vision and design are often tied up in the person of its leader—in Abercrombie's case, longtime CEO Michael Jeffries, who was let go by the board in

2015. It is also true that no service design archetype is more at risk from drinking its own (artisanal) Kool-Aid and going too far. Sometimes "too far" means getting so out in front of its customers that few can keep pace; for others, "too far" means trying to spread the magic into markets or industries where the company has no right to win and lacks an intuitive feel for customers. In most markets, there's a natural limit to the size of the Trendsetter customer base, and companies seeking growth are better off pursuing a share of wallet strategy than trying to expand the market. They should be very leery of acquisitions, particularly given the importance of culture in delivering a Trendsetter experience.

Smart Trendsetters offer value beyond "snob appeal" or brand identity to justify their higher prices, provided those extras connect with its core value proposition. "There's more to the company than just one aspect of our business model," says Dave Gilboa, co-CEO of Warby Parker, which donates money to nonprofits to cover the cost to distribute to people in low-income countries as many glasses as it sells. "If we portrayed ourselves just as eyewear experts and took more of a clinical medical approach, I do not think we would have attracted the same customers because we think our brand stands for fun and creativity and doing good in the world."

*   *   *

The Utility

* Often regulated, sometimes bureaucratic, we deliver essential services to lots of people—and do it well, considering.

* We are a public trust.

* We may be the only game in town.

* "We're the Ma Bell of ____."

Utilities are private, often-regulated companies serving the public good, providing essential services. On the Monopoly board, they are Water Works and the Electric Company, but they are also the phone company, your cable provider, your Internet service provider. From the standpoint of service design and delivery, government services like the post office, public transportation, and public schools fall into the Utility archetype, too. Indeed, a service (gas, electricity, water, Wi-Fi) that is publicly provided in one city might be sold by a private company in another.

AT&T
The Boston Globe
Chicago Transit Authority
Comcast
General hospitals
La Poste
Pacific Gas & Electric
Public schools
U.S. Postal Service

Hospitals have utility-like characteristics. Though taxi owners are entrepreneurial, the taxi industry as a whole is a Utility. These days, you might even include a city's surviving major daily newspaper as a Utility, because of its role as the community's hearth. The *Boston Globe* is a pillar of the city and of Red Sox Nation's distant colonies. Certainly when the *Globe* botched the rollout of a new home delivery service, the public reacted with dismay comparable to what it displays when Eversource (the electric company) has a power failure or the T goes down (see Chapter 12).

HOW THE UTILITY CREATES AND CAPTURES VALUE

As far back as John Stuart Mill, economists identified Utilities as natural monopolies. These arise when the cost of building and maintaining a system (like an electrical distribution network) is so great that it makes no sense to build a rival. A new example: cell phone towers, two-thirds of which are owned by just two companies in the United States. The resulting economies of scale and network effects—the fact that a value of a network grows geometrically as it gets bigger—make Utilities seemingly impregnable. Hence the common practice of regulation, to restrain monopolists from misbehaving, for example, price-gouging customers who have no alternative.

Utilities capture value as monopolies; they create it because their service—power, water, communication—is the substrate of many other industries. They create value in other ways, too. They set standards, such as for electrical current, the width of railway rails, safe wiring in homes and offices. The Financial Accounting Standards Board, a private group, makes rules that are recognized by the Securities and Exchange Commission as well as the accounting profession. Every business benefits from public education and public health. Last but not least, Utilities are a source of value for conservative investors, "widows and orphans" stocks because regulators see to it that they make a reasonable profit.

SERVICE DESIGN AND THE UTILITY

Most Utilities cannot choose their customers, and often customers cannot choose their Utilities. "Just because people do not have choice about being your customer does not mean that great customer service does not matter," says Charles V. Firlotte, CEO of Aquarion Water Company, the largest investor-owned water utility in New England, which delivers water to about 700,000 people in Connecticut, Massachusetts, and New Hampshire. "It takes a lot to build trust and it can be lost easily."

Almost of necessity, they become bureaucracies, with all the strengths and weaknesses that implies. Utilities have big customer service workloads. They must visit every mail slot, teach every child, and run power to every home, shop, skyscraper, church, and factory. They need robust back-office capabilities. Scale and flexibility are uneasy bedfellows, but the best Utilities use technology to create a single view of the customer and put that record in front of whoever answers the phone. It is not easy being that person, since Utilities often can only give limited authority to frontline workers. They need to be carefully chosen, trained, and supported.

As public trusts, Utilities cannot cut private deals. Transparency, then, is a pillar of service design for the Utility. Though Utilities cannot refuse customers, they can segment them; but the segmentation should generally be based on the Utility's cost, not on what the market will bear. Indeed, the perception of limited value for high cost has hurt cable companies; 15 percent of millennials surveyed for Salesforce's Connected Subscriber report "cut the cord" in 2015; 56 percent of cord cutters among all age groups did so because of costs.

A Utility's service design needs clear policies and robust dispute resolution. These may be quasi-judicial and bureaucratic—which in turn means a Utility must balance due process with empathy. Empathy also creates opportunities for the kind of design-led innovation that starts by reimagining customers' journeys to make them better. The Transportation Safety Administration's TSA PreCheck program is a good example of customer-friendly innovation by a Utility; it is noteworthy that the agency's watchwords, emblazoned on patches worn by employees, are integrity, team spirit, and—surprise—innovation.

Stakeholder management is critical in the service design of a Utility, which operates in a more complex ecosystem than almost any other company. So are crisis management capabilities, policies, and playbooks. People will forgive disruptions caused by an "act of God," such as Superstorm Sandy in 2012. But God help you if you take too long in restoring service—or if customers feel you caused the problem.

TRAPS AND PITFALLS

Many Utilities appear to believe that customer focus means getting better at explaining things rather than getting better at listening. Where many Utilities fail, Firlotte says, is not in the delivery of the actual service: "Far too many Utilities are not focused on service because they have taken the customer base for granted," he says. On the American Customer Satisfaction Index, industries that fit the Utility archetype all rank below average; the best of a mediocre lot are classic Utilities—gas, water, and electric—we'd guess because they are most likely to be held to a level of service by regulators.

Even when a Utility is not deaf, it may be tone-deaf. Consider Time Warner Cable's on-time guarantee: "The On-Time Guarantee is our promise that we'll show up on time for installations and service appointments, because we understand nothing is more frustrating than waiting around for an appointment. That is why Time Warner Cable was the first company in the industry to introduce the On-Time Guarantee." Yet in the next sentence the company hedges: "Contact us for the details of your area's On-Time Guarantee policy." Does "on-time" mean something different in your area? (Coincidentally, Tom was editing these pages in upstate New York while his hosts were waiting for the cable guy. Time Warner had promised he would appear between noon and 1 p.m. He arrived at 10:15 a.m.)

Utilities' other Achilles' heel is taking their business model as much for granted as they do customers. Rooftop solar, streaming video, mobile telephony, storefront urgent care clinics, Lyft and Uber: Name a utility and you can find a recent, serious threat of disruption. It is inherently difficult to build a capacity for innovation and experimentation in a business whose core job is to be absolutely reliable, but the Utility will have to learn.

CHAPTER 10

Designing for Customer Capital Growth: When One Plus One Equals Three

In any transaction, there's a two-way exchange of value: As the seller you get money, your customer gets something in return—a room for the night, a package shipped, a medical test. Each of you puts something in and each takes something away. But ideally you both leave something behind: knowledge of each other's skills and preferences, the option to work together again, the trust on which a relationship is built or flourishes. These are the elements of customer capital. Every time you and a customer have a positive experience, your customer capital grows; every bad experience diminishes it.

Customer capital is one of a triad of intangible assets that together comprise intellectual capital. The others are human capital (the collective skills and knowledge of the people who work for your company) and structural capital (intellectual property, processes, tools, and other intangibles that are not embodied in people or relationships).

These are not assets in the traditional sense; they appear on no balance sheet and there is no generally accepted way to measure their worth. But they are assets in every other way: You can manage them, leverage them, borrow against them, and make money from them. Crucially, intellectual capital is the heart of a company's strategic differentiation. Some companies have unique assets like oil fields, but almost all other tangible assets can be had by anyone with enough money. Capabilities and relationships, however, are unique.

Though customer capital accrues in all businesses, services are uniquely rich in it, because of the customer's active participation in creating value—even if it is something as simple as telling the barber to take a little more off the sides.

Just as services offer greater opportunity to build capital, the risk of destroying customer capital is especially high in services. If you start off on the wrong foot, or you put a foot wrong at a critical moment of the customer's journey, it is hard to recover. The old adage about it being cheaper to keep a customer than gain a new one is true (provided you have the right customer—which we explored in Chapter 4). At every moment, therefore, you need to know whether you are making deposits or withdrawals in the customer capital account—and whether your customer is investing alongside you.

Deposits or Withdrawals?

Every opportunity to build customer capital is also a chance to destroy it. An example: companies that expect customers to do more of the work themselves, whether it is checking themselves out at the supermarket or filling their own beverage cup; or no longer interacting with human beings (executing their own stock trades; paying bills online). Companies have derived considerable cost savings from these moves to automation and pushing work off onto the customer.

You can accrue customer capital with such moves as long as the customer benefits, too. You will seek in vain for any way to get live help from an actual human at Amazon, points out Boston College business school dean Andy Boynton; to him, that is just fine. "I've tried to find a way to call them; forget it. But on the parameters that matter to Amazon and to me that is not important," says Boynton. "It is fast, it is reliable, it is cheap, I can find stuff."

Being cheap, fast, and reliable—and technology-driven—is a service design choice for Amazon, just as is L.L.Bean's model of having a forthright, confidence-inspiring customer service rep to talk you through an exchange. When Boynton deals with Amazon, deposits are being made into the customer capital account because of the ease of the transaction.

Outsourcing to customers is a plus if:

* It saves them—not just you—time or money

* It makes dealing with you more convenient (the way ATMs eliminated "bankers' hours")

* It allows them to engage with you on their terms rather than through a protocol or formula you have established

But it can be a minus if:

* You are just fobbing off work, with no tangible benefit to the customer (self-checkout at a bricks-and-mortar store)

* You add complexity (a complicated interface or a tiresome phone command system)

* You erect barriers (making it difficult for customers with complex problems to speak to a person)

Designing for Capital Gains

What are you doing about your customer capital? Are you growing it, or are you living off it? Are you actively managing it, or letting it fend for itself, like money in a checking account? Are you leveraging it, as you would any other kind of capital, or are you contenting yourself with mediocre returns?

Many companies will give the "right" answer—we're growing it, managing it, leveraging it—but have little to show for it. Airline loyalty programs were an early attempt to ascribe specific value to customer relationships—you are silver! gold! platinum!—but there is next to no evidence that they have created genuine loyalty, let alone goodwill. (It does not help that airlines regularly debase the value of the "currency" in frequent-flyer accounts.)

But service design offers specific, demonstrable ways to grow, manage, leverage, and profit from customer capital. Because service design links customers' experiences to your strategy, it builds the value of relationships in four ways:

* By enabling you to design and open feedback channels, so that your customers are continually and continuously helping you serve them better

* By creating opportunities for you to solve problems together

* By enabling you to innovate together, collectively designing testing, and rolling out new offerings

* By providing a framework with which you can bring a customer into your extended enterprise, co-creating with them so that they become partners as much as they are customers

Customer capital is intangible, but it nevertheless leaves its mark on your financial statements. You may own the intellectual property associated with your brand, such as logos and trademarks, but the brand itself lives in the minds of the public; its value is largely determined by customer capital. Advertisements and actions help people construct that brand, but Disney is "the happiest place on earth" only if visitors walk out smiling.

Customer capital shows up in customer loyalty, in the likelihood that today's customer will be tomorrow's; in the value customers offer by becoming de facto adjuncts of your marketing department—fans on Facebook, references for new clients, sources of word of mouth.

Finally, you can use customer capital to serve all customers better, because good customers make you better. They become part of your extended business ecosystem, working with you both directly and indirectly to solve problems, collaborating with you to innovate, and becoming real business partners in a co-creative relationship.

The idea of working with customers in an explicit way to create value together is fairly new. The term *co-creation* was first used in 2002 by C. K. Prahalad and Venkatram Ramaswamy. "Most of the time, managers are so preoccupied with operating efficiently that they don't even think about value in terms of the consumer's experience," they wrote. "The consumer typically has little or no influence on value created until the point of exchange when ownership of the product is typically transferred to the consumer."

Those days are gone. Customers are not merely buyers who pick from options presented to them, as if on an episode of *The Bachelor*. They participate with you to shape what you sell and they buy. Even in the area of corporate social responsibility, Harvard Business School strategist Michael Porter advocates for what he calls "shared value"—a strategy in which companies consider social gains to be part of their value proposition, not a charity to be funded from the profits they make elsewhere.

Design is what makes it happen. Deciding whether, where, and how to tap into customer capital is a fundamental choice you will make in service design and delivery.

Who's on Top?

Customer capital is jointly but not necessarily equally owned. In this as in most relationships, one "shareholder" may have majority ownership—or at least enough power to make the other knuckle. In Tom's first book, *Intellectual Capital,* he wrote: "When information is power, power flows downstream to the customer."

Looking back, that statement seems too black and white. Information is still power, that is for sure. But in today's transparent, interactive marketplace, power surges back and forth like the tide in the Bay of Fundy, now running in favor of buyers, who can whip out cell phones and compare prices up and down the avenue, now turning to favor sellers, who drop cookies, collect data, and know so much about their customers that in some cases they have even inferred that women were pregnant before they told their families.

Tension between buyer and seller is inevitable, but it need not be zero-sum. In Porter's Five Forces model, the relative power of buyer versus seller is one factor determining profitability. If customers have a lot of bargaining power they will drive prices down; insurers do that with drug prices because they control high volumes of purchases, for example. If it is the other way around—buyers have few choices, or the cost of switching is high—sellers can charge more.

These tensions do not have to be destructive of value. SD^2 presents the opportunity to convert the energy of interaction into a source of value for each and for both. Customers' and sellers' increasing knowledge of each other can even lead to a fundamental redirection of companies' investment away from marketing and toward service, says Amazon founder and CEO Jeff Bezos: "the world is getting increasingly transparent . . . information perfection is on the rise. If you believe that, it becomes strategically smart to align yourself with the customer. You think about marketing differently. If in the old world you devoted 30% of your attention to building a great service and 70% of your attention to shouting about it, in the new world that inverts."

Consider the relationship Edmunds struck up with auto dealers with its Price Promise program. Price Promise is an online tool that gives customers the lowest price local dealers are offering—and a guarantee that the shopping experience will be haggle-free, which some may equate with hassle-free. A customer enters his or her zip code and what kind of vehicle they want; Edmunds finds the closest matches from local dealers who choose to participate in the program. Shoppers get a Price Promise certificate (printed or online) that they bring with them to the dealer. Dealers get serious shoppers in the door and can close sales faster because neither they nor the shoppers are passing prices back and forth. And Edmunds builds capital with both sides of its market—car shoppers and car sellers.

Four Platforms for Co-Creating Customer Capital

Co-creating customer capital may be as simple as improving feedback loops or as complex as inviting customers to create products for you (think Frito-Lay's wildly popular "Do Us a Flavor" contest). It can involve a service design in which you get ever more intimate with each customer (as with Stitch Fix) or one in which you partner with suppliers to learn more about your customers than you could alone. The results can be as basic as improvement in your service, as dramatic as innovation in what you offer, or as significant as a constantly escalating and evolving ability to deliver on your value proposition.

There are four platforms for co-creating capital.

Designing for Customer Capital Formation

Four levels of interaction

Level One: Feedback	Level Two: Problem Solving	Level Three: Innovation	Level Four: Business Model
• Periodic and real-time feedback • Two-way customer service dialogue • Social monitoring • Analytics	• Joint problem-solving teams • Agile project management • Service level agreements	• Lead customer involvement in new service development • A/B testing • Predictive modeling	• One size–fits–one value proposition • Full customer engagement in designing service provided

Customer comments
Corrective action

New offerings grounded
in customer insight

Full co-creation of
offerings and value

LEVEL 1: FEEDBACK

Companies have always had the ability to talk *at* customers—en masse, and in a static way, through advertising and other forms of marketing. And while customers have always had the ability to talk about you—indeed, word of mouth has always been a powerful force—they can now talk back. The customers' voice has been amplified through social megaphones like Facebook, Pinterest, Instagram, etc. And there are also conversations happening over which you have little control and are not participating in. "Social media and sites like Trip Advisor are the eight-hundred-pound gorilla. They have not just given the consumer a voice; they have elevated the standards of hospitality because they hold everyone in our industry accountable every single day," says McDiarmid of the luxury hotel the Wickaninnish Inn.

But just as customers' ability to talk to and about you has vastly grown, so has your ability to communicate with them. You can talk to them one-on-one; through groups; join them on the platforms and channels they are using to talk with each other; and, thanks to analytics, you can draw much smarter inferences from their behavior than you could before.

Most companies have some formal process to collect customer feedback. Not all do, however: Customer satisfaction measurements are novel in professional services. They are only just beginning in health care, as Medicare is starting to require hospitals to track customer experience as well as the technical quality of care, but odds are your doctor has never systematically inquired about patient experiences, asked what could be improved, or even tracked basic metrics like how often he or she is on time.

But there is a big step between collecting customer feedback and integrating it into service design to make your business better. Sophisticated companies elicit three different kinds of feedback: pulsed, periodic, and persistent, in the language of Christopher Meyer of Strategic Alignment Group.

* **Pulsed** feedback comes from a special study: a focus group to examine a new logo, a research project to discern the car rental habits of urban millennials, a test of a new service to find out why it is performing differently than expected. In some ways, pulsed studies resemble old-fashioned market research.

* **Periodic** feedback is just that—quarterly account reviews, user-group surveys, telephone- or Web-based studies. These may focus on particularly valuable customer segments, or examine customer attitudes or behavior with an eye toward uncovering the unmet needs of current customers.

* **Persistent** feedback is the corporate equivalent of a Fitbit, a constant stream of data about daily operations. It is chiefly valuable for identifying trends or problems in the current business. Ideally it should be unobtrusive—the fact that Tom gets a "how did we do?" survey after every Delta flight is annoying, given that he flies Delta at least twice a month; even worse, the survey questions are exactly the same, whether the flight was on time, delayed, or canceled.

    Persistent feedback is particularly useful when it is tied to measures of backstage performance: Shake Shack's computers time-stamp every order when it is entered and again when the kitchen hands it off to be picked up. Thus the chain has, among other data, a complete backstage record of how long orders take, and can identify busy times when staff might need to be added, see which menu items create logjams, compare times at different locations, correlate the stats, or use them to spot problems early.

The key to feedback is determining which pieces of it are relevant, practical, and worth acting upon, which is where data and analytics come in. Your customers supply you with no small amount of data about themselves, directly through information you ask them for, from the information you collect from your interactions with them, and indirectly through your ability to track their history with you.

In the aggregate, this forms Big Data. Big Data is not about who can build the biggest haystack; it is about finding the needles that allow you to create value for as many customers as possible while also making individual customers feel their specific needs are being met.

Finding needles in haystacks does not require a lot of computing power. "Guest cards have always been the lifeline of our industry," says McDiarmid of the Wickaninnish Inn. "You need to respect that the customer's perspective may not individually be right but collectively they always tell you what you should or should not do." "The Wick," as the inn is known, delves deep into this data, tracking observations and ratings, and comparing the ratings year-to-date from the previous year. The insights received are no less valuable because of their low-tech origins. "Ninety percent of the changes we've made at the inn are because of what we learn from the comment cards," says McDiarmid. "Our guests are staying in all of our rooms, three hundred and sixty-five days a year, giving us both data we couldn't get otherwise."

The Power of Peersuasion: A Special Kind of Feedback

An important form of feedback comes from what we call "peersuasion": customers' influence over each other, especially when it is amplified via social media. This is both a form of customer capital and a by-product of it; customers are not only creating *with* you, they are also creating *for* you, most notably with regard to your brand. Good word of mouth has long been a manifestation of strong customer capital but it is now exponentially more important—and also measurable thanks to social media.

Some statistics show the power of peersuasion:

* A dissatisfied customer will tell between 9 and 15 people about their experience.

* Around 13 percent of dissatisfied customers tell more than 20 people.

* Negative interactions with a business are spread to twice as many people as positive ones.

* People are twice as likely to talk about bad customer service experiences as they are to talk about good experiences.

* 67 percent of people spend money after getting recommendations from their friends on online communities like Facebook and Twitter.

* Happy customers who get their issue resolved tell about 4 to 6 people about their experience.

Potential customers pay a lot of attention to what your current customers say. Studies by Reevoo, a British firm that helps companies collect and post customer reviews online, show that three out of five customers read online product and service reviews and that customer reviews are trusted twelve times more than what a company says about itself. Thus when customers tell customers, they are helping you build the confidence that is a key component of customer capital.

Your goal is to leverage and harness the power of peersuasion. For Stitch Fix, it has been a key driver of growth. Founder Lake says the benefits go beyond saving money on marketing, and carry more weight than advertising. Focus groups indicate there is confusion around the practicality of Stitch Fix's service and hesitation to spend $20 (the fixed price of the styling service) for possibly nothing more than trying on clothes that a stranger has selected for you. "I hear people say, 'Why would I hand over twenty dollars when I have no idea what's coming and who my stylist is?'"

LEVEL 2: PROBLEM SOLVING

As barriers between you and your customers have broken down, customers inevitably—albeit perhaps not justifiably—feel more empowered. Mark Ingwer, a business psychologist and the author of *Empathetic Marketing*, asserts that "satisfying the control needs of the consumer, more than any individual need discussed in this book, holds the most potential for a company to build loyalty to a brand, product, or service through intrinsic motivation, which is the internal sense of satisfaction with the purchasing process and the resulting purchase."

How much control to give the customer is a tricky question. Asks Francis Gouillart, CEO and cofounder of the Experience Co-Creation Partnership, "When does co-creation reach a tipping point where the customer is distorting your product and your service; constantly trying to bend them to suit their needs?" Gouillart, whose consulting projects include a transformation of La Poste, the French post office, says a happy medium is reached when "it makes sense to change your practices and offerings in such a way that it is not about stretching to the point of distortion but encompassing and meeting a need."

Such was La Poste's experience with co-creation. Like many postal services around the world, La Poste found itself losing customers—and revenue—in a world where people increasingly rely on digital communication. In 2009, under the direction of then-CEO Jean-Paul Bailly, La Poste turned to co-creation to redesign its services.

Jacques Rapoport, who headed the division that was in charge of the post office locations, had read about co-creation and was intrigued by the notion that service could be redesigned in partnership with the customers, according to Gouillart, who worked on the project.

Among the first decisions: to start small in terms of both scale and ambition. Three post offices with very different customer bases were selected as the "laboratories": one in a city, one in a suburb, and one in the rural village of Amplepuis, northwest of Lyon.

"We advocated a very limited top-down view here: We coached them on having only three or four very high-level service indicators at the top," says Gouillart. "More than that would have been too daunting and does not allow for the kind of experimentation that needs to take place."

While the transformation initiative ultimately brought about greater efficiency and new sources of revenue for La Poste throughout the country, one of the first—and most significant—results was changing the hours of service. And it all started in Amplepuis, with a population just over 5,000.

The village had the open-air markets every Wednesday and Friday. The post office opened at 9 a.m.—when the market was already in full swing. Both La Poste employees and customers suggested that the post office open at 7 a.m. on those days, to accommodate the needs of the people who worked at the market.

That nut was harder to crack than one might think, given a long French tradition of centrally controlled, dirigiste management and strong unions hardwired to insist on rigid work rules in part to counteract the top-down hand of management. The solution that broke the shell: to let employees decide how they should allocate their 35 hours of mandated weekly work—basically a spreadsheet on the wall.

LEVEL 3: INNOVATION

The first two levels of building customer capital—feedback and problem-solving—are about working with customers to improve your existing business. The next two levels are about bringing them into the tent to help you change your business, starting with level 3, innovation. In Chapter 8 we discussed the importance of innovation at every link in the service value chain, and how advanced companies conduct real-time experiments with customers to test new services, service and interface changes, and the like. We should make two additional points here.

The first is that technology, and particularly the app economy, will make co-creative innovation more common, whether companies invite it or not. Your ability to maintain sole control of your intellectual property is seriously compromised in a world of mash-ups and open source software; so when it comes to customers building stuff on top of your stuff, you're better off embracing it than wrestling with it. The "Internet of Things"—the proliferation of devices connected to the Internet—will only accelerate the process. According to IDC, by 2018 there will be 22 billion such devices installed, which will drive the development of 200,000 new IOT apps and services—a number that far outstrips the capabilities of "traditional" IT sources.

The second is that building customer capital is possible at every point in the service value chain: Just as your customers co-create with you, you can co-create with the companies whose customers you are, or might become. A great proponent of the power of co-creation is A. G. Lafley, the two-time CEO of Procter & Gamble, who brought hundreds of designers onto the P&G payroll and instilled design thinking throughout the organization. As a result, the nexus of innovation at P&G began to move out of the lab and into consumers' homes and in relationships with outside researchers—a model the company called *connect and develop* as opposed to *research and develop*.

In one project, P&G employed a team from Continuum, the Boston-based design firm, to watch people at work in their homes and learned that they were spending as much time cleaning their mops as they were cleaning their floors. From that insight—voilà—came the company's wildly successful Swiffer line of household cleaning products.

Driving Innovation Together

One company that is ahead of the co-creation curve is Edmunds, the automotive information platform. "Our goal is to reduce the friction among shoppers, dealers, and manufacturers and to help transactions take place," says Avi Steinlauf, CEO of the privately held company. "When you talk about a triangle we are in an interesting space."

In 2013, as mentioned earlier, Edmunds launched "Hackomotive," an offspring of its internal hackathon. "Folks from our IT department found them useful, so for us the next logical step was to invite teams from the outside to see if we could come up with innovative ideas in the auto shopping space," remembers Steinlauf.

Edmunds made Hackomotive enticing with judges and real prize money. In 2014, first prize went to CarCode, a start-up whose technology enabled SMS texting, allowing dealers to centrally manage all of their texting rather than relying on just one individual's phone. The CarCode team won not just $20,000 but the interest of Steinlauf and Edmunds, which eventually bought the start-up. "CarCode fit our goal of providing the best, easiest experience for shoppers and dealers, regardless of platform," says Steinlauf.

He points out that like other shoppers, potential car buyers want the convenience of mobile shopping and the ability to showroom. Car shoppers can text participating dealers questions, including "do you have such-and-such a car in stock," and get photos. CarCode is being offered to all of Edmunds's dealer partners at no extra charge, and participating dealers receive text message leads from Edmunds .com. They also have the opportunity to add a "Text Us" button on their own mobile sites, which drives increased levels of engagement from car shoppers.

LEVEL 4: BUSINESS MODEL

Co-creation is not only a powerful tool to improve customer experience; it can become a strategy in and of itself, a way to bring your customers "inside" as your partners in building a more valuable, profitable enterprise.

For online stylist Stitch Fix, customer capital is a critical component of its business model. Founder Katrina Lake and her stylists pride themselves on personalizing each "fix"—a box of five items—from price points selected by clients, for a styling fee of $20 applied to purchase. Stitch Fix depends on constant customer feedback to give that personalized touch. And it is working. Says Lake: "Women tell us all the time, 'I went to a store and tried on twenty pairs of jeans and I couldn't find one that fit. Stitch Fix sent me one pair and they fit. You must be a wizard.'"

The wizardry comes from the combination of engineering and empathy. Every client begins her relationship with Stitch Fix by filling in a detailed style profile; the data feed into an algorithm that is then interpreted through the personal touch of a stylist. Clients are paired with a stylist chosen for "compatibility," based on the profile. "Your" stylist (Patricia became a client while doing research for the book) sends a note with pictured suggestions about how to wear/accessorize each item in the fix, and will include suggestions related to previous fix(es) as well.

The Stitch Hitch: You and your stylist never even directly email each other, let alone talk, Skype, or text. There are several reasons for that: One is economics. "It does not make sense to spend forty-five minutes on the phone to sell you a $38 tank top," says Lake. Another is that saving customers time is part of Stitch Fix's value proposition. Finally, Stitch Fix's extensive data—both about a specific customer and customers in the aggregate—make it unnecessary. "We ask for a lot of data, but it is the right data," says Lake. "Even when we schedule that first fix for a customer, we have a leg up because of the four-plus years of data and millions of data points that we have to better understand how our customers and products are really interacting."

But the data is only as good as the stylist's use of it. "It is hard to imagine that the stylist could be anywhere near as effective without the algorithm, or the algorithm alone could be anywhere near as effective as the two of them together," says Lake. The effectiveness depends on the customer's willingness to share a fair bit of information not just at the beginning but all along. Customers are asked to give feedback on every item in every fix, whether they keep it or not.

If Lake and her stylists do their jobs right, and if customers give them useful feedback, every "fix" a stylist sends will be a little more perfect than the one before, and both buyer and seller will be the better for it. (The company, founded in 2011, does not release sales figures—which have been estimated at above $200 million annually—and it has attracted enthusiastic followership and impressive leadership, including COO Julie Bornstein, former CMO and chief digital officer of Sephora.)

Customer capital is more than a virtuous circle; it is a spiral. As the relationship between you and your customer deepens, the value to both of you increases, and as customers' expectations grow, so does your ability to meet them. "When we ask customers to leave feedback about their fix, we know we are raising the bar in terms of what it will take to make them happy because they expect the stylist to pay attention and use it for their next fix," says Lake. "We're asking our customers to partner with us, which puts the responsibility on us to constantly make their experience better."

At its best, co-creation leverages your and your customers' shared interests, needs, knowledge, and skills to elevate your interactions to the level of a delightful experience for the customer and a profitable one for you. It is the recognition that one plus one equals three, that what you can do in concert is more potent than what you can do solo—indeed, it's the recognition that customers are a source of more than money.

CHAPTER 11

The Virtuous Circle:
Corporate Culture and Service Design

We have a mission statement that we want to be the employer, the investment, and the service provider of choice," says Charles V. Firlotte, CEO of Aquarion Water Company. A water utility might be "the last of the great monopolies," as Firlotte says, but it cannot succeed unless it works for staff, stockholders, and customers—which means having a culture that is nothing like the stolid bureaucracies of yore.

When Firlotte took over as CEO in 2003, customers' complaints were high, and their frustration was exacerbated by their not being able to find someone in the company who could answer their questions. "We had an antiquated company information system," he recalls. "Our customers would call the call center when there was a problem, so the customer service people knew more of what was happening in the field than field employees did."

Today Aquarion's company information system facilitates information exchange between field employees and call center representatives. A focus on customer service training and observance of key metrics has resulted in a dramatic drop in complaints. For several years running Aquarion has outperformed all other utilities in Connecticut for having the lowest rate of customer complaints.

"There is a strong, enduring correlation between what happens on the outside and what happens on the inside," says Firlotte. "If you walk into a manufacturing facility and you see sloppy housekeeping, dollars to donuts I can tell you product quality, service delivery, and the state of employee and industrial relations are all probably troubled. The same is true in service."

Few executives are as candid or as critical about their own operations and cultures as Firlotte. Indeed, it seems that everyone says (but perhaps does not truly believe) that their company has a culture that serves both employees and customers well: "Our employees love us—and we love them!" "We really care about our clients!" Some of these executives mean what they say and are correct. Some mean what they say but are wrong. And many secretly believe that something is wrong with their culture, slowing them down, infecting the place, hurting results. It is hard to delight your customers when your culture and your value proposition are not in harmony.

Corporate culture has many definitions—perhaps the most broadly understood and widely accepted of which is "the way we do things around here." This hints at the inseparable link between culture and service design. Design should determine behavior— what you do at every interaction with customers, what must be done behind the scenes to prepare for those interactions—and behavior shapes culture. "You create culture through design. Use design to create the instances, rituals, spaces, and tools that make up a culture," says Tim Brown of IDEO.

We advocate creating what we call a service culture. A service culture isn't servile. It is about making sure that *your culture lines up with your customer's expectations and reinforces your ability to deliver on those expectations.* This chapter will show you how to create a strong, virtuous circle between service design and a service culture—the way things are done, and the way they should be done. By doing so, you all but ensure that you end up with the culture you want.

Cultures do not emerge in a vacuum. They serve a purpose and, generally, come into being in response to stimuli from the boss. A boss who is constantly looking to pin blame on people should not be surprised if a defensive, "don't look at me" culture comes into being. According to Stan Slap, consultant and author of, among other books, *Bury My Heart at Conference Room B*, "A culture exists to protect itself, so it will adapt as needed for survival and self-preservation."

But if dysfunctional cultures are the result of management behavior, so are vibrant, functional ones. If self-preservation is tied to delivering the right customer experience, you are using the power of culture rather than fighting it.

A vibrant culture aligned with strategy can differentiate you as both an employer and a vendor—especially in services, where value is often delivered person-to-person. Travelers are drawn to Southwest Airlines not only for its low prices but also for its reputation as being a place where everybody chips in and is cheerful—a culture that is manifested in the jokes (funny or not) flight attendants customarily broadcast before takeoff. Salesforce's founder/CEO Marc Benioff explicitly links his company's open culture with its business success: "That is the product that we sell, trust. Customers work with us because they trust us, and employees work for us because they trust us." Customers flock to Nordstrom expecting exemplary service. Who hasn't heard the story of the customer who returned a set of car tires to the clothing retailer? The fact that the legend endures despite probably being apocryphal makes it an example of the most powerful artifact of culture—a myth.

There are many myths about culture itself, the most insidious of which is that the way to change a culture is to address it head-on. Do not blame your culture, warns Jon Katzenbach, the renowned expert on teams and the informal organization: "Just as you typically cannot argue someone out of a deeply held belief, you cannot force people to change the way they think and feel about their work." Instead, Katzenbach urges, you should identify specific behaviors to change that solve real problems and deliver real results. Their thinking—and your culture—will then start evolving in ways you want.

Another dangerous myth: Great cultures are all the same, full of warmth and collegiality. It ain't so. A great culture is defined by its ability to work equally well for customers and staff. A fast-charging, relentlessly cost-conscious shop like Amazon has been criticized for a fast-charging, relentless culture—maybe rightly, though company and employees have offered strong rebuttals—but no one would suggest that working at Amazon should be like playing in the Puppy Bowl.

Design helps define the parameters in which your employees operate, what they can and should do to deliver a delightful customer experience. Good service design translates customer expectations into employee expectations, and carries, therefore, the quasi-moral authority of the customer's voice. A service-oriented culture is the residue of design, not the consequence of managerial cheerleading or whip-cracking. If you get the design right, and reinforce it with policies, processes, incentives, and attaboys, the culture will come along. When service is properly designed, employees are not bucking the system when they do the right thing.

It does not work to try it the other way around. Culture is notoriously hard to change, precisely because it *is* the way thing get done—and have been getting done for some time. Starbucks's Howard Schultz is just one of legions of CEOs who have said some variation of "Culture trumps strategy." In Schultz's 2012 book, *Onward: How Starbucks Fought for Its Life without Losing Its Soul*, he wrote: "Like crafting the perfect cup of coffee, creating an engaging, respectful, trusting workplace culture is not the result of any one thing. It is a combination of intent, process, and heart, a trio that must constantly be fine-tuned."

Intent, process, and heart: Set the right expectations and incentives; design the right workflows and jobs; demonstrate leadership to set the right examples. With those working, the culture will, like your service design, be a source of differentiation. "There are roughly

46,000 accounting firms in America and the majority of them are providing very similar services," says Wayne Berson, chief executive officer of BDO USA. "So you've got to separate yourself based on who you really are as a firm. And that gets down to the culture and the core values and what it is that you stand for."

Service design identifies the moments of truth in your interactions with customers, develops employee activities that create the experience your strategy calls for, and designs them in such a way that they make employees' lives easier and customers' experiences better. When that happens, your company culture becomes a sail pulling your strategy forward, not an anchor holding it back.

What Defines a Good Service Culture?

Companies rightly boast when they make one of the "great places to work" lists that have proliferated in recent years. Prospective employees are right to check out what people say about a company on social media or sites like Glassdoor. Culture is frequently judged by the quality and quantity of employee perks (Free snacks! Sushi bar in the cafeteria! Bring your pet to work! Unlimited sick days!) rather than how well employees are supported in doing their jobs.

But the best-stocked corporate pantry cannot compensate for the absence of the basics. If you want to know whether you have a good culture for service, judge it by these things:

* **Clarity:** Do employees understand your value proposition and how it is manifest in customer experience? Is there a clear connection between your customers' experience and the behavior you expect (and reward) from employees?

* **Understanding:** Do your employees know what they need to do at every step of the customer journey to deliver that experience? Do they know which touchpoints are most critical?

* **Leadership:** Is senior management both engaged and engaging in providing delightful experiences? Do they pad their wallets while preaching frugality? Do they know and celebrate people lower in the ranks—men and women who exemplify the behavior they want?

* **Transparency:** Do employees at all levels have visibility into the issues that affect their—and your company's—ability to serve customers/clients? Are customers/clients able to see the link between your employees' behavior and your value proposition?

* **Uniqueness:** How can you ensure that your corporate culture underscores what makes you different, instead of undermining it?

* **Relationship:** What kinds of internal relationships (competitive, egalitarian, etc.) do you want to foster? What kinds of customer relationships (cool, warm, etc.) do you want to foster?

* **Empathy:** Do employees throughout the company hear the "voice of the customer" directly or indirectly and whenever decisions are made? Does service design start with customers, or with internal activities?

Executives often treat culture as something apart from the business of doing things and making money. They focus on strategy and operations, then do "the culture piece." That is a mistake. The ligaments of your culture are laid alongside the lines of your organization chart and service design map. Your culture comes to life, bone to its bone, when the phone starts ringing and you decide who will answer it, what you will do for the caller, and who will get the credit. Culture is the sinew that determines how your organization moves.

You should apply the principles of service design, therefore, to develop the instances, rituals, spaces, and tools that constitute a culture.

The First Principle: The Customer Is Always Right . . . Provided the Customer Is Right for You. In Chapter 4, we talked about encouraging the customers you want and discouraging the ones you do not. It is important to recognize that all kinds of cultural forces push against your ability to do this: people's natural desire to please a customer; the preference for saying yes instead of no; long traditions of celebrating the salesperson who sells the most widgets instead of making the most profit; the squeaky wheel getting the grease.

There is no simple prescription. You do not want to reward employees for being rude to customers any more than you want to convey the idea that because the customer is right, your employee is wrong. Go through your incentives and rituals and do an audit to see if you are celebrating or incentivizing the wrong behavior, or doing things in service of the wrong customers. What would or should be done differently in recognition that you are selecting and segmenting customers? And what would or should be done differently when you have the right ones?

The Second Principle: Don't Surprise and Delight Your Customers— Just Delight Them. Consider the ideas we discussed in Chapter 5: Excellent service begins by getting the basics right, so that you can meet the expectations you set every time; it is the product of customer experience and technical excellence; it feels inevitable.

The process begins with expectations, which are the bar your company and culture must clear. Customer expectations need to be translated into employee expectations. Even the most able, skilled, competent employees cannot succeed if they do not know what they should—and shouldn't—be doing. "Our managers spend a lot of time on the floor—our approach is shoulder to shoulder," says Nordstrom's Ken Worzel. "Even if you are selling a lot, if you don't delight people, you won't last. We remind people all the time that this is what we win on. It is fragile."

Consistency across the organization is also critical. This means objectives and measurements need to be aligned. You should not design metrics just to track the activities of an individual department, but instead so that you can manage touchpoints and stages of the customer's journey. If salespeople are incented on customer satisfaction, but call center support is measured on reduced call times rather than call resolution or satisfaction, you're going to have conflicting objectives, poor outcomes, and a poor customer experience.

The principle of delight should shape whom you hire. This is not about technical competence, which can be acquired. It is about something more intrinsic. Are their motivations and values in line with your company's? Recall from Chapter 3 how Enterprise Rent-A-Car recruits extroverted "people people," whom it pays on commission: These are offstage design choices that help ensure that its culture supports its onstage activities. Subscription airline service Surf Air (see Chapter 5) acts similarly: "We rejected pilots who had hours of experience because they didn't have the right cultural fit, which is a thick skin, an eye for service, and a humble heart," says Justin Hart, the airline's vice president for customer acquisition. "Because of the way our business is structured with highly personalized service, even the pilots have to know your favorite drinks and snacks."

The Third Principle: Great Service Must Not Require Heroic Efforts on the Part of the Provider or the Customer. Think about a service provider on a granular level—meaning individual employees. A good service culture works for employees as much as for customers—because services are delivered, mostly, by people, whether consultants, colorists, or cooks. A design change that makes life better for customers but worse for employees will flag—the culture will kill it, often by going into a passive-aggressive mode that makes it almost impossible for management to respond. The employee culture, designed for survival, will adapt as needed, so it is critical that senior management set the right tone.

Culture is codified and conveyed by stories, and these telltale moments can help everyone see what behavior you want. Slap cites a case in point: In the wake of Hurricane Katrina in Louisiana, Progressive Insurance made a radical decision to scrap more than 5,000 vehicles it insured that had been deemed total losses from floodwater damage. The other choice: subjecting the *E. coli*–infected cars and trucks—and by extension Progressive employees—to a cleaning process that would have made the vehicles eligible for resale. Reselling the vehicles might have cost less, but money wasn't the point. "The reasons are simple," said Juan Andrade, claims general manager for the region. "We do not want our people working around those cars and we do not want them back on the road."

The Fourth Principle: Service Design Must Deliver a Coherent Experience Across All Channels and Touchpoints. Everyone who interacts with a potential client or customer has a responsibility to help deliver the experience you have promised regardless of their decision-making authority—and regardless of where in the organization they reside. A Classic company—the Ritz-Carlton hotel chain, for example—needs reservation agents and telephone salespeople as courteous as any concierge. Cultural cognitive dissonance occurred at Mobile Mini when it improved the quality of its storage containers product (a good thing, to be sure) but hadn't addressed its issues around pickup and delivery.

Think of how Apple's brand image and product designs are manifested in its people—not just the designers and supply-chain folks in Cupertino, but the technical support at Apple Care and salespeople in its retail stores. Apple employees need to embody the experience the company encases in its products and touts in its ads. Before Apple CEO Tim Cook famously hired former Burberry CEO Angela Ahrendts as senior vice president for retail and online in 2014, he had hired British retailing executive John Browett to run retail.

Browett's tenure lasted just seven months. Cook told *Fortune* magazine in 2015 that Browett was "not a cultural fit" for Apple. It was reported that Browett alienated the retail staff with moves to cut hours and benefits. Apple has wrestled with how much to pay store employees, generally offering more than the run of retailers (but taking criticism for not paying enough), knowing that its strategy depends on a service design that, in turn, depends on in-store employees (see Chapter 12).

Apple also knows what happened to electronics retailer Circuit

City, which accelerated its descent into bankruptcy by replacing its commission sales staff with hourly employees in 2004, then three years later firing 3,400 of the most experienced (read: most expensive), replacing them with a minimum-wage force. As Ahrendts told *Fortune*: "If you're going to employ people anyway, why not make them the differentiator?"

The Fifth Principle: You're Never Done. Every company's culture has an innovation gene waiting to be expressed; often it is turned off by work rules and policies—especially policies that strip front-line workers (so important for service) of initiative and autonomy. But even in these, a spirit of customer-centered improvement can be brought to life. "The hallmarks of a leader and a service-oriented culture are an ethos of curiosity and experimentation, where there are as many questions as answers; more 'what if' kinds of conversations than declarations of certainty," says consultant and author Matt May, who brought that spirit of innovation to life in the Los Angeles Police Department.

Intent: Culture and the Principles of Service Design and Delivery

As part of May's work with Toyota University, he saw the value of "what if" in one of the most unlikely places: the Los Angeles Police Department. In the early aughts, the LAPD found itself demoralized and operating under the supervision of the U.S. Department of Justice under a 2001 consent decree imposed largely because of corruption in LAPD's ranks. "If you do not have the luxury of sweeping in and brooming out all your executives, so to speak—which the LAPD didn't even though a new chief of police was on the horizon—where do you begin?" May asks rhetorically. Looking for some help, the LAPD turned to Toyota University.

"This is a culture that did not have a process of innovation," says May of the LAPD. "It was 'do as I say and do as I say now,' because when you are in survival mode the last thing on your mind is experimenting. So where could we possibly begin to think about change?"

The easiest place to start was with the non-sworn parts of the LAPD: employees who wear a badge, but are not sworn police officers. They do not have police training or carry guns; they book arrestees, operate the jails, and do other behind-the-scenes work. "The process of transformation began in the jails. We would show them how with little changes they could make vast improvements," he says. One improvement came in speeding up the time it took to process arrestees.

The sworn officers were, in effect, the "internal customers" for the booking process, and the change improved their experience, because it got them back on the street looking for bad guys much faster than before. That caught the attention of the sworn officers, who started asking questions, and eventually the culture of experimentation migrated from being among the non-sworn officers to the sworn ones; a cultural shift had occurred.

Inspired by Toyota's techniques for continuous improvement, May and his team worked out an arrangement with LAPD's top brass that went like this: If a team devises an experiment that it can run within one deployment period (28 days), that has a plan and measure of success, and that team members can run on their own time with no additional head count or money, the brass had to say yes. "We taught them a process for improvement," May recalls, "and little by little, team by team, things changed."

Process: The Power of Design and Action

Two generations ago, a young scholar named Steve Kerr, then at The Ohio State University but later chief learning officer for General Electric and Goldman Sachs, wrote a classic article whose title perfectly captures its thesis: "On the Folly of Rewarding A, While Hoping for B." How can a company expect executives to take a long-term perspective if promotions and bonuses are based only on near-term results? Kerr asked. We would echo him: How can a company expect exemplary service if it punishes people who deliver it, puts obstacles in their way, or sets goals that pull against it? Delivering great service is about the process, not merely the product or result, and the process often involves a lot of people.

Many companies save money by trying to automate the human factor out of service design, for example with self-checkout at stores (see the next chapter). Even then, you cannot escape culture. On the one hand, customers will expect to have the same feeling (warm and fuzzy; or brusque and efficient) from machines as from people. But ironically, customers will also expect the same level of service from people as they get from machines—they'll want a bank branch officer to be as quick and reliable as the ATM in the lobby.

"We view every customer interaction as a chance to add to or subtract from the brand experience," says Rob Weisberg, CEO of Invaluable, the online auction marketplace. The map of your customers' service journeys (see page 249) will show you who interacts with customers and whether those interactions are at critical points. It is up to you to learn, then, if the people who are interacting at critical points have both the *ability* to influence the customer's experience and the *incentive* to do the right thing.

"One of the core values we have is that customer service and customer experience is owned by everyone," says Weisberg. For Invaluable, that means not just hiring people who share that mindset but empowering everyone and anyone to solve customers' problems. "In our business, you might have someone panicking because he or she made an accidental bid," he says. "We make sure that the first person a customer speaks with has not only the responsibility but the authority to solve the customer's problem."

As Weisberg knows, all the good intentions in the world will not empower frontline employees if you haven't created the right service design. The front line cannot help if it does not have both information and authority. "I'll have to connect you to someone else" and "I'll have to check with my manager"—these are marks of a failure of service design.

A service-oriented culture empowers people by learning from everything, including mistakes, and by being willing to learn from everyone. "Everybody is an expert in their own way," says SCAD's Victor Ermoli. "If you have five years of answering the phone in customer service, or five years of listening to customers at the cash register, nobody knows more than you. You are not the only person with knowledge, but that knowledge has to be valued and put to use."

At BDO, employees are encouraged to have a "bedside manner" that includes what Berson calls "professional skepticism." He recalls one situation where a partner raised a red flag about a potential client because of behavior that suggested a cultural incompatibility with BDO. "Part of our strategic plan is built around leadership and accountability," he says. "That partner alerted us to a potential problem down the road. We were concerned enough to take action." By not just listening to but acting on employees' feedback, the company is sending a message to employees about what's important and encouraging the behavior it wants.

Rewards and punishments can support or erode a service design. Do you hail the hero who parachutes into a disastrous situation and fixes it—like Red Adair, famous for putting out oil well fires—but not celebrate the engineer who makes sure that disasters never happen in the first place? Do the "creatives" in your company snipe at the "suits," and the suits sneer in return? Do people get promoted for the customer delight they deliver, or only for delivering the numbers in their plans and budgets? How do you maintain the right balance between encouraging creativity and punishing sloppiness? Most important: How does your company make time for empathy—for walking in customers' shoes—and reward it?

Heart: Leadership, Service Design and Culture

A service-oriented culture demands a specific type of leadership; what we call service leadership. If servant leadership, an idea popularized by Robert Greenleaf in 1970, is about respecting employees, service leadership is about being a strong advocate for the customer as well as employees.

Service leadership demands a constant focus on finding a better way to serve both customers and employees. "We've always been a service-oriented business and it was a natural evolution for us to realize that we need to be as focused on our people as we are on our clients," says Abby Gold, chief human resources officer of Weber Shandwick.

Another aspect of service leadership is never being satisfied with the status quo. If you do not have leadership that is always striving for improvement then you're not going to have the culture of service running through the veins of the firm.

How do leaders act? A powerful example of service leadership was the way Shake Shack CEO Randy Garutti handled the company's great french fry shakeup. The casual burger, fry, and frozen custard chain (which went public in 2015 after humble beginnings as a food cart in Manhattan's Madison Square Park in 2004) decided in 2013 to switch from frozen, crinkle-cut fries to hand-cut, fresh ones. It was a big investment. The switch involved redesigning kitchens, retraining staff, and rethinking logistics: Having fresh potatoes on hand was a different matter than storing frozen ones. Garutti saw the fresh, hand-cut fries as an upgrade in taste and quality.

Only one problem: Customers didn't agree. Sales of fries, which had been the chain's best-selling menu item, fell. Garutti thought customers just needed time to adjust to the change. They never did. "It took six months before I would admit that I made a mistake," Garutti told *Fast Company* magazine. "We didn't fully appreciate the simple, tactile pleasure and the emotional attachment our fans have to the crispiness, the ridges and pure joy that these fries bring to guests of all ages," Garutti wrote on Shake Shack's website when he announced the change. "It is humbling to know that so many people care so deeply about our menu."

Within a year of the switch to the fresh, hand-cut fries, Shake Shack brought back the beloved crinkly fries—but also used the occasion as an opportunity for improvement. The fries were still frozen, but Shake Shack worked with the manufacturer to remove artificial ingredients and preservatives. By retreating and moving forward at the same time, Garutti sent a powerful message to customers and employees alike about the company's commitment to natural, top-quality ingredients—its "anti-chain" ethos.

Brazilian cosmetics company Natura used a serious service crisis to send a strong message internally. Natura had always sought zero-defect delivery performance, meaning no missing, late, or broken items. In late 2011, the company missed its mark. Ninety-nine percent of orders were accurate, but that meant that 20,000 Natura consultants—many of whom were low-income women—had to explain problems with orders to their customers just before the all-important Christmas season. With the snafu, Natura had broken its promise to its customers and its consultants. "Any missing box, and any complaints matter," customer service director Ricardo Faucon said later. That Christmas, every disappointed customer got a hand-signed letter of apology and some kind of gift.

The performance problem didn't hurt the company's profits: In 2011, Natura had its best year to date. But the real issue was how to show employees that more than profits were at stake. If there were no consequences, what was to stop the company from accepting lower standards? Company policy dictated that bonuses could be given only if the company met its goals in profits, environmental sustainability, and quality of service. Because of the service failure, no executives received bonuses for a year of record profits.

The withheld bonuses were both a carrot and a stick: There was

a renewed focus on improving and redesigning logistics and fulfillment. In 2012 and thereafter, the company's service performance
was back to its previous standards.

*   *   *

Like so many things, culture is simple but not easy. At its core,
service leadership and creating a service culture come down to the
people you hire, what you expect of them, and what you want to be
known for as a company. BDO USA is also applying a keen eye to
shifting demographics in the workplace. "You now have multiple
generations that are working together and that is impacting how we
service clients and how we structure our teams," says CEO Wayne
Berson. "We are increasingly finding that building teams with di-
verse backgrounds, coming from different generations, is enabling
us to deliver the best value to the clients. It allows us to leverage the
different perspectives and skill sets that each team member brings
to the table."

What you stand for as a company is a question you have to answer
as both a service provider and as an employer. The answer to one will
determine the answer to the other, and vice versa. "Our clients are
our calling card, but to employees, we needed to be able to tell them
what we stand for from a people point of view," says Abby Gold of
Weber Shandwick. "When we're trying to bring talent into the organization, they want to know what our programs and policies are,
what do we do about flexible working arrangements, what can they
expect?"

Ultimately, a service culture is about show, not tell. "We are generally reluctant to spend a lot of time trumpeting how great we are at
service," says Nordstrom's Ken Worzel. "We'd rather be focusing on
keeping employees centered on the customer rather than ourselves."

CHAPTER 12

The Full Circle: The Service-Product Connection

A t this book's beginning, we described how much of what is known about management and design comes from industrial companies. The export of knowledge to services companies was often awkward, occasionally successful. ThedaCare and Virginia Mason are two of many hospitals that adopted the Toyota Production System, for example. But the flow rarely went the other way, from services to industry. In the early 1990s, General Electric rolled out a project to study and learn from best practices at other companies, looking at outfits like electronic components maker AMP, Chaparral Steel, Ford, Hewlett-Packard, and Xerox. As one GE executive put it, "People who make turbines do not think they can learn anything from David's Cookies."

Ironically, at that point GE was midway through a transition from a company that in 1980 got 85 percent of its revenues from manufacturing to one that, by 2000, was 75 percent services. IBM was following a similar path, as we discussed in Chapter 2. By 2004, Rolls-Royce, GE's rival in the aircraft engine business, got half its revenue from services. In 2010, according to the Economist Intelligence Unit, one out of four manufacturers was offering design services; one out of five offered maintenance services, and about the same number offered additional consulting services. Forty percent of electrical equipment makers offered design services.

When it comes to learning, the student has become the teacher—in management circles the "services transition" is studied not only as a macroeconomic phenomenon but as a passage individual companies must navigate. Some jargoneers have given it a perfectly horrid name: servitization.

In this chapter, our focus shifts to the ways goods-making companies can design services, work more effectively with their existing service arms, or become partners with service businesses. Companies like GE and IBM no longer manage themselves according to an arbitrary distinction between goods and services—not if they want to deliver a consistent experience to customers or strong value to investors. Your opportunity to delight your customer can no longer end at the loading dock. You have some responsibility for the customer's experience—and your customer will insist that you accept it, ready or not. The principles of service design and delivery are not only available to manufacturers; they are necessary.

Hybrid Vigor

When services study manufacturing, it is often to learn how to achieve economies of scale by standardizing offerings (making services more like products) or automating work (making service delivery more like an assembly line). When it is the other way around, it is frequently because manufacturers hope services companies can show them how to increase flexibility, customize, and personalize—without giving up scale economies. The process of "servitization" (we will stop using the term now) can be much more sophisticated than that: At its best, it can help companies forge a direct link to their customers and acquire for themselves the revenues, profits, and customer capital that middlemen had accrued.

A study of 348 German companies shows that "hybrid innovations"—where a company introduces product and related service innovations simultaneously—produce more revenue and profit than product or service innovations alone. An example: the lighting system at Amsterdam's Schiphol Airport. Philips and an energy services company called Cofely own and manage the lights; Schiphol pays for the light it uses—not unlike the software-as-a-service model many tech companies offer. Philips and Cofely believe they can cut energy costs in half through a combination of new technology and innovative design—and will pocket the profits.

Leased cars, leased software, leased lumens: The line between services and products, blurry already, will become blurrier still. In a world of connected devices—the Internet of Things—virtually every product will have an IP address and the ability to communicate. Caterpillar and an analytics company called Uptake have created predictive diagnostics tools so customers can monitor equipment, plan maintenance, and improve uptime. Your refrigerator will tell you—or your grocer, or Amazon—that you are running low on orange juice and Greek yogurt, and order it if you wish. Is that a product or a service? Your orthopedist will X-ray your pelvis and send the data to a room down the hall from the operating room, where a 3-D printer will make your new, one-of-a-kind artificial hip while you're being prepped for surgery. Is that a service or a product?

You do not have to invoke science fiction to see how service design helps manufacturers succeed. Just swing by your local Apple Store. The success of Apple Stores is justly legendary—they have the highest sales per square foot of any shops in history, beating Tiffany's by better than three-to-two. But when the first Apple Store opened in 2001 (five months before the release of the first iPod), a number of pundits prophesied catastrophe—one predicting that it wouldn't last two years. Doubters said Apple was opening stores only because Macs didn't thrive with the usual retailers—Best Buy, Circuit City, and a host of smaller shops.

The story of the Apple Store—from Steve Jobs's meticulous attention even to the staircases to modeling the Genius Bar after the concierge desk at the Four Seasons hotel chain—is well known. But why did it work? Of course physical design is part of the magic, but the real secret is the way every aspect of retail service design expresses and extends the design of Apple's products, giving consistent, elegant form to the entire customer journey—shopping, buying, owning, tech support.

Apple, a Trendsetter in our service design typology, has always prioritized customer experience over technical computing power. A few months before opening the first Apple Stores, Steve Jobs told the Macworld trade show, "Buying a car is no longer the worst purchasing experience. Buying a computer is now No. 1." Apple wrested control over customer experience from mass-market chains, which weren't passionate about the product, and Mac-fanatic shops, which were inconsistent. Apple's 2011 Form 10K, filed with the Securities and Exchange Commission—the last such form Jobs would have personally overseen—includes a remarkable section called "Business Strategy" that explicitly connects the company's product strategy to its service design.

It begins by saying that the company is "committed to bringing the best user experiences" with hardware, software, and services together, and specifically states that its stores are designed and staffed to "simplify and enhance" its products, viewing "direct contact with customers" as an essential part of demonstrating its products' advantages. Store, service, software, stuff: It's all one experience. It is arguable that Apple's integration of customer experience has been of greater value to shareholders than its integrated "closed system" of hardware and software. Certainly the company's resurrection and transformation did not begin until it combined service design with product design—a stunning example of hybrid vigor.

Stunning, but far from unique. Lexus swept into the American car market in 1989, becoming the number-one luxury import in just two years and the top luxury car, import or domestic, in just eleven.

Lexus delivered a brilliantly designed one-two punch of product and service. Thanks to the Toyota Production System, Lexus was able to build luxurious and defect-free cars for less than Mercedes, BMW, Lincoln, and Cadillac, because Lexuses needed less inspection and rework. The company funneled the savings into building a dealer network entirely separate from Toyota's existing one, and offered such attention-getting (and customer-winning) services as free pickup, drop-off, and loaner-car services in the event that a car needed to go into the shop.

Other luxury marques have fought back in recent years—particularly the German car companies. Audi has outpaced Lexus in styling and performance and chipped away at its service edge, further evidence that innovation is an endless journey (see Chapter 8). But Lexus's extraordinary ascent, in an industry where market share generally changes slowly, is further evidence of how manufacturers can use well-designed services to woo, wow, and win customers.

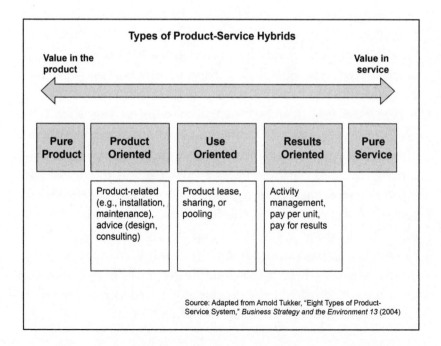

Types of Product-Service Hybrids

Value in the product → Value in service

Pure Product	Product Oriented	Use Oriented	Results Oriented	Pure Service
	Product-related (e.g., installation, maintenance), advice (design, consulting)	Product lease, sharing, or pooling	Activity management, pay per unit, pay for results	

Source: Adapted from Arnold Tukker, "Eight Types of Product-Service System," *Business Strategy and the Environment 13* (2004)

Well Being, Being Well

Natura Cosméticos is a company with $2.7 billion in sales, commanding about a quarter of the cosmetics market in Brazil, with a unique customer interface: She is your neighbor. In Brazil, five other Latin American countries, and France, 1.7 million people, mostly women, work as "consultants" selling makeup, toiletries, and other bath and beauty products door-to-door; they are the face of the company, quite literally.

Technically speaking, Natura is a manufacturer; it has 6,500 employees, laboratories, a factory, and a high-tech warehouse that ships 61 million orders a day directly to customers. But the business model is designed from the customer back. "We are driven by two passions: products and relationships. Everything oscillates around that," says R&D director Victor Fernandes. Natura is not a factory with customers outside, but a meticulously designed customer experience—a service surrounding a factory.

That experience is summed up in the company's tagline, *Bem Estar Bem*—"Well Being, Being Well." That slogan is meant to express the company's deeply held belief that it has not only a social mission—the well-being of people and the environment—but also a profit motive.

Bem Estar Bem manifests itself in four interlocking ways. The first is personal contact—neighbor-to-neighbor, woman-to-woman. The second is the product line, which Natura has grouped into four concepts, each of which expresses a value that has to do with life experience more than physical beauty: Ekos, whose ingredients are sustainably harvested from Brazilian forests ("look after yourself; look after the world"); Chronos, a line designed not to cover wrinkles but to celebrate beauty at any age ("each woman has her own story"); Mamãe e Bebê, a matching line of toiletries and products for mothers and babies ("the deepest love"); Tododia, for everyday beauty ("to cherish every moment of the day").

Third, prosaic but awesome, is the ability to distribute millions of small orders—a shampoo, two lipsticks, and a mascara—error-free and economically. Failure there would cause chaos in the warehouse and also tie up consultants' time apologizing and fixing mistakes. Having recovered from its 2011 stumble (see Chapter 11), Natura now enters, picks, ships, and delivers with 100 percent accuracy. So advanced is the warehouse that Natura is on track to staff it with 30 percent of employees who are developmentally or physically disabled—another way its social mission shows up in operations.

The fourth element is continuous innovation—new products, along with seasonal promotions for existing ones, are presented in a catalogue published every three weeks, which gives the consultant a reason to ring doorbells. Natura's open and networked innovation strategy includes partnerships with more than 200 organizations, in Brazil and elsewhere (including MIT), as well as a co-creation program open to customers, consultants, and the public. Together these partners have helped in 60 percent of Natura's innovation projects.

"The most important capability of Natura has to do with relationships. Instead of giving everyone red jackets or pink Cadillacs, we try to treat everyone as individuals, and allow them to be themselves," says Alessandro Carlucci, CEO until 2014 and now chairman of Business for Social Responsibility, a nonprofit group. "There are several ways in which the values are made tangible. One way is through the products. Another way is through the services, like supply and logistics."

It's the Journey, Stupid

Customers care little about the distinction between maker and seller. Their loyalty is earned by the entirety of their experience, not just one part of it. In health care, it is good to know that a provider follows the book in terms of treatment protocols—but the real question is whether the patient recovers fully and retains quality of life and didn't have to go through hell in the process. Whatever the offering, and whatever the arrangement between goods producer and service provider, the important point is to develop and design a customer journey that delivers the value you promise.

We wrote about the importance of critical customer interactions in Chapter 3—the touchpoints that make an experience memorable or one a customer wants to forget. But as we said and have emphasized throughout this book, it is not enough to succeed *just* at make-or-break moments. Research by the McKinsey consulting firm confirms the importance of managing the customer journey as a whole. According to the consultants, "Performance on journeys is 30% to 40% more strongly correlated with customer satisfaction than performance on touchpoints is—and 20% to 30% more strongly correlated with business outcomes, such as high revenue, repeat purchase, low customer churn, and positive word of mouth."

Products or services that have or seek a strong emotional connection to customers need to be especially alert to the impact of value-chain partners on the experience they want customers to have. For manufacturers and their customers, shopping and technical support are emotional as well as practical considerations. The connection works the other way, too, from service to product. When a restaurant says it uses Niman Ranch beef or pork, it is using a product attribute to validate its service excellence. The Finest Carrier, a Southern California company that specializes in transporting classic, antique, and racing cars, assures customers, "We use only the finest equipment."

Consider the calamity that briefly befell the *Boston Globe* in late December 2015 when the paper, technically a manufacturer, switched to a new contractor for home delivery service. The contractor, a California company, botched the job, hiring too few drivers and designing such bad delivery routes that one columnist—who like many of his newspaper colleagues pitched in to deliver the Sunday paper to more than 150 routes—said the maps looked like what you would get "if you handed an Etch-a-Sketch to a really drunk guy and told him to turn the knobs." The newspaper staffers' heroics reflected their understanding that, for readers, there was no boundary between the product and the service.

For days, paper and contractor pointed fingers at one another, but ultimately, as owner John Henry (who also owns another local institution, the Red Sox baseball team) wrote in an apology to readers, "Your carrier is, in fact, often the public face of our company. When I purchased the Globe two years ago, more than half the subscribers who were not renewing their subscriptions told us it was due to delivery service issues. . . . Before I arrived, the *Globe* had moved away from operating its own delivery service. That was a mistake. . . . We began to look for an alternative delivery service."

That move caused the New Year's debacle, from which the *Globe* has largely recovered, thanks to swift action—and the dividends of customer capital. The paper switched delivery partners on December 28, 2015. By January 4, 2016, half the routes were back in the hand of its previous distributor; the transition was 100 percent completed by March 14. Ironically, by April 1, customer complaints about delivery were lower than they had been before the December 28 move. Subscribers who canceled received free papers; after five weeks 50 percent had returned, and as of May 2016, the paper reported it was bringing back 10 percent per week. "There is a difference between losing a customer because they hate the product and losing a customer because you can't get them the product they love," says CEO Mike Sheehan. "You can recover from the latter fairly quickly."

The two lessons: Consumers pay to experience the whole play, not just your role in it; and manufacturers have just as much to lose—or win—from service design and delivery as do services companies themselves.

Easier Said than Served

To be clear: We are not saying that manufacturers should integrate downstream into services (for example, that the *Globe* should manage delivery itself); nor are we saying that manufacturers should avidly add value-added services to their offerings; nor are we saying that services companies should integrate upstream and become producers of goods. You can find companies that have succeeded with each strategy (Apple in retail, GE and Rolls-Royce aircraft engines in servicing the aircraft engines they make, Netflix in producing movies and television series).

You can also find failures, some of them calamitous. In 2009, Xerox paid $6.4 billion to buy Affiliated Computer Services in an attempt to add technology outsourcing services to its copier and document-management capabilities. The move ended up sucking resources from the core and not returning them in the form of sales synergies, and in 2016 the company announced that it would split itself in two, essentially splitting itself into product and service companies.

Manufacturing-service hybrids are enormously complex. Start with the fact that most manufacturing is done in a few central locations, while most services need to be deployed in many, often far-flung places. Add to that the organizational difficulty of optimizing both the mass production (which products like) and the customization (which services demand); the fact that you now have to coordinate many more points of contact with each of your customers; the fact that managing inventory for manufacturing (where you want parts to arrive just in time) is almost the reverse of manufacturing inventory for maintenance (where you need to stockpile them just in case, including for products you no longer make); and the fact that not every product wants to have a "solution" tacked on to it.

Similar tensions exist not just across the services-manufacturing divide but within manufacturers and within services companies. Often they result from companies trying on the one hand to sell to or serve many customers in fairly simple transactions (where volume rules), and, on the other hand, serve or sell to a few customers in complex transactions (where customization rules). Such was the case, as outlined in Chapter 3, when retail broker Charles Schwab attempted to integrate the wealth management services of U.S. Trust.

It is almost impossible for a company to be equally good at both volume operations and complex services, consultant Geoffrey Moore argues in a brilliant article titled "Strategy and Your Stronger Hand." The two business models are inherently in conflict and one or the other is likely to dominate. The difficulties extend from customer experience back to the counting room. Measurements like return on assets may accurately assess a capital-intensive factory but be meaningless for an intellectual-capital-intensive service business, whose assets are desks, computers, and, most important, people and relationships. You calculate productivity using different inputs and outputs. It is exceptionally difficult to evaluate budget requests for product-service hybrids, and harder still to compare them to product-alone or service-alone proposals. Incentive pay may be harder to mete out.

In sum: A manufacturer that adds services without understanding the economics, organization, and design requirements has upped the number of ways it can disappoint customers and shareholders alike. Yet—regardless of who owns whom and whatever the business model—there is every reason to design an end-to-end customer journey together: When companies are connected, "It is not our responsibility" makes no more sense as an excuse to a customer than "It is not my department" does if only your company is involved. When the journeys are not co-designed, products may suffer, services may suffer, and the customer almost always will suffer.

The service design map thus becomes bigger. For service companies that deal in goods, like distributors and retailers, it reaches back into the factory and forward into repair and service. It has feedback and feed-forward loops that cross company boundaries if they need to. Offstage, information gleaned from service calls feeds back to manufacturing and feeds forward to product development. Real-time sales data course through the organization to fine-tune purchasing, production, distribution, and marketing. Onstage, cocreation is encouraged in as many places as possible.

Companies that do not deal in physical goods also have an extended map, often one that involves other service providers, as we saw in Chapter 7. If the first map goes horizontally from one stage of the journey to another, this one goes vertically as well, to include multiple providers at each stage. With this large map, the well-designed service company is able to understand the full dimensions of a customer's experience, craft customer expectations more intelligently, and develop ways to work constructively with other companies for the common good of wooing, wowing, and winning customers.

CHAPTER 13

First Steps, Next Steps

Tell Ryanair's Chief Marketing Officer Kenny Jacobs that he's an exemplary convert to the religion of service design and delivery, and he laughs—an easy laugh, not a self-conscious one. Few companies could rival Ryanair's long-held reputation for delivering a lousy customer experience. Indeed, even in an industry often criticized for being deaf to customer needs and complaints, Ryanair stood out. In 2007, the *Economist* described the low-cost Dublin-based airline as "a byword for appalling customer service," citing its "jeering rudeness towards anyone or anything that gets in its way."

Ryanair offered seemingly impossibly cheap flights throughout Europe, opening up the possibility of air travel to millions of people. The company took almost a perverse pride in its reputation for meanness in every sense; CEO Michael O'Leary even mused publicly about charging passengers for using lavatories. The Hobbesian strategy of operating flights that were not only cheap but short, nasty, and brutish worked—until it didn't.

After years of rising profits, Ryanair issued a profit warning in September 2013; it saw its net income for 2014 fall to 522.8 million euros, from 569.3 million euros in 2013. As Ryanair watched its profits drop, low-cost competitor easyJet saw its profits double. Not coincidentally, in late 2013 O'Leary said, with an Irish forthrightness, that the company had to "stop unnecessarily pissing people off."[*]

The person charged with figuring out how to do that was Jacobs, who joined the company in January 2014 after thirteen years in food retailing. Jacobs told one of us his thinking at the time was, "It is either going to be the worst or the best job that I've ever had in the customer marketing space."

Shortly after joining, he drafted Ryanair's new marketing slogan: "Always Getting Better"; the three words also served as a rallying cry; a manifesto for change. "The things you need to do to get it right are always obvious," says Jacobs. "That said, how you execute change to the benefit of improving the customer experience is harder to do than people think."

The challenge for Ryanair was to stay true to its value proposition—the fact that it is a Bargain, and a rock-bottom Bargain at that, is the one thing that earned it any favor from customers—while figuring out how to improve customer experience. "We were at a crossroads," Jacobs remembers. "We had pushed things too far in certain areas in terms of having a reputation and a model that were too rough around the edges. That led to a look in the mirror and we said, 'Right, how do we keep low fares, how do we keep the cost advantage and the great returns for shareholders, but how do we rapidly and very significantly improve the customer experience?'"

The airline focused on three key aspects of the journey: the digital experience, with a more user-friendly, intuitive website; the airport experience, with more streamlined, efficient operations; and the inflight experience, allowing people to bring on luggage and offering assigned seats (for a fee). Notice that:

* each addresses a major *Ow* moment in one of the three principal phases of a trip by air

....

* Michael O'Leary also said in the same article, "Business books are bullshit and are usually written by wankers."

* none is untrue to the airline's low-price promise

* the cost is minimal; indeed, each can save the company effort and money—giving the company a win-win: better service, lower cost.

If anything, says Jacobs, "we've become the even more ruthless price leader with a love of innovation, digital, and a relentless pursuit of a great customer experience." The airline isn't chasing customer's hearts, but their minds. "I don't want customers to say, 'I love Ryanair,'" says Jacobs. "We want people to say, 'This is a commoditized, functional experience getting from Dublin to London, from London to Madrid.'"

By the end of fiscal 2015, Ryanair was carrying 19 more passengers per flight than it had two years earlier, confirmation to Jacobs that the airline is living up to its pledge of "Always Getting Better." The initiative has more than paid for itself. "We've reduced our cost per customer over the last two years, which is why shareholders love us. Those nineteen extra passengers help subsidize our initiatives, and I do not think we would have them had we not changed our approach to customer experience."

*   *   *

We have used the metaphor of the service journey throughout this book. It is fitting, then, that we should end with the story about Ryanair, whose very business is journeys. Studying and writing about service design has been a journey for us, too, as it has been for many business leaders, and as it is, we hope, for you. Service design presents an exciting opportunity to explore something that is new to management thinking, new to business practice, new to many business leaders. It was a journey of confirmation and discovery, of realization and recognition.

Like us, many of the companies we researched—some of which we have written about; others which have provided context, background, and confirmation—were experiencing a dawning awareness of how design thinking, and service design in particular, can transform businesses, improve relationships with customers, and help companies shape their destinies.

For some, service design was a consciously constructed connective tissue between strategy, business plan, and operating system. A whole section of the Edmunds website showcases the role of design thinking in the company and its approach to business. Other leaders are service designers who had never heard the term before we talked with them; like Molière's Monsieur Jourdain, they had been speaking prose without knowing it. Some came to service design from other management disciplines, such as lean management; others started by trying to figure out what "customer-centricity" means, and found themselves in the business of design without knowing it.

Allow us to summarize what we discovered along the road.

The way to manage customer experience is to think of it as a journey that you and your customer take together. This journey has many steps—many touchpoints—each of which is important. But it is not a series of discrete interactions or transactions. It is something more seamless, something that makes sense, something that feels, as Continuum's Jon Campbell put it, "inevitable." It has a beginning, middle, and end.

It is a shared journey: You and your customer are companions along the way. You cannot manage your customers' journeys if you do not keep up with them by managing your internal handoffs so that you deliver the experience you promise at every moment. You cannot manage the journey if your culture, incentives, and organizational design get in the way.

Others join the two of you on the journey—ecosystem partners that you may not be able to control but cannot afford to ignore. The services Edmunds provides to car buyers are greatly enhanced by its deliberately designed work with dealerships, and everybody—buyer, Edmunds, dealer—wins.

Your hope is that the end of each journey marks the beginning of a new one for you and your customer. The customer's repeat business is a reflection of the value that you give and that you create together. You must never lose sight of the customer's value to you and of the importance of that value exchange and the joint accumulation of value.

*   *   *

Empathy is the starting point of the journey and must be your constant companion—your Jiminy Cricket—as you design the customer's experience. Empathy allows you to understand what the customer is experiencing, to anticipate even those needs and desires that customers have not put into words, and to translate these into actions through your design and delivery. Empathy liberates you to do the innovation and experimentation and continuous improvement that are necessary for excellence in service design and delivery, because it allows you to walk in your customers' shoes, and understand their needs even when they are unspoken.

Remember the demented watch salesman—"Want a watch? You don't like this watch? I've got another watch . . ."? Empathy reminds us not to flog watches, but to learn why customers need to know the time of day. If you are truly committed to excellence in SD^2, you need to design from the outside in. Even if you design and provide a service that is notably insensitive to customers' feelings (indeed, that was what Ryanair originally did), you need to know what customers need and what they perceive about you.

Empathy also reminds us that customers are individuals, not segments—people, not "the customer." At ThedaCare, Lori personifies the customer: Sometimes the patient, sometimes the patient's mother, spouse, or daughter, Lori is always there. Her name is invoked at team meetings. Real-life Loris regularly participate in meetings at the hospital to discuss problems and vet new ideas. Lori is a way of making sure that design, processes, and treatment are not for the convenience of staff or physicians or insurers or any of the other participants—but that the science, the skill, and the health care system are arranged for the benefit of Lori and her loved ones.

Every company needs a Lori, or several Loris. We called them "use cases" in Chapter 6. But it is even better when you call them by name.

*   *   *

Empathy must be reined in by expectations you set and meet. Empathy unbridled can lead you to wanting to do all and be all; expectations keep you and your customer in line. Expectations are promises you make; therefore they must be promises you keep. They need to be visible and articulated equally well internally and externally.

Because expectations are promises, setting them has to begin by understanding your capabilities—what they are, and what they must be to succeed every time. What are the half a dozen things you do (or must do) better than anyone else so as to do something for customers that rivals cannot match? Natura, recall, combines managing and supporting a vast direct-sales force, rapid-fire innovation, the ability to manage brand families, an extraordinary distribution system, and an ecological ethos—capabilities that collectively define what customers can expect and that are essential to meeting expectations. They also define what customers should not expect—fancy packaging of the sort designed to stand out on a drugstore shelf, for example.

Or consider Surf Air. For frequent California business travelers, Surf Air promises to deliver the hassle-free experience of private aviation at or below the cost of normal commercial travel. That is a lofty expectation, but Surf Air achieves it as much by what it does not do as by what it does—it does not fly out of major airports, does not offer a frequent-flyer program, does not connect to national route systems, does not offer multiple classes of service. We could not have asked for a better experience getting from the Bay Area to Los Angeles, flying Surf Air from San Carlos to Hawthorne.

Your ability and willingness to meet customer expectations are powerful indications of whether you do in fact have an actual design to your service.

*   *   *

Service design and delivery are a strategic discipline. When service design began, with the work of Lynn Shostack and others, it emphasized bringing to disorderly services the tools and operational discipline that manufacturers had deployed for several generations. When that engineering mindset interacted with design thinking a generation later, service design became as much a creative tool as an operational one. In both senses, however, service designers' sanctum sanctorum, the holiest of holy places, has been a team room whose walls are covered with Post-it notes, flowcharts, and diagrams.

It needs to be a boardroom discussion, too. In service businesses, even more than for product companies, the three foundational questions of strategy—where to compete, what to sell, how to win—are inextricably bound up with design. This is because your customers are with you, in your presence, when you create value through services. You design the arena in which you meet, whether it is physical space like a hotel lobby or operational space like processes your bankers use when working with clients.

Use strategy to determine SD^2; use SD^2 to execute and reinforce strategy. Your goal is to design and deliver a delightful experience to your customers in arenas where you have the right to win. Your senior executives—up to and including the board—should be reviewing the SD^2 Report Card (which we show you how to make in the Appendix), comparing it to previous performance and to the service design profile of your competitors, and discussing how design can make you distinctive and unbeatable.

*   *   *

Coherence, consistency, and alignment need to be designed into your service offering, or they will be frittered away in the delivery. There are many reasons to stray from strategy, most of which look good at the time. The natural desire to emulate a rival's success; misaligned incentives; customers who ask for what you should not—you know—give; the competing interests of different companies in the same service value system; internal competition between functions or business units, each with its own goals; the pressure to grow—all of these can pull you off course. For these reasons, you must understand which customer interactions are most critical—and get company-wide agreement on the list and empower leaders to enforce adherence to that agreement. As much as possible, you should map and measure customer journeys as a whole, not just at each touchpoint, so that you can reward for the whole and not just the parts.

Doing this will help you set priorities, too. There is, and always will be, an almost infinite list of ways to improve customers' experience. You cannot know where to begin or how to allocate your resources without knowing which *Ahhh*s and *Ow*s are most important to the successful completion of a customer's journey with you.

Furthermore, by attending carefully to service design both onstage and backstage, you can make reliably delightful service the natural thing for employees to do. Everything about Dunkin' Donuts is designed to make it easy to give customers what they want and get them on their way quickly, from the items on the menu to the machinery that employees use to the design of the shops themselves.

If employees have to buck the system to do what is right for customers, they will, before long, stop doing what is right—or only a few heroes will do what's right while the rest stand passively by. But if doing the right thing is natural, employees will do it without being told. Leaders at Mobile Mini, you will recall, track a "Customer Effort Score" that asks how easy the company is to do business with. We have not yet seen a company that asks *employees* to rate how easy it is for them to do right by *customers*. But we think it would be a good idea.

* * *

Responsibility for customer delight belongs to everyone. It is not just the job of frontline employees, who interact directly with customers and in many cases actually create the service you sell; nor just the role of marketing, which tries to understand what customers want; nor just the role of customer service, which tries to solve problems customers encounter. In a truly customer-centric organization, everyone is arrayed around the customer and everyone can contribute to the success of the journey you are on together—even, you will remember, the folks in finance who send out the bill.

This is easy to say and easy to agree on, but exceptionally difficult to do. One reason it is hard: the ordinary but powerful pressures of maintaining internal harmony. We like to imagine someone coming to work in the morning to discover two urgent messages, each saying, "Call me the minute you get in." One is from a major customer; one is from his boss. Which should he answer first? And in your company, which would he?

The second reason: Many employees see or hear customers indirectly and distantly, if at all. Managers sometimes try to substitute the notion of "internal customers" to create a sense of accountability for people deep in the back office or far upstream in production, but internal customers are no substitute for the real thing. Your service design map (which we show you how to create in the Appendix) is an important way to draw direct *and measurable* connections between backstage work and onstage experience.

* * *

In many ways SD² is simple, but its simplicity must not hide the fact that it is a never-ending process. You are never done; by the same token, it is never too late to begin.

It is simple in that the principles that guide it—the five principles we have outlined—are logical and rooted in good business and management practices. In some ways, excellence in service is, or should be, simpler than excellence in manufacturing, because it begins, not with science or technology of a hulking great factory, but with a handshake: the moment you and your customer meet each other, seal the deal, or say thanks when you are done. What could be simpler?

What could be more complex? Every customer is different from every other customer. Each customer is different from one touchpoint to another, or from one journey to the next. Moreover, the environment in which you are interacting changes around you both, particularly as information technology advances.

You are never done, therefore, because customers' needs and tastes will evolve, as will your own ability to meet them. Ideally one should not widely outpace the other.

It is never too late to begin, but the choice never to begin is a mistake. As more companies become aware of the importance of service design and delivery, as services—many of them largely commoditized—become a larger segment of the economy, as customers have fewer reasons to be loyal and more ways to discover competitive or alternative solutions to their needs, businesses that do not embrace the opportunity to differentiate themselves through design will suffer.

You do the wooing and the wowing, but ideally you and your customer both win.

APPENDIX

....

Tools for the Journey

We have made the case for service design as a strategic discipline—that is, as a way to make better strategic decisions and to execute them more effectively. But service design is also a very practical approach to problem solving. Its tools and methods can help you find the root causes of customer dissatisfaction and uncover new paths to delight customers. They can improve your success rate with new customer offerings. Service design is a management tool, like project management, lean management, predictive analytics, benchmarking, and others. It can help you cut costs; it can improve alignment between sales and marketing and between operations and support staff.

The universe of service design practitioners is one of whiteboards and conference room walls covered with multicolored Post-it notes, of field trips to watch customers in action, of ideation sessions, rapid prototyping, and iterative experimentation. Every year, scores of service designers earn advanced degrees in the subject.

In the pages that follow, we will describe a number of tools and methods to help you sharpen your service design thinking and will outline several specific projects to put thinking into action. We have made no attempt to be comprehensive; this is not an MA in a box. Several excellent toolkits exist in print and online—we list a few at the end of this section.

Instead, we have developed—and in a few cases adapted—tools and projects that extend the logic of this book. The first group comprises two basic tools that amplify the thinking in the first part of the book, "Service Design in Context." We ask you to begin by creating a baseline—a Service Design Grade Point Average—by which you can measure your current competence at service design and delivery, and against which you can measure progress. We will also show you how to weight the scores on your report card to emphasize what elements of SD^2 are most important to your value proposition.

Then—and this will come as no surprise to students of the field—we show you a prototype for a map of the service journeys on which you take customers. You will want to develop your own version of this map—probably iterated with those walls full of Post-its; what we are describing is an example from which you can build.

The second section proposes seven service design improvement projects, from identifying and strengthening critical customer interactions to building customer capital. Each of these picks up a key theme of the book. Several of them focus on one of the five principles of SD^2—such as the project for creating cross-platform excellence. Individually and together, these seven projects will go a long way toward improving your ability to woo, wow, and win.

Finally, we include a section of tools and diagnostics (about measuring the value of a customer, diagnosing product-service conflicts, etc.) that we believe will be especially useful as you undertake your SD^2 journey. They are aimed at eliciting insights and diagnoses and sparking discussions, so that you undertake your service design journey with a good idea of where to go and what to do. We encourage you to find others that are useful to you or to develop your own: This is a new field, and you can be among its innovators.

Basic Tools

WHAT'S YOUR SERVICE DESIGN GRADE POINT AVERAGE? THE SD² REPORT CARD

To plan a successful service design journey, you must know your starting point. The SD² Report Card will provide you and your teams with a baseline by which you can evaluate your current competence in service design and identify areas for improvement. You can do this by scoring each business unit or service line on each of the ten elements of SD² excellence we outlined in Chapter 1 (see p. 20.)

Rate each element on a five-point scale. We like using 0 to 4 rather than 1 to 5—zero meaning, "We do not do this at all," four meaning, "We're world class." This way, you have a five-point scale (which statisticians like), but you can combine the results into a Grade Point Average—for example, a 3.2, equivalent to a B+.

To get a more accurate and nuanced result, complete the report card with a team whose members come from different parts of a business—the customer service desk is likely to have a different perspective on these issues than the sales director or the head of operations. You can get further perspective by using the report as the basis for customer surveys or focus groups. You can also get valuable information by getting input from people who "should" be customers (right profile, for example) but are not.

Your result is a starting point—your baseline. From it, you can begin to identify where to apply service design techniques to raise your grade and improve your business, and which service lines or business units have best practices you can propagate internally. You can also complete a report card for your competitors, and compare your results to theirs.

YOUR SERVICE DESIGN AND DELIVERY REPORT CARD

	BUSINESS UNIT OR SERVICE LINE A	BUSINESS UNIT OR SERVICE LINE B	BUSINESS UNIT OR SERVICE LINE C
CUSTOMER FACING (0 = POOR; 4 = EXCELLENT)			
Empathy: Did we take into account what it would be like to be the customer?			
Expectation: Are we and customers both clear about what customers should (and should not) expect?			
Emotion: Do we understand our customers' emotional stake in the experience we provide? Have we accounted for it in our design and offering?			
Elegance: Is our offering clean, simple, easy to work with—nothing superfluous, nothing omitted? Are we easy to do business with?			
Engagement: Do we track all points and types of interaction with our customer?			
COMPANY FACING			
Execution: Are we able to deliver on our value proposition every time?			
Engineering: Are our processes and delivery robust? Are our operations lean? Is any engineering done at the expense of the customer's experience?			
Economics: Is the service well priced? Does the customer get value for money? Are we earning an acceptable profit?			

	BUSINESS UNIT OR SERVICE LINE A	BUSINESS UNIT OR SERVICE LINE B	BUSINESS UNIT OR SERVICE LINE C
Experimentation: Do we have processes for continuous improvement? Do we conduct experiments to try out new things? Do we regularly introduce new offerings with a good success rate?			
Equivalence: How well satisfied are we, as the seller?			
TOTAL			
AVERAGE (SD² GPA)			

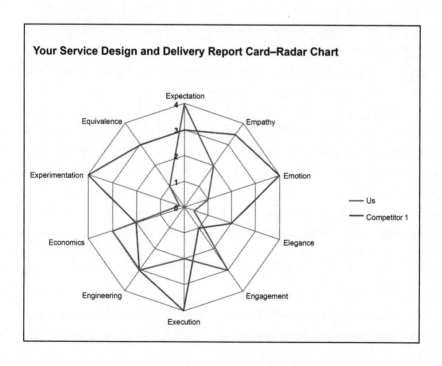

If you are fond of radar charts (as we are) it is possible to use them to display these data so as to compare your company with its competitors, or to make analyses of strengths and weaknesses across the various business units or service lines.

SCORING WHAT IS MOST IMPORTANT TO YOUR CUSTOMERS

The ten elements of the scorecard, you recall from Chapter 5, can be divided into two groups, one measuring the quality of the customer's experience, the other technical excellence. Both matter—but which matters more? Delighting customers depends on reliably executing what matters for them and for you. Are experience and excellence equally important? Is it 60/40 in favor of customer experience? Maybe it is 30/70 in favor of excellence?

With some thinking and a little arithmetic, you can manipulate your report card to put more emphasis on which of its ten elements is most important to your strategy and value proposition—like giving more weight to the grade you get in a major academic course than your grade in gym or shop. A weighted GPA will help you judge how to invest your time and money to design and deliver delight to your customers.

Learn what matters. You can do this internally, with a discussion among colleagues, making sure to include people from all parts of the organization. Better still, involve customers and others in the conversation:

* Which elements of the report card do sales reps emphasize when calling on customers?

* Which does your service team discover when dealing with complaints?

* When customers describe why they do business with you, which elements do they most mention?

* When they describe why they stay?

* When they explain why they have left?

* How would you score your competitors on the ten elements?

* How do customers score your competitors on the ten elements?

* What do the ratings of independent sources (J.D. Power, etc.) imply about you and your competitors in terms of the ten elements of SD²?

Feed these data into your report card, and sort the responses into "excellence" and "experience" piles. Where is the preponderance of opinion?

Now, factor in two strategic elements: What is the nature of the critical customer interactions you identified in Chapter 3—experiential, technical, or a mix of both? Also, which of these categories gives you the biggest chance for differentiation? Every airline must meet standards for technical excellence—those are necessities; their opportunity to differentiate is greatest in the experiential realm. The reverse may be true for another business—cybersecurity services, for example. While you are looking for an overall weighting between experience and excellence, take note of any individual element that is of overwhelmingly high importance—expectation-setting, for example, or economy.

Create a weighting. This needn't be mathematically precise, but *it must be agreed upon.* You are looking for a rough figure—60/40, 40/60—that every relevant function or department accepts. You need this consensus to minimize conflict when teams set priorities.

Now, return to your original scorecard, and apply the weighting. The original scorecard offers a maximum of 40 points: 4 x 5 in experience, 4 x 5 in excellence. You now need to reapportion the points according to the weighting. If experience is more important than excellence, it should count for 25 of the 40 points, say. The gap between the definition of delight and your current performance will widen or narrow accordingly, and the greater, more urgent part of your efforts should be devoted to those gaps.

MAPPING THE CUSTOMER JOURNEY

The essence of design thinking is to work on multiple solutions to a problem in parallel, rather than working in a linear sequence. Service design requires similar dexterity: looking at things from the customer's perspective, taking into account just about every possible outcome, and coming up with empathetic solutions that deliver on a company's strategy. It requires an understanding of the experience you aim to deliver (on which you just scored yourself), and then examining and mapping every point of contact (often called touchpoints) between the customer and company, recognizing that each is an opportunity to make the customer say either *Ahhh* or *Ow*.

The essential tool in service design is a map. The purpose of a map is to mark out all interactions between a company and its customers. Because service is a journey, the map must start before service begins (with advertising, for example) and continue after it is over (such as by receiving customer feedback and learning from it). Because services are handshakes, the map needs to depict both sides of the relationship—buyer as well as seller. And because services are experiences, a map should attempt to capture not just the actions and transactions, but also the reactions: the *Ahhh*, the *Ow*, and the *Wow*.

It is easy to make a map too complex. It is also easy to make it too simple, looking only at actions and processes. A good map should do eight things:

* Define the overall experience you intend to design and deliver: your value proposition and what makes you distinctive

* Offer proof points—that is, measures by which you and your customer will test whether the promised experience occurred

* Identify the touchpoints between you and your customer

* Describe the actions you take that the customer sees

* Describe what happens that the customer does not see

* Note where other companies or organizations participate in the journey

* Capture the promises you make at various parts of the journey

* Help you monitor the experiential and technical quality of your work.

What we describe here is a skeletal version of your customer journey map. Each company's map will be unique, of course. Ideally, developing the map should be a cross-functional, group project. A big wall and stacks of multicolored Post-it notes help. Over time, you will elaborate your map—zeroing in on particular touchpoints or stages of the journey (for example, a hospital might have different maps for oncology, maternity, and other patients). You might also develop much more comprehensive views of your backstage processes than we have sketched here. (Some service designers distinguish between a customer journey map and a service design blueprint—which is the detailed look "backstage.")

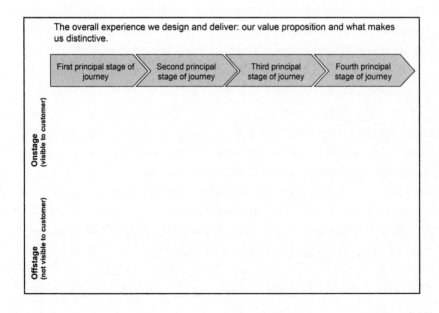

For starters, let's get the main points right.

Your template should look like the one on the previous page. Use as many or as few principal stages of the journey as are correct for your business.

Let's illustrate the process using Singapore Airlines as an example. Singapore Airlines' parent company operates four services: Singapore Airlines itself, two Asian regional brands (SilkAir and Tigerair), and low-cost carrier Scoot. We will focus on the flagship service, though some capabilities (mostly behind-the-scenes services like IT and maintenance) are shared by all four.

Define the overall experience you intend to design and deliver: your value proposition and what makes you distinctive. Offer some proof points.

The definition should be one sentence that is clear and jargon-free. For Singapore Airlines, it might be something like this:

Singapore Airlines provides international travel of the highest standard of elegance, comfort, and style.

As for proof points: The airline has been designated "Best airline in the world" by *Condé Nast Traveler* 26 out of 27 times. All its flights are international—Singapore is a city-state less than thirty miles across—and many are long-haul. First-class passengers drink Dom Pérignon; in business class, they settle for Taittinger. The company mission statement says, "Singapore Airlines is a global company dedicated to providing air transportation services of the highest quality and to maximizing returns for the benefit of its shareholders and employees," and it has been one of the few consistently profitable airlines in the world.

Identify the touchpoints between you and your customer and map actions you take that the customer sees.

What do customers see when they fly on Singapore Airlines? You might map it like this, with four basic stages and a set of touchpoints, some that vary by class of service, some that may not apply in all cases, and some that are provided by others.

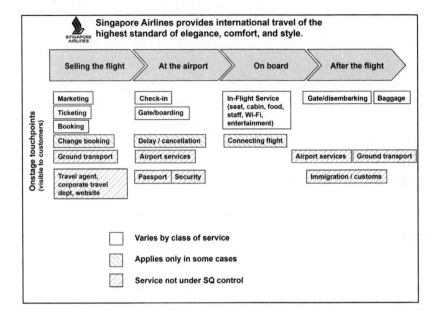

Describe what happens that the customer does not see. Now elaborate the behind-the-scenes activities that support what happens with the customers.

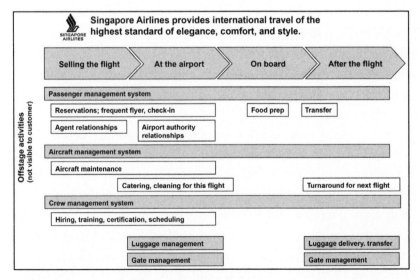

As you complete the map, you will add a row for partners and intermediaries—such as airport management, security services, cus-

toms and immigration authorities—that affect the customer's journey.

At any or all points you can go deeper, elaborating the map to show
all the details onstage or behind the scenes. Your goal is to identify
ways in which you can optimize touchpoints—while also delivering a
coherent, satisfying, and delightful overall journey.

There are many examples of service design maps and blueprints
on the Web. You can look to them for further inspiration. The Service Design Tools website, www.servicedesigntools.org (retrieved in
early 2016), includes customer journey maps and blueprints. There
are also many service design blueprints on Pinterest.

Seven Service Design and Delivery Improvement Projects

The report card and map are basic tools of service design—the first
to provide a baseline and identify areas of excellence or weakness, the
second to give an overall shape and picture to the journey your customer takes. It is not enough to visualize the architecture or admire
the problem, of course. Design thinking generally and service design
in particular are holistic; problems and opportunities are not best
addressed by taking them apart and dealing with them piecemeal.
So where to begin?

The projects that follow are manageable; you can define scope
and deliverables and do all the other things that project management and agile project management ask. But they are also broad and
holistic; they deal with cross-functional issues and with themes that
will occur over and over in your business. They are also repeatable:
Once you complete any one of these projects, you can start another
of the same kind, just as the crews that repaint the Golden Gate
Bridge no sooner come to the far end of the bridge than they return
to the beginning.

1. IDENTIFY AND STRENGTHEN CRITICAL CUSTOMER INTERACTIONS

Not all interactions with customers are of equal importance. As we described in Chapter 3, many touchpoints are common transactions: They will not win a customer to your side—though they can cost you customers if you get them wrong. A handful of other interactions are moments of truth. They are critical because they define who you are (for example, how a full-service bank manages multiple relationships with a customer), or because they come at particularly important moments for a customer (for example, how an insurance company handles a claim).

Critical interactions deserve special attention. The framework that follows will help you identify and improve them.

* Identify three or four (no more) reasons customers prefer you. Look for intangibles rather than specific service offerings: "We're the low-cost provider"; "we are the most innovative"; "we have unique advantages in terms of location." These are often manifestations of your archetype.

* Identify events in a customer's relationship with you where those reasons-to-buy are manifest: "how fast we get up to speed"; "how closely we listen to customers' financial needs"; "how effectively we cross-sell."

* Locate where these happen on your service journey map— noting that they can happen in more than one place. (For example, on Singapore Airlines, a differentiator would be the in-cabin experience, but not ticketing.)

* Identify whether these are triggered by you (you reach out to the customer) or triggered by the customer (customer asks, you then convert the ask to a pivotal event).

* For each of these, devise a plan to

  ▪ Make it even more what you want it to be (Bargain, Classic, etc.).

- Make it defensible—create entry barriers.

- Connect across silos (functions, service lines, ecosystem partners).

- Fully understand customer needs, including involving the customer in co-creation of value.

* Identify segment essentials (see p. 52)

  - Locate where these happen on your service journey map.

  - Identify whether these are triggered by you or triggered by the customer.

  - Evaluate your ability to deliver on these using the 10 E's of the Service Design/Delivery Scorecard.

* Identify table stakes (see p. 52)

  - Locate where these happen on your service journey map.

  - Identify whether these are triggered by you or triggered by the customer.

  - Evaluate your ability to deliver on these using the 10 E's of the Service Design/Delivery Scorecard.

* Identify nonessentials—the distractions (see p. 55).

  - Locate where these happen on your service journey map.

  - Identify whether these are triggered by you or triggered by the customer.

  - Add up the cost of these distractions and calculate the impact of dropping them.

2. IMPROVE HOW YOU MANAGE CUSTOMER EMOTIONS

Every customer comes into the service environment, from barbershop to bank office, with emotions that color his or her expectations.

Understanding these emotions can help you develop a more effective service design—one that is more likely to delight customers and to strengthen your business. If you know your customers' emotions, you can recognize critical customer interactions more clearly; know better whom to hire and how to train them; and even design services with the specific intention of transforming your customer's emotions into something else. Buying a cup of coffee in America was a low-commitment deal until Howard Schultz and Starbucks designed a café vaguely modeled on what he had seen in Italy and suffused the whole experience with new emotions.

It is useful to look at customers' emotions in several dimensions.

INTENSITY

COOL ←——————→ **WARM**

How much emotion is the customer likely to have? Is the customer in a hurry? Do you want to change the intensity? If so, how would you do it? For example, you might want to calm someone calling your complaint line or warm up someone at the beginning of a sales call.

COMMITMENT/IDENTIFICATION

HIGH ←——————→ **LOW**

Does the customer feel intense commitment to you? Identify with your brand? Are there ways you can take a generic offering and brand it (as Starbucks did)? Can you identify opportunities to convert indifference into loyalty (for example in handling an insurance claim)?

PURPOSE

BUSINESS ←——————→ **PLEASURE**

Is the customer spending his or her own money or the company's? Misunderstanding the customer's purpose and mindset can be as grave a faux pas as wearing a business suit to a barbecue. How do you design a mixed-use environment (such as an airport)?

INTIMACY

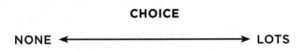

LOW-TOUCH ←——————————————→ HIGH-TOUCH

Does the customer want a personal touch or would she rather serve herself? Would you like to automate service to save money, or personalize it to increase the chance to sell more? Can you design separate tracks for each?

CHOICE

NONE ←——————————————→ LOTS

Is the customer a Free Agent ("I hear you have the best steak in town") or a Captive ("Is this the line for the DMV?")? Can you design ways to help Captive customers feel more at ease?

By understanding your customers' emotions and how you want to respond to them, you can begin to develop specific changes in service design. Service design students at the Savannah College of Art and Design may include a section about emotions on service-journey maps (it runs alongside the onstage activities), showing what they are—and what they can be—at different stages of a customer's experience.

3. DO MORE BY YOUR MOST VALUABLE CUSTOMERS

Designing for the customer that is right for you is first and foremost a strategic exercise in understanding the economics related to your customers. As always, this is a two-sided coin: Does the customer get value for money? Are you earning an acceptable profit? The answer to both of these questions must be yes.

Beyond the economics, however, two other elements of the Service Design Report Card come into play: *equivalence*—understanding your satisfaction in other-than-monetary terms—and *expectation*. Ultimately, your strongest tool for managing the conflicting desires and challenging economics of your customers is to set expectations in such a way that you can profitably serve and delight the customers you want.

Economics. There are many ways to measure customer profitability. We present one later in this section (see p. 266) but you should select the tool that most suits your business. Whatever you use, it will be more useful for service design if it gets you granular data: You should be able to look at different customer segments and different touchpoints and determine where you (and your customers) are adding value and incurring costs. Some kind of activity-based approach will give you the most useful information, though these can be complicated to use.

You want to analyze profitability by line of service as well as by customer. Are you making money on investment banking services but not on loans? From booze but not from burgers?

Armed with this information, you can

* Look for opportunities to create service bundles—encouraging unprofitable customers to add on services that make money for you

* Alternatively, unbundle: use à la carte offerings and pricing to change the customer and service mix

* Eliminate or outsource services that do not make money for you—perhaps finding ecosystem partners who can make money at something you cannot profitably do (see Chapter 7)

Equivalence enters your thinking as you account for the investments you make to acquire customers and to retain them. Quantify them if you can. If not, think back to the "Customer Bestiary" (see p. 77); collect information from marketing, sales, operations, and service teams: Which customers and which service lines appear to be just more trouble than they're worth? Where do you need to work extra hard to find customers whom you then struggle to retain? Which customers are, simply, exhausting? Even in the absence of financial information, these insights can point you to customers or service lines that are long-term losers, or (if they're profitable) that need to be reengineered so that you can deliver them without burning your organization out.

Using these insights,

* Create pricing and marketing cues that drive "bad" customers away

* Manage customer acquisition costs, shifting your marketing activities toward more profitable customers or lines of service

* Manage retention costs, so that you are investing to retain only customers that work for you

* Reengineer backstage work processes to eliminate or reduce the *Ow*s that your staff endures

Expectation-setting is the third element of delivering the right service to the right customers. What you learn from the first two exercises should help you determine how to set and manage customer expectations. At American Express, green, gold, and platinum cardholders see a schedule of benefits and a corresponding price list. Fidelity Investments and others in that industry offer different services depending on the amount of assets a customer parks with them; they also have separate, explicit lists of offers and service policies for individuals whose employers contract with Fidelity for employee wealth-management services. Sometimes companies do not make such explicit distinctions among clients—particularly in B2B situations, the segmentation is likely to be implied rather than stated outright.

Openly (by creating segments like green, gold, or platinum) or tacitly consider how to

* Create tiers of service, for example, with automated services for the lower end, a personal touch at the high; or, in businesses like professional services, with associates serving less important clients or overseeing more commoditized service offerings and partners handling the bigger, more complex deals

* More clearly set and communicate what you are offering, so that customers come in with expectations you can reliably and profitably meet

* Devise perks and paths to encourage low-end customers to move to premium ranks

* Develop clear guidelines for employees—particularly account managers and in the front line—setting out the degree of flexibility they have when it comes to serving marginal customers

* Examine customer requests and employee complaints to see if they reveal promising opportunities—for example, are you turning down customers to do something that could become a profitable new line of business for you?

4. MAKE IT EASY FOR CUSTOMERS AND EMPLOYEES—REGARDLESS OF CHANNEL OR PLATFORM

When you make it hard for customers to work with you, they leave. When you make it hard for employees, they take shortcuts—and customers leave. And when offerings across multiple channels create more confusion than value, you have turned what should be a sponge into a leaky hose. In Chapters 6 and 7 we discussed the importance of eliminating the need for heroics and of creating cross-platform coherence. Separately and together, projects to turn those principles into reality will pay you great dividends.

Reduce customer effort. People try to measure customer service in many ways: How quickly was the call answered? Was the customer's problem resolved on the first call? Was the customer satisfied by the result? Would you recommend us to others? These are good questions, but they skirt around the central issue: How much of a pain are you to deal with? In our experience, it is better to measure something directly than to try to infer it from indirect measurements, but not until 2008 did anyone propose asking straightforwardly, "How easy was it to deal with the issue you had?"

That measurement, a Customer Effort Score (CES), was developed by the Corporate Executive Board, which studied interactions with call centers—that is, customers who had some kind of question or problem. Their research showed that reducing customer effort has a greater impact on customer loyalty than going above and beyond to make up for a problem with refunds, discounts, or other extra effort. The CEB's basic question asks about service calls: "To what extent do you agree or disagree with the following statement: 'The company made it easy for me to handle my issue.'" (Mobile Mini, you will recall from Chapter 6, uses the Customer Effort Score.)

The CEB has since developed several tools (available on its website https://www.cebglobal.com/sales-service/effortless-experience/bonus-materials.html, registration required) to look at other aspects of customer effort, such as an audit tool for websites, call centers, and interactive voice response systems. The tool asks questions like whether information on the website is written in customer (not company) language, whether navigation is optimized for the customers you most want, whether customers can track an order online, whether phone numbers are easy to find, etc.

The CEB's Customer Effort tools are valuable but limited. First, they focus on the customer service function itself—a good place to start but inadequate given that companies are wasting customers' time all along the length of the service journey. Second, the CES itself is better suited to companies with lots of transactions or customers than it is to, say, professional services firms; but every company can and should develop some sort of index of effort. The question should be broadened beyond customer service to ask generally, "How easy are we to do business with?"

Ease of doing business extends to making reservations on the

Web, getting your doctor on the phone, understanding your insurance claim statement, or making it easy for the procurement team to have a total view of your activities with a customer. To design this measurement, make sure you are asking about issues customers tell you are most important. In complex services—engineering, professional services, consulting, etc.—surveys will be of limited use in eliciting hard-to-do-business information: You'll need to sit down and talk—and do the numbers. In these industries, the problem and its solution may lie in the training and behavior of individual partners or executives rather than in design per se.

Reduce employee effort. The flip side of customer effort is employee effort: Remember, the Second Principle holds that no heroic efforts should be required by the customer or by employees.

If a measurement of employee effort exists, we have never seen it. Engagement scores, yes—plenty of them, whose business purpose is largely to see whether employees put in extra effort and to find ways to reduce turnover among valuable employees. Other studies convincingly show that employees are happiest and most productive when they can achieve (and be recognized for) a continuing stream of "small victories" and other signs of progress. But, again, why not ask straight out?

The generic question is "How easy is it for you to do right by a customer?" That question should be asked of frontline people such as sales reps, technical support staff, account managers, and anyone else who comes into direct contact with customers. It can be broadened and deepened, however, depending on your business:

* How easy is it for your employees to know where to direct a customer's query?

* How easy is it for marketing and sales to develop leads?

* How easy is it to line up staff, equipment, and other resources to get started on a project for a new customer?

* For an existing customer?

* What policies, incentives, procedures, or habits make cross-functional teamwork difficult?

* What other internal requirements create hurdles for you in serving a customer?

Create cross-platform ease of use. The Fourth Principle (the principle of coherence) asks companies to do two difficult things: deliver end-to-end excellence in each channel or platform; and allow a customer to switch from one channel to another seamlessly, without losing a step. The first is a *multichannel* experience: It recognizes that Patricia might prefer to talk to someone on the phone, Tom to get self-service on the Web; Tom might like the print edition, Patricia the Web version, and you the edition you reach by clicking on a friend's link on Facebook.

The second is an *omnichannel* experience: Can a customer begin a transaction on the Web and complete it in the store? If he does, will you—the seller—be able to pick up in the new channel where you left off in the old one? The quest for omnichannel excellence reminds us of Super Mario–type video games, in which a player must leap from platform to platform and level to level to avoid oncoming obstacles and threats.

In the Tools and Diagnostics section below we present a checklist that will help you audit your multichannel and omnichannel excellence, and then plan improvements.

5. ANSWER TWENTY-ONE QUESTIONS TO STRENGTHEN END-TO-END INNOVATION

Innovation in services often differs from innovation in goods-producing companies. As we describe in Chapter 10, it is likely to be underemphasized, with many units and functions not recognizing that they, too, can develop and deploy new or better customer experiences. For the same reason, service innovation may also be chaotic. It is likely to be highly decentralized (at least in comparison with manufacturing) and therefore prone to entropy—with different innovation projects starting in different places in the company, often unbeknownst to top management and going off in different and even incompatible directions.

The IBM service sciences center's agenda for research in services—quality, productivity, innovation—provides a framework within which to think about designing innovation into the way your company operates (see Chapter 2).

With these in mind, here are twenty-one questions to help you raise your game in innovation:

Review each backstage touchpoint.

1. Quality: Where do errors occur? What non-value-adding inspections take place?

2. Productivity: What steps or processes can be combined or eliminated?

3. Innovation: What changes in technology can be applied to change what we do at this touchpoint?

Review each onstage touchpoint, paying particular attention to critical customer interactions.

4. Quality: What do customer complaints or criticisms reveal about our work?

5. Productivity: Where do customers wait or waste time?

6. Innovation: What changes in technology can be applied? What customer-owned technologies can we leverage?

7. What additional value can we create at each touchpoint?

8. What customer behavior do we see that surprises us?

Look beyond the borders of your map.

9. Are we defining the customer journey too narrowly?

10. What other customer needs can we address?

11. What touchpoints have we overlooked?

12. Who else is making money off the same customer journey?

Develop innovation processes.

13. Is there a formal innovation process for ideation?

14. For selection?

15. For execution?

Make a list of 20 or more innovations—ranging from big (new service offerings) to small (a new checkout process on the website).

16. Where on the value chain (on the map) did these innovations occur? Are there clusters where many innovations happen, and deserts where few occur?

17. Who was involved in these projects?

Take your last innovation project.

18. Where did it originate? Who was involved in the process, and in what roles?

19. Is there an explicit role for service designers in our innovation process?

20. Where and how do we conduct experiments?

21. What measurements do we use to evaluate innovation projects?

We will return to the subject of innovation in the Tools and Diagnostics section, with a framework for measuring the return on innovation in services (see p. 270).

6. DESIGN FOR CUSTOMER CAPITAL GROWTH

Great SD^2 feeds into and feeds off of customer capital: It is both an input and a result of making sure your customers get the experience you want them to have. Everything you do in service design builds customer capital, but you can also manage it explicitly if you:

* Reimagine the role your customer can play in creating his or her *entire* experience (beyond the moment of transaction or any one touchpoint)

* Engage in continuous communication *between* you and your customer, rather than static interaction or talking *at* your customer, resulting in insights you both can use

* Enlist your customers in an active "peersuasion" community of customers who are your best critics and most ardent Evangelists

* Apply analysis of data both big and small, directly and indirectly supplied, to give your customer an experience that is either appropriately personalized or deeply meaningful to him or her

* Involve customers directly in value creation

Recall the four platforms for customer-capital formation: feedback, problem solving, innovation, and co-creation (see Chapter 10). The map you created—where you outlined the touchpoints and what happens behind the scenes, what your customer sees, and how and when your customer encounters and interacts with you—is valuable in determining where to find opportunities for each of these, and which you should develop and which not:

* Where can you add real-time or periodic feedback?

* Where can you engage customers (individually or in groups) in removing bottlenecks?

* Where can you innovate with customers (recalling the importance of "innovation in the wild")?

* Where can you insert opportunities for customers to customize or configure your offering? Even small customization tools— such as the chance to select one's own seat on an airplane— create goodwill.

Full-on co-creation involves more than individual touchpoints or stages; it involves the entirety of the journey. It is not possible in all cases or for all customers. (An airline or other regulated business has limited opportunities for co-creation.) But the project will repay you many times. To do it, apply the "DART" framework— Dialogue, Access, Risk Assessment, Transparency—developed by C. K. Prahalad and Venkat Ramaswamy in their pioneering work on co-creation.

Tools and Diagnostics

1. HOW TO MEASURE THE VALUE OF A CUSTOMER

What is a loyal customer worth? Given the proverbial extra dollar, would you invest it in finding new customers or retaining current ones? Which new ones? Which current ones? Oh, and which experiences are worth most?

There are many ways to measure the value and profitability of a customer. A Google search on "How to measure customer profitability" will turn up excellent approaches. The method that follows, similar to the one in Tom's first book, *Intellectual Capital* (New York: Doubleday Currency, 1997, p. 242), measures the net present value of a customer. Again, you can find several ways to do this but this approach is particularly useful for service design, because it asks you to identify sources of cost and income that design can affect. The math is not difficult, though the data may be hard to find.

* First, decide on a meaningful period over which to track customers—a few years for a children's retailer, decades for a mortgage banker—then calculate the profit they generate each year you keep them. This may vary by business unit or customer.

* The second step is to calculate the profit customers generate each year you keep them. This, too, will vary by segment or line of business.

  ▪ Begin by subtracting the cost of acquiring and retaining customers. For the first year, this will include advertising, commissions, etc.—all the costs of bringing in new business. In subsequent years, you will have costs, too, such as customer service, time spent maintaining relationships, freebies, and the like. Overall, though, retention costs should be lower than acquisition costs, and should continuously decrease. If the cost of retention increases, something is wrong in your business.

  ▪ Next, add the revenue from sales (minus the cost of goods). This should grow over time as satisfied customers return for more. Add margin growth (the cost of serving customers should decline), incremental sales (checking account, savings account, auto loan, mortgage loan . . .), and the value of referrals.

  ▪ To visualize these data, you will want to create a simple bar chart for each business or customer segment, with one bar for each year that tots up the different kinds of revenue and subtracts the cost. You are hoping to see each bar higher than the one that came before.

* Third, calculate customer "life expectancy," which is your

churn rate—the percentage of customers (again, by line of business and segment) who leave each year.

* Finally, calculate the net present value of a customer. Pick a discount rate. We recommend choosing your target return-on-assets rate, because loyal customers are assets. Apply it to each year's profit, adjusted for the likelihood that the customer will leave.

If your discount rate is 15 percent, in year one your NPV will be *profit/1.15*. The next year, the NPV is *(year-two profit x retention rate)/1.15²*, etc., until you come to the end of the meaningful period you established at the beginning. The sum of years 1 through *n* is the net present value of all the profits you can expect from the customer during his or her time with you. In theory, it is what you could get if you sold the customer (or the line of business) to someone else.

You can use this information in many ways. It can reveal which customers are most valuable to attract and whether you are spending too much or (more likely) too little to retain your most valuable customers. You can connect these data to what you know about *Ahhh* and *Ow* moments—places where you win a customer's loyalty or lose it. You can then design experiments and, based on experiments, changes, with pretty sure knowledge of what customers will be worth to you. You can also be more strategic in designing pathways to attract customers to deal with you across multiple lines of business and platforms, thereby increasing your share of their wallet.

2. HOW TO MEASURE CROSS-PLATFORM CAPABILITY

Forrester Research developed a valuable "maturity model" showing how companies progress from multichannel to omnichannel service as they move from operating in channel-specific silos; then integrating across channels, then leveraging insights to optimize marketing, and finally orchestrating "real-time contextual marketing." We

DIAGNOSING CROSS-CHANNEL COHERENCE

	YES	NO	NOTES
WITHIN EACH CHANNEL OR PLATFORM			
Can you deliver a complete, end-to-end customer journey in each channel/on each platform (i.e., does a customer have to switch channels whether or not she wants to)?			
Do customers leave a channel for another (or drop off)? (E.g., do customers book with you on the Web but use the phone to check on the status of an order?)			
Is each channel reliable? Are they comparably reliable?			
Do you regularly hear significant complaints in one or more channels? In all channels?			
In each channel is your cost-to-serve equal to your industry best? Equal to the best regardless of industry?			
Does each channel have a dashboard? Are the dashboards comparable to each other, or are they apples and oranges? Do they measure what is most important to your best customers? (See the Report Card weighting tool, p. 247.)			
ACROSS CHANNELS OR PLATFORMS			
Can customers begin a journey on one channel or platform and switch to another without significant effort on their part?			
Can customers switch channels/platforms without significant effort or cost on *your* part?			
Can you identify your most valuable customers regardless of channel?			
Do you have a single view of the customer internally?			
Can you offer personalized customer experiences?			
Are navigation, look and feel, and quality of brand experience the same on all platforms and channels? Does each "feel like you"?			
Can you measure end-to-end experience and excellence by journey, regardless of channel? Can you analyze by line of business and customer segment?			
Can you conduct experiments and develop or deploy innovations across all platforms simultaneously?			

believe this is more useful as a diagnostic than as a plan for action. These days, if you first build and optimize individual channels or platforms, you're likely to create more work down the road when you try to integrate them than if you had built omnichannel capabilities from the start.

The table on page 269 provides some questions (some of which are derived from Forrester's work) to ask yourself.

3. HOW TO MEASURE RETURN ON SERVICE INNOVATION

Measuring innovation is an inexact science; measuring innovation in services is not only inexact but, relatively speaking, untried. Traditional measurements of innovation derive from the world of manufactured products; they include percentage of sales from new products, percentage of products that meet financial targets, and return on R&D investment.

These are fine as far as they go. But they have limited relevance to services, where many innovations start not in a laboratory funded by an R&D budget but with an IT team that improves a user interface or on a marketing team that develops a service offering specially designed for a customer segment.

Service innovations, according to a pair of Australian scholars, can be classified into five types: new business model, new customer interface, new offering, new process or system innovation, and new channel to market. The first type is rare, so we have not included it in the table on page 271. You can use the grid to measure innovation effectiveness. You should custom-design a grid for your business, but a generic form might look like the one on the next page.

4. HOW TO CREATE A CUSTOMER CAPITAL DASHBOARD

Customer capital is a jointly owned bank account where you and your customers are constantly making withdrawals or deposits. We described how to measure the value of a customer (p. 266), but there is no real way to quantify the value of the customer capital account.

FRAMEWORK FOR MEASURING
SERVICE INNOVATION

	CUSTOMER INTERFACE INNOVATION	NEW SERVICE OFFERING	PROCESS OR SYSTEM INNOVATION	NEW CHANNEL
% of revenue from new markets				
% of revenue from innovations in the last X years				
Success rate for innovations (return on investment vs. a preset hurdle rate)				
Increase in revenue from core customer segments				
% of revenue from new customer segments				
Royalty or licensing revenue				

Still, there are other and additional ways by which to keep tabs on your customer capital: You can know whether and how fast it is growing and you can design interventions that will increase the deposits and reduce the withdrawals.

A service-oriented company should construct a dashboard. Yours should be unique to your company (at least until such time as there exist Generally Accepted Accounting Principles for intangible assets). Here are some straightforward measurements—and some that have a bit of a twist:

* *Rate of customer churn—renewal and defection rates.* These should be tracked overall, by line of business, and by channel or platform.

* *Customer engagement.* "Engagement" is frequently used to measure activity on a website or in digital and social marketing— what percentage of emails were opened, how many tweets were retweeted, how many Web pages a user looked at. These are fine measurements, new and unique to the digital world, but there are analogue ways to gauge engagement that can be even more valuable. Among them:

  ▪ share of wallet (are customers bringing more and more of their business to you?)

  ▪ activity (is someone who used to buy airline tickets from you every fortnight now buying less than once month? In many businesses, such as health clubs, there is a strong correlation between renewal rates and recency of activity. But in any business, declining activity signals customer capital depletion. [Hiya, Orbitz!])

  ▪ number of customers entering into automated relationships (electronic bill paying, automatic stock replenishment, etc.)

  ▪ age of receivables

* Gross margin by length of customer relationship. (It should rise.)

* Customer acquisition costs. (They should fall.)

* Ratio of leads generated to deals closed. (They should fall, too.)

* Economic vitality of customers. Are your customers the best in the business? Are they growing faster than their direct competitors? Is your business with them growing at least as fast as their business overall? Do they have strong balance sheets? If you are a key supplier to growing, industry-leading customers, you have a valuable asset.

Remember, you should not just be thinking about your customers. You are the customer of your suppliers. A comprehensive audit of customer capital will therefore look upstream as well as downstream.

5. HOW TO DIAGNOSE PRODUCT-SERVICE ISSUES

"We cannot fix it for you; you'll have to send it back to them."

"I can sell you a new one."

"That is the manufacturer's warranty, not ours."

"It must have been damaged in shipping."

"We're not responsible for repairs we do not do."

"There's nothing wrong with the product—the installation was done wrong."

"I don't know why they told you we can do that."

Customers hear comments of this kind all too often—attempts by one company to blame another for a customer's bad experience. The finger-pointing occurs even when the product and service are offered by the same company; it may happen behind the scenes, out of the customer's view, but it happens nonetheless.

Solving these problems requires finding causes, not assigning blame. When services and products do not connect, the root cause usually can be found in one of three areas: poor service design and delivery; poor product design or performance; or poor customer management. You can use the table on p. 274 as a diagnostic to learn the cause of problems—and hence to understand how to fix them.

* * *

We said at the beginning of his book that service design and delivery carry the potential to transform your company—that SD^2 is not just a set of methods and tools but a way of refining strategy, sharpening execution, and building relationships with customers that are long-lasting, valuable assets, not merely transactions. Accordingly, we developed and chose tools to create a connection between the boardroom and the team room.

WHEN SERVICES AND PRODUCTS
DO NOT CONNECT: A DIAGNOSTIC

PROBLEM CLUSTER	SYMPTOMS	POSSIBLE CAUSES AND DESIGN FAILURES
Poor service design and delivery	Bad handoffs internally	Functional or P&L silos—no single face to customer
	Bad handoffs among partners in extended value chain	No shared map of customer journey; unaligned or misaligned incentives; antagonistic relationships with suppliers/distributors
	Consistent complaints about user experience	Services teams/units lack power to influence design or pricing
	Little or no innovation in service	Product-centric view of innovation; inadequate accounting or measurement of service profitability
Poor product design and performance	Frequent product defects	Weak customer feedback loops; separation of R&D and manufacturing from service and repair
	Rigid or slow product development process	Weak customer feed-forward loops; lack of "agile" methods involving customer in new product/service development
	Uncompetitive pricing	Pricing determined by production cost, not customer value; bloated cost structure
Poor customer management	Selling to the wrong customers; bad debts	Customer risk and profitability ignored or mismanaged
	Excessive customer churn	Failure to identify critical customer interactions and work across businesses/functions to relieve pain points or add value
	Misallocation of resources among customer segments	Inadequate maps of customer journeys, especially backstage
	Problems in "relationship" or "solutions" sales	No single view of customer, no company-wide goals for major customers or customer segments; disconnect between sales, ops, and service
	Gaps between customer expectations and company goals/actions	Wrong customers; misaligned incentives across backstage functions; inadequate collaboration/ co-creation with customers

You—if you are a senior leader—can use these frameworks, dashboards, project ideas, and tools to chart and deploy service design thinking, and keep track of the benefits. You—if you are a service design practitioner—can use them in a similar way: to show how your brick-and-mortar work builds and buttresses the cathedral of your company's strategy.

As we said, these tools do not stand for the full panoply that designers use. You can find these resources in many other places. Here are a few of them:

* Marc Stickdorn and Jakob Schneider, *This Is Service Design Thinking: Basics, Tools, Cases* (Amsterdam: BIS, 2010) provides just what the subtitle says. The authors also created a website, http://thisisservicedesignthinking.com/, that includes useful tools, including a "service design canvas" that is a very good downloadable version of a journey map.

* Ben Reason, Lavrans Løvlie, and Melvin Brand Flu, *Service Design for Business: A Practical Guide to Optimizing the Customer Experience* (New York: Wiley, 2015) is a similarly excellent collection of practical tools and methods for service design.

* Service Design Tools is a valuable website, http://www.servicedesigntools.org/, developed by Roberta Tassi of the department of industrial design at Politecnico di Milano in Italy. It contains an open collection of tools, such as blueprints, use cases, and many more.

* Two Belgian design firms, Namahn and Design Flanders, created an excellent Service Design Toolkit website, http://www.servicedesigntoolkit.org/.

* The United Kingdom's Design Council has studied and published extensively on the topic of service design especially for the public sector; it makes available a selection of tools useful

in all contexts at http://www.designcouncil.org.uk/sites/
default/files/asset/document/Design%20methods%20for%20
developing%20services.pdf.

* More than two dozen schools offer advanced training in service design, and each of them, in turn, has tools used by their
students. The Service Design Network maintains a list of these
academies at https://www.service-design-network.org. Membership in the network is not free, but the list of schools is.

In addition, of course, a growing number of design consultancies—
Continuum, IDEO, others we have referred to and others we have
not—have sophisticated tools and methods.

An important part of what they know—and what we have written—is that service design must be done and delivered in the field,
by studying customers in their natural habitat, by experimenting
and prototyping in real time in the real world. You cannot succeed
in service design without tools. But the tools you use are only as
good as the projects in which you employ them. And those projects are only as useful as the strategic journey they advance. Start,
resume, or keep on with your own journey. We hope this book is a
useful and welcome companion for you.

ACKNOWLEDGMENTS

Any book is an act of co-creation, involving scores of people. In our case, they include the executives and others who gave us their time and shared their stories and insights, the friends and family who gave up their time so that we could work on the book, our colleagues, the publishing team that supported, kibitzed, edited, challenged us, and ultimately brought this book into being, and many more.

Tom would particularly like to thank Dean Anil Makhija of the Fisher College of Business at The Ohio State University, along with his colleagues at the National Center for the Middle Market, Doug Farren and Alicia Ritchey, for their support and understanding while this book was being developed. Aravind Chandrasekaran, Shashi Matta, and Peter Ward of the Fisher College faculty gave us helpful advice, insight, and introductions. Niko Canner, Ken Favaro, Jon Katzenbach, Art Kleiner, Nadia Kubis, Paul Leinwand, Cesare Mainardi, and Josselyn Simpson of Strategy&—Booz & Company as it then was—helped shape Tom's thinking in this book in ways he hopes they will recognize; Natasha Andre was and remains indispensable. Kate Pugh, director of Columbia University's Information and Knowledge Strategy program, was a terrific thought partner, too.

Patricia specially wants to thank Crystal Berg for her administrative support; Chenoa Taitt and Laura Stephens for their unfailing support and infallible wisdom; Laura Pollock and the team at Third Street Partners for giving her a home away from home; Bruce Weinstein for his encouragement, advice, and infectious enthusiasm; Barbara Henricks McDougal, Andrew Morrissey, Mukul Pandya, Tony Plohoros, Cortney Stapleton, and Greg Winter for their professional advice and for opening doors; Ian and Kevin, Lenny from Maxwell's, Nick, and the staffs at numerous businesses of all kinds who have not only exemplified the best in service design and delivery but also taught her about the true value of customer capital customers and the responsibility in co-creating memorable experiences. There are far too many to name but she would nevertheless like to single out the folks at Bobby Van's, Sfoglia, Paola's, and Heidi's House.

Dozens upon dozens of people gave generously of their time and prodigiously of their insights and experiences. We apologize to anyone whose name we accidentally omitted; a violation of at least one principle of service design, we are certain.

We are indebted to Gail Heyman, Cathy Calhoun, Abby Gold, Fred Lindeberg, and Michael Wehman of Weber Shandwick; Avi Steinlauf, Paddy Hannon, Michelle Schotts, Mark Holtoff, and Rachel Rogers from Edmunds; Paula Wallace, Victor Ermoli, and Danny Filson of the Savannah College of Art and Design; the leadership team of Mobile Mini, including Erik Olsson, Rob Loy, and Kelly Williams; John Toussaint, Helen Zak, Dena Tarkowski, Jenny Redman-Schell, Kim Barnes, Kevin Hartz, Jim Matheson, and Bill Mann of ThedaCare; at Continuum, Jon Campbell, Toby Bottorf, Gretchen Rice, Anthony Pannozzo; Karen Kaplan and Brent Feldman from Hill Holiday; a Warby Parker group that included Neil Blumenthal, Dave Gilboa, Lori Krauss, Kaki Reid, Ruthie Thier, and Olivia Tresham; Jeff Potter and Justin Hart from Surf Air; and Jim Spohrer, Paul Maglio, and Ray Harishankar of IBM, and Paul Horn who was there when services science began (and is now at New York University). In addition, we would like to thank Olivier Aries, Dan Ariens, Wayne Berson, Mary Jo Bittner, Andy Boynton, Robert Bustos-McNeil, Tim Brown, Michael Cargill, Sylvie Charbonnier,

John Cooper, John Costello, Mark Demich, Elena Evgrafova, Peter Fader, Jon Fine, Charles V. Firlotte, Erin First, Frances Frei, Michelle Gerdes, Glenn Goldman, Francis Gouillart, Brandt Handley (who introduced us to Surf Air and arranged for us to fly on it as his guests), Sandy Hillman, Tom Hubbard, Kenny Jacobs, Walter Kiechel III, Katrina Lake, Robert Marston, Roger Martin, Matthew May, Charles McDiarmid, Lenny Mendonca, Anil Menon, Christopher Meyer, Chris Moschovitis and Anna Murray, Francois Nader, Ellis O'Connor, Andrew Palladino, Helen Patrikis, William Powell, Bruce Rosenstein, Ira Sager, Bill Saporito, Mohan Sawhney, Len Schlesinger, Mike Sheehan, Stan Slap, Eddie Smith, Danny Stern, Robert Sutton, Jill Totenberg, Rob Weisberg, and Ken Worzel.

At Harper Business, Hollis Heimbouch has been enthusiastic, quick, constructive, to the point, and appropriately firm; we have both been on her side of the editor's desk and know how lucky we are to have worked with her and her team, including the patient, efficient, and very helpful Eric Meyer and Brian Perrin. Tom Pitoniak was deft, detailed, and delicate in his copy editing. Jim Santo designed and built our website, www.woowowwin.com. Jim Levine has been everything an agent should be: wise, thoughtful, streetsmart, and a true advocate. Mark Fortier has been energetic and effective with marketing support.

Friends and family deserve a special shout-out. Amanda Vaill, Pamela, and Patrick Stewart were generous with insights, boundless with patience, and unstinting in support. Ann, Regina, Kathleen, Jim O'Connell, and the late William J. O'Connell are to be thanked for their patience and understanding in pursuit of this project. Tom Gilbert, Denise Menelly, Carol Butler, Eileen Houck, and Sue Ross are among the many who served as reminders of how important it is to keep one's sense of humor, and Rick Menelly was a generous reminder of the importance of keeping one's sense of self.

Finally, collaborating on this book—sometimes at long distance, sometimes face-to-face—would have been a lot harder without Skype and, particularly, Dropbox. There were times when we cursed them both for being imperfect and our network providers for not always being instantaneous; but they truly did make it possible for us to play one piano with four hands. Tools are only as good as the people who wield them, of course. Therefore, hokey though it may be, Tom would like to thank Patricia for being a great collaborator; and Patricia would like to thank Tom for being just as good as she.

—TAS & PO'C

Notes

Introduction

3 "a human-centered approach": Tim Brown's definition is quoted, inter alia, at https://www.ideo.com/about/. Retrieved April 27, 2016.

6 service-dominant logic: Robert F. Lusch and Steven L. Vargo, *Service-Dominant Logic: Premises, Perspectives, Possibilities* (Cambridge: Cambridge University Press, 2014).

Chapter 1: The Road to "*Ahhh!*"

15 "Membership gives people something": Interview with Jeff Potter, CEO, Surf Air, August 13, 2015.

19 A large and growing: For summary of the research, most led by Thomas Gilovich of Cornell University, see James Hamblin, "Buy Experiences, Not Things," *Atlantic*, October 7, 2014, http://www.theatlantic.com/business/archive/2014/10/buy-experiences/381132/. See, for example, Amit Kumar and Thomas Gilovich, "Some Thing to Talk About? Differential Story Utility from Experiential and Material Purchases," *Personality and Social Psychology Bulletin*, June 1, 2015.

19 it is not enough just to fix the parts: Alex Rawson, Ewan Duncan, and Conor Jones, "The Truth About Customer Experience: Touchpoints Matter, but It Is the Full Journey That Really Counts," *Harvard Business Review*, September 2013.

21 "Service design is a system": Interview with Victor Ermoli, June 17, 2015.

22 comparing it to Amazon.com: Catherine Palmiera, "To an Analogue Banker in a Digital World," *strategy + business*, August 27, 2013, http://www.strategy-business.com/article/00206?pg, retrieved January 30, 2014.

23 *Uncommon Service*: Frances Frei and Anne Morriss, *Uncommon Service: How to Win by Putting Customers at the Core of Your Business* (Boston: Harvard Business Press, 2012).

23 Lexus: See Wikipedia entry, http://en.wikipedia.org/wiki/Lexus, retrieved February 2, 2015.

23 commercial airlines spend more than $10 billion: SITA Aero, "The Potential of Collaboration: IT Trends Survey, 2013—An Airline View," http://www.slide-share.net/tknierim/how-airlines, retrieved April 28, 2016.

26 an enormous $190 billion: Annie Lowrey, "Study of U.S. Healthcare System Finds Both Waste and Opportunity to Improve," *New York Times*, September 11, 2012, http://www.nytimes.com/2012/09/12/health/policy/waste-and-promise-seen-in-us-health-care-system.html.

26 400,000 lives: Blue Cross/Blue Shield of North Carolina, "Why Does Health Care Cost So Much," 2016, http://connect.bcbsnc.com/lets-talk-cost-2013/the-cost-problem/waste/posts/cause-medical-errors/, retrieved April 29, 2016.

26 Overall, the institute estimates: Alan B. Krueger, "A Hidden Cost of Health Care," *New York Times*, February 9, 2009, retrieved November 29, 2013, http://economix.blogs.nytimes.com/2009/02/09/a-hidden-cost-of-health-care-patient-time/?_r=0.

26 Most hospitals find it difficult to improve: Claire Senot and Aravind Chandrasekaran, "What Has the Biggest Impact on Hospital Readmission Rates," *Harvard Business Review*, September 23, 2015.

27 Her Majesty's Inspectorate of Constabulary: Richard Alleyne, "Frontline Police Spend Half Their Day Filling Out Forms," *Telegraph*, July 2, 2008, http://www.telegraph.co.uk/news/uknews/2235915/Frontline-police-spend-half-their-day-filling-out-forms.html, retrieved April 29, 2016.

28 almost three times more murder: 2014 FBI statistics for 2014 collected at https://en.wikipedia.org/wiki/List_of_United_States_cities_by_crime_rate_%282014%29, retrieved April 29, 2016.

Chapter 2: The Service Design Revolution

32 10 percent of its revenue: For an excellent discussion of Blockbuster versus Netflix, see http://amitadeshpande.blogspot.com/2010/12/netflix-vs-blockbuster.html.

32 U.S. airlines: IdeaWorks and CarTrawler, "Airline Ancillary Revenue Projected to Be $59.2 Billion Worldwide in 2015," http://www.ideaworkscompany.com/wp-content/uploads/2016/04/Press-Release-103-Global-Estimate.pdf, retrieved April 20, 2016

33 It wasn't long: For information on design history see, inter alia, the Industrial Design History website of Auburn University, written by Bret H. Smith: http://www.industrialdesignhistory.com/timelineproducts.

34 In the United States, four out of five: U.S. Bureau of Labor Statistics, "Industry Employment and Output Projections to 2022," *Monthly Labor Review*, December 2013, http://www.bls.gov/emp/ep_table_201.htm.

34 "These are not necessarily busboys": Kenichi Ohmae, *The Borderless World: Power and Strategy in the Interlinked Economy* (New York: HarperCollins, 1990).

34 but that December, *Fortune* magazine: John Huey, "America's Hottest Export: Pop Culture," *Fortune*, December 31, 1990.

36 Customers do not own a service: The pioneering (and still superb) description of services-as-experiences is G. Lynn Shostack, "Breaking Free from Product Marketing," *Journal of Marketing* 41, no. 2 (April 1977): 73–80, http://www.jstor.org/stable/1250637.

37 "Designing Services That Deliver": G. Lynn Shostack, "Designing Services

That Deliver," *Harvard Business Review*, January 1984, http://hbr.org/1984/01/designing-services-that-deliver/ar/1, retrieved February 3, 2014. For customer loyalty, see among others Frederick F. Reichheld, "Loyalty-Based Management," *Harvard Business Review*, March–April 1993, http://hbr.org/1993/03/loyalty-based-management/ar/1.

37 "break free": Shostack, "Breaking Free from Product Marketing."

38 a surge of interest in … loyalty: See for example Frederick F. Reichheld and W. Earl Sasser, Jr., "Zero Defections: Quality Comes to Services," *Harvard Business Review,* September-October 1990.

38 According to Tim Brown: Interview with Tim Brown, June 11, 2015.

39 Big Blue had been a big player: Bernardo Bátis-Lazo, "A Brief History of the ATM," *Atlantic*, March 26, 2015.

39 ceding the business: Geoffrey Colvin, "The Wee Outfit That Decked IBM," Fortune, November 19, 1990.

39 In 2003: IBM 2003 annual report, ftp://public.dhe.ibm.com/annual report/2003/2003_ibm_ar.pdf.

39 For Paul Horn: Interviews with Paul Horn, June 15, 2015; Robert Morris, July 30, 2015; and James Spohrer, October 19, 2015.

40 "Icons of Progress": http://www-03.ibm.com/ibm/history/ibm100/us/en/icons/, retrieved November 21, 2015.

40 eightfold return: See Spohrer's LinkedIn profile: https://www.linkedin.com/in/spohrer, retrieved November 21, 2015. There he writes, "Successful service research must: 1. Improve the firm's existing value propositions (existing service offerings); 2. Help the firm create new value propositions (new service offerings); 3. Help the firm acquire, divest, in-source, out-source (portfolio of service offerings-internal and external); 4. Help the firm's customers/partners improve their capabilities in all the above areas; 5. Create patents and enhance the firm's IP assets with all the above; 6. Create papers and enhance service knowledge with all the above."

41 dramatically cut the percentage of bags: SITA, The Baggage Report 2015 Air Transportation Industry Insights, https://www.sita.aero/globalassets/docs/surveys—reports/baggage-report-2015.pdf#page=1&zoom=auto,-48,842 http://www.sita.aero/resources/type/surveys-reports/baggage-report-2015.

41 "Agile software development" principles: These were first enunciated in the 2001 "Manifesto for Agile Software Development," http://agilemanifesto.org/, retrieved November 23, 2015.

41 "We have well-tested, scientific methods": Stefan Thomke, "R&D Comes to Services: Bank of America's Pathbreaking Experiments," *Harvard Business Review*, April 2003.

42 IBM's pretax profit: "Icons of Progress," http://www-03.ibm.com/ibm/history/ibm100/us/en/icons/, retrieved November 21, 2015.

42 three generations of management consulting: For an illuminating and entertaining history of the consulting industry, see Walter Kiechel, *The Lords of Strategy: The Secret Intellectual History of the New Corporate World* (Boston: Harvard Business Press, 2010).

Chapter 3: Service Design and Your Strategy

47 "[t]he very first thing they always said": Interview with Cathy Calhoun, September 29, 2015.

48 Michael Wehman: Authors' interview with Michael Wehman, September 29, 2015.

49 Weber Shandwick's 2004 billings: The Holmes Report, 2015, http://www .holmesreport.com/ranking-and-data/world-pr-report/agency-rankings-2015/ top-250, retrieved December 2, 2015.

50 "wide selection": https://www.schwab.com/, retrieved December 4, 2015.

51 it reserves full person-to-person: Schwab in 2000 bought the high-end wealth management company U.S. Trust. The combination did not work well, and Schwab sold off the business six years later.

51 "the industry too often gets in the way": Charles Schwab Annual Report, 2014.

51 "through a national network": David J. Collis and Michael G. Rukstad, "Can You Say What Your Strategy Is?," *Harvard Business Review*, April 2008.

51 The firm's website: https://www.edwardjones.com/index.html, retrieved December 5, 2015.

52 Research by the A. T. Kearney consulting firm: "Using Pivotal Customer Events to Create Value," A. T. Kearney, 2015, https://www.atkearney.com/ documents/5472320/6218530/34969_PCE+Whitepaper+2015+v4_Report.pdf /7f10f532–6f93–4c4f-987d-7ff2a24b1380, retrieved December 9, 2015.

53 "Companies were spending": Interview with Robert Bustos-McNeil, May 11, 2015.

54 For Virgin Atlantic: http://www.virgin-atlantic.com/us/en/travel-information /airport-guides/london-heathrow/clubhouse.html, retrieved December 9, 2015.

57 Theodore Levitt cited McDonald's: Theodore Levitt, "Production-Line Approach to Services," *Harvard Business Review*, September–October 1972.

58 "We hire from the half": Quoted in Meghan Busse and Jeroen Swinkels, "Enterprise Rent-a-Car," case study, Kellogg School of Management, revised March 21, 2012.

59 a substantial body of research: See James L. Heskett, Thomas O. Jones, Gary W. Loveman, W. Earl Sasser Jr., and Leonard A. Schlesinger, "Putting the Service-Profit Chain to Work," *Harvard Business Review*, March–April 1994; for fast-food restaurants, WaWa, for example, see Neeli Bendapudi and Venkat Bendapudi, "Creating the Living Brand," *Harvard Business Review*, May 2005.

Chapter 4: The First Principle: The Customer Is Always Right—Provided the Customer Is Right for You

66 In that crowded space: Leslie Patton, "Dunkin' Donuts Tests Mobil Ordering in Bid to Catch Up with Starbucks," Bloomberg Technology, November 18, 2015, http://www.bloomberg.com/news/articles/2015–11–18/dunkin-donuts-plays -catch-up-to-starbucks-with-mobile-ordering.

66 When the American Customer Satisfaction Index: http://www.fool.com

/investing/general/2015/07/18/can-you-guess-americas-favorite-coffee-shop-hint-i.aspx, retrieved December 14, 2015.

66   "The customer is always right": See, inter alia, http://www.phrases.org.uk/meanings/106700.html.

69   If you're not convinced: Amy Gallo, "The Value of Keeping the Right Customers," *Harvard Business Review*, October 29, 2014, https://hbr.org/2014/10/the-value-of-keeping-the-right-customers/.

70   "It is really important": Interview with Peter Fader, May 26, 2015.

Chapter 5: The Second Principle: Don't Surprise and Delight Your Customers—Just Delight Them

83   Orphan drugmaker NPS Pharmaceuticals: Interview with Francois Nader, June 19, 2015.

87   "A good experience": Interview with Jon Campbell, March 13, 2015.

87   "You earn people's loyalty": Interview with Michelle Shotts, June 12, 2015.

88   "I don't care about a free snack box": Interview with Charles McDiarmid, June 5, 2015.

88   96 percent of unhappy customers: "50 Facts About Customer Experience," http://returnonbehavior.com/2010/10/50-facts-about-customer-experience-for-2011/, retrieved May 14, 2015.

88   A dissatisfied customer: Ibid.

88   It takes 12: Ibid.

88   "When service design": Interview with Victor Ermoli, June 16, 2015.

89   In a bank McKinsey studied: Marc Beaujean, Jonathan Davidson, and Stacey Madge, "The Moment of Truth in Customer Service," *McKinsey Quarterly*, February 2006.

89   "For the first two years": Interview with Katrina Lake, December 6, 2015.

89   "When you've earned": Interview with Erik Olsson, June 25, 2015.

90   Scott Cook, founder of Intuit: Carmen Nobel, "Clay Christensen's Milkshake Marketing," Working Knowledge, February 14, 2011, http://hbswk.hbs.edu/item/clay-christensens-milkshake-marketing, retrieved October 14, 2015.

90   buying milk shakes: Clayton M. Christensen, Scott Cook, and Taddy Hall, "Marketing Malpractice: The Cause and the Cure," *Harvard Business Review*, December 2005.

91   "You do market research": Interview with Len Schlesinger, March 13, 2015.

91   Johannes Hattula: Scott Berinato, "Putting Yourself in the Customers' Shoes Does Not Work: An Interview with Johannes Hattula," *Harvard Business Review*, March 2015.

92   Such was the case: Simon Glynn, "The New Customer Centric," http://www.mediapost.com/publications/article/195380/the-new-customer-centric.html?print#axzz2fMhyqkE1, retrieved April 4, 2015.

93   McDonald's: Bryan Gruley and Leslie Patton, "McRevolt: The Frustrating Life of the McDonald's Franchisee Not Lovin' It," Bloomberg, http://www.bloomberg.com/features/2015-mcdonalds-franchises/, retrieved September 16, 2015.

94   "We suggest to them": Interview with Rob Loy, June 25, 2015.

95   "Whatever your job description": Interview with Kenneth Worzel, July 14, 2015.

96   Dunkin' Donuts has what: Interview with John Costello, October 1, 2015.

96   "The questions that we ask": Interview with Cathy Calhoun, September 29, 2015.

97   transformation of customers into heroes: Interview with Victor Ermoli, June 17, 2015.

97   Randall Stephenson, the CEO of AT&T: Quentin Hardy, "Gearing Up for the Cloud, AT&T Tells Its Workers: Adapt, or Else," *New York Times*, February 13, 2016, http://www.nytimes.com/2016/02/14/technology/gearing-up-for-the-cloud-att-tells-its-workers-adapt-or-else.html?_r=0, retrieved February 14, 2016.

98   "We were fortunate that": Interview with Erik Olsson, June 25, 2015.

98   "you're running laps in a race": Interview with Jeff Potter, July 9, 2015.

Chapter 6: The Third Principle: Great Service Must Not Require Heroic Efforts on the Part of the Provider or the Customer

100   "*episodic* excellence": "The End of Customer Service Heroes," interview with Frances Frei and Anne Morriss, HBR Ideacast, February 2, 2012, https://hbr.org/ideacast/2012/02/the-end-of-customer-service-he, retrieved December 21 2015.

100   orderlies and nursing assistants: Daniel Zwerdling, "Hospitals Fail to Protect Nursing Staff from Becoming Patients," National Public Radio, February 4, 2015, http://www.npr.org/2015/02/04/382639199/hospitals-fail-to-protect-nursing-staff-from-becoming-patients, retrieved December 18, 2015.

101   "The number-one waste": Interview with Dr. John Toussaint, M.D., March 11, 2015.

101   Improving patient experience: Interview with Aravind Chandrasekaran, July 23, 2015; Claire Senot and Aravind Chandrasekaran, "What Has the Biggest Impact on Hospital Readmission Rates," *Harvard Business Review*, September 23, 2015, https://hbr.org/2015/09/what-has-the-biggest-impact-on-hospital-readmis.

102   "the Mercedes of storage": Interview with Erik Olsson, June 25, 2015.

103   Customer Effort Score: See Matthew Dixon, Karen Freeman, and Nicholas Toman, "Stop Trying to Delight Your Customers," *Harvard Business Review*, July–August 2010, https://hbr.org/2010/07/stop-trying-to-delight-your-customers.

103   "Chief Officer of Pain Points": Interview with Kelly Williams, June 25, 2015.

104   "lean consumption": James P. Womack and Daniel T. Jones, "Lean Consumption," *Harvard Business Review*, March 2005.

104 with no small amount of difficulty: See https://en.wikipedia.org/wiki/ 1-Click, retrieved December 22, 2015.

106 highest-quality, lowest-cost: Interview with John Toussaint, March 11, 2015.

107 ThedaCare's Collaborative Care model: See Leonard L. Berry and Jamie Dunham, "Redefining the Patient Experience with Collaborative Care," *Harvard Business Review*, September 20, 2013, and ThedaCare Center for Health Care Value, https://createvalue.org/collaborative-care/.

108 450,000 patient visits: American Medical Group Association, "ThedaCare Physicians: New Delivery Model," *Group Practice Journal*, July/August 2010.

109 "We want lab work turned around": Interview with Jenny Redman-Schell, September 23, 2015.

Chapter 7: The Fourth Principle: Service Design Must Deliver a Coherent Experience Across All Channels and Touchpoints

115 Bank of America deposits: Bank of America 4Q 2015 investor presentation, January 19, 2016, p. 3, http://investor.bankofamerica.com/phoenix.zhtml ?c=71595&p=quarterlyearnings#fbid=knFUfVg4rtN, retrieved February 19, 2016.

115 "omnichannel consumers": "IDC Futurescape: Worldwide Retail 2015 Predictions—It Is All About Participation Now," IDC, November 2014.

115 Merrill Lynch brought in: Michael Wursthorn, "Merrill Contributes More to Bank of America's Bottom Line," *Wall Street Journal*, January 15, 2015, http:// www.wsj.com/articles/merrill-lynch-contributes-more-to-bank-of-americas -bottom-line-1421342758.

115 a drop in the bucket: Bank of America, 2014 annual report, p. 7.

115 At SunTrust bank: "Delighting Customers at SunTrust: How Multichannel Banking Mobilizes Financial Well-being," Kony Inc., Innovator Series Brief, 2013, http://forms.kony.com/rs/konysolutions/images/Kony-CS-ISB-SunTrust .pdf, retrieved March 9, 2016.

116 one health insurance company: David Meer, "When Big Data Isn't an Option," *strategy + business*, May 19, 2014, http://www.strategy-business.com /article/00250?pg=all

118 "Advertising or communications used to be": Interview with Karen Kaplan, March 13, 2015.

118 Forrester Research found: Lori Wizdo, "Buyer Behavior Helps B2B Marketers Guide the Buyer's Journey," October 4, 2012, http://blogs.forrester.com/lori_ wizdo/12–10–04-buyer_behavior_helps_b2b_marketers_guide_the_buyers_ journey, retrieved March 1, 2016.

119 TD Bank Checking Experience Index: https://mediaroom.tdbank.com/ checkingexperience, retrieved February 7, 2016.

121 "If I can control how costs": Conversation with HBS dean Kim B. Clark, 2004.

121 According to Marvin Ellison: Teresa Lindeman, "Department Stores Must Innovate to Survive," *Columbus Dispatch*, July 26, 2015, http://www.dispatch

.com/content/stories/business/2015/07/26/1-department-stores-must -innovate-to-survive.html, retrieved March 3, 2016.

121 low-price Rack stores: Susan Thurston, "Nordstrom Gained 1 Million Cus-tomers from Its Nordstrom Rack Stores," *Business Administration Information*, August 26, 2015, http://www.businessadministrationinformation.com/news/cus-tomers-nordstrom-rack-sales.

122 "Retail's Hottest Spring Trend": Pymnts.com, February 26, 2016, http:// www.pymnts.com/news/retail/2016/retails-hottest-spring-trend-store-closures/, retrieved April 29, 2016.

124 Nordstrom.com returns: Mark Brohan, "E-commerce for Nordstrom Ac-counts for 19% of Total Sales," *Internet Retailer*, February 20, 2015, https://www .internetretailer.com/2015/02/20/e-commerce-nordstrom-accounts-15-total -sales, retrieved March 2, 2016.

125 "My mission for": Interview with Mike Sheehan, March 24, 2015.

Chapter 8: The Fifth Principle: You're Never Done: Iterate, Create, Anticipate, and Innovate—And Repeat All Steps as Needed

131 "In ten years that store will be worn out": Les Wexner remarks at annual investor meeting, 2015, http://edge.media-server.com/m/p/djgbtg3x, retrieved January 2, 2016. These remarks were made about thirty minutes into the meeting.

132 "You'd think innovation": John Cerni, CEO Cerni Motor Sales Inc., http:// www.middlemarketcenter.org/events/2014-access-ge-executive-education-program.

132 explosion of service innovation: Data in this paragraph from Sara Jerving, "Bank Tellers Battle Obsolescence," *Wall Street Journal*, November 14, 2014, http://www.wsj.com/articles/bank-tellers-battle-obsolescence-1416244137, re-trieved December 30, 2015; Steve Kummer and Christian Pauletto, "The History of Derivatives: A Few Milestones," EFTA Seminar on Regulation of Derivatives Markets, Zurich, May 3, 2012; derivatives data tracked by the Bank for Interna-tional Settlements, http://www.bis.org/index.htm.

132 Take communications: Data in this paragraph from Email Statistics Report, 2013–2017, editor: Sara Radicati, http://www.radicati.com/wp/wp-content /uploads/2013/04/Email-Statistics-Report-2013–2017-Executive-Summary.pdf, retrieved December 30, 2015; https://about.usps.com/who-we-are/postal-history/ first-class-mail-since-1926.htm, retrieved December 30, 2015; "At JPMorgan, Voicemail Deemed Obsolescent," Reuters, June 2, 2015, http://www.reuters.com/ article/us-jpmorgan-expenses-voicemail-idUSKBN0OI2HZ20150602, retrieved December 30, 2015.

133 "We want to be the ones who continually": Interview with Avi Steinlauf, June 12, 2015.

134 "well into nine figures": Sramana Mitra, "Unicorn in the Making: Avi Steinlauf, CEO of Edmunds.com," http://www.sramanamitra.com/2015/03/08/ unicorn-in-the-making-avi-steinlauf-ceo-of-edmunds-com-part-7/, retrieved Jan-uary 7, 2016.

136 "To be able to build value": Interview with Andy Boynton, February 18, 2015.

137 "But where does the lobby begin?": Interview with Victor Ermoli, June 17, 2015.

137 Tim Brown recalls: Interview with Tim Brown, June 11, 2015.

137 "It is not the consumer's job": Quoted in Steve Lohr, "The Yin and Yang of Corporate Innovation," *New York Times*, January 26, 2012, http://www.nytimes .com/2012/01/27/technology/apple-and-google-as-creative-archetypes.html?_ r=2&ref=technology; "you've got to start with the customer experience": Steve Jobs at a 1997 Apple developer's conference, video at (among other places) http://www.imore.com/steve-jobs-you-have-start-customer-experience-and-work -backwards-technology, retrieved January 12, 2016.

138 "need seekers": Barry Jaruzelski, Volker Staack, and Brad Goehle, "The Global Innovation 1000: Proven Paths to Innovation Success," *strategy + business*, Winter 2014, http://www.strategy-business.com/article/00295?gko=b91bb, retrieved January 8, 2016.

138 In the middle market: National Center for the Middle Market, Cherry Bekaert LLP, and Michael Leiblein, "Organizing for Innovation in the Middle Market," 2015, http://www.middlemarketcenter.org/research-reports/ innovation-processes-tools-middle-market-companies, retrieved January 8, 2016.

138 "Keep the Change": IDEO, "Keep the Change: Account Service for Bank of America: A Service Innovation to Attract and Retain Bank Members," https:// www.ideo.com/work/keep-the-change-account-service-for-bofa, retrieved April 4, 2016.

139 "Because a service": Stefan Thomke, "R&D Comes to Services: Bank of America's Pathbreaking Experiments," *Harvard Business Review*, April 2003.

139 "Services are not milled in prototype": Interview with Toby Bottorf, March 13, 2015.

140 Intuit ran experiments: Andrea Meyer, "Intuit Is High-Velocity Experiments," HBS Working Knowledge, August 12, 2012, http://www.workingknowl edge.com/blog/intuits-high-velocity-experiments/, retrieved January 10 2016.

140 "Always be in beta": Craig LaRosa, "Our Economy Is Mostly Services. How Do You Design Great Service Experiences?," Continuum blog post, February 28, 2012, http://continuuminnovation.com/our-economy-is-mostly-services-how -do-you-design-great-service-experiences/#.VplM01KqHoY, retrieved January 15, 2016.

141 Dave Thomas: R. David Thomas, *Dave's Way: A New Approach to Old-Fashioned Success* (New York: Zondervan, 1994).

141 Wendy's has used: Maureen Morrison, "How to Create a Successful Limited-Time Offer," *Ad Age*, July 22, 2014, http://adage.com/article/best-practices/prac tices-create-a-limited-time-offer/294230/, retrieved January 13, 2016; "Wendy's Ignites Fast-Food Battle with Bundled 'Value' Deals," *Columbus Dispatch*, January 7, 2016.

142 "we want to be on trend": Gretchen Goffe, "Ideas on Innovation from the Middle Market: How Innovation Models Affect a Firm's Ability to Capture the Value It Creates," National Center for the Middle Market, 2014, http://www.mid dlemarketcenter.org/Media/Documents/lessons-in-innovation-from-the-mid dle-market-1_NCMM_Innovation_Research_Report_FINAL_WEB.pdf.

142 product life cycle: The original, classic description of the product life cycle is Conrad Jones and Sam Johnson, "How to Organize for New Products," *Harvard*

Business Review, May–June 1957; it is unaccountably missing from *HBR*'s online archive.

142 paraphrasing Theodore Levitt: Theodore Levitt, "Exploit the Product Life Cycle," *Harvard Business Review*, November–December 1965, https://hbr.org/1965/11/exploit-the-product-life-cycle.

143 "The mindset around innovation": Interview with Matthew May, February 23, 2015.

143 Kaiser Permanente: "Unpacking Design Thinking: Test," blog post at Knowledge Without Borders, August 13, 2014, http://knowwithoutborders.org/unpacking-design-thinking-test/, retrieved January 17, 2016.

143 "Those who are responsible": Jeroen P. J. de Jong and Patrick A. M. Vermeulen, "Organizing Successful New Service Development: A Literature Review," SCALES-paper N200307, EIM Business and Policy Research, 2003.

Chapter 9: Service Design Archetypes

148 "I do not look": Interview with Mark Holtoff, June 12, 2015.

149 "One Stop Shop": Phrase Finder, http://www.phrases.org.uk/meanings/one-stop-shop.html, retrieved January 17, 2016.

150 one common experience: We owe the phrase to the strategy and consulting firm. See http://www.strategyand.pwc.com/global/home/what-we-think/cds_home/toolkit/cds_way_to_play/way_to_play_tool, retrieved January 17, 2016.

151 "If we do not sell it": http://www.adslogans.co.uk/site/pages/gallery/if-we-don-t-sell-it-you-won-t-need-it.8611.php, retrieved January 17, 2016.

152 "two-sided markets": For an excellent discussion of how two-sided markets work and how to compete in them, see Thomas R. Eisenmann, Geoffrey Parker, and Marshall W. Van Alstyne, "Strategies for Two-Sided Markets," *Harvard Business Review*, October 2006.

153 "Whenever we're facing": Julia Kirby and Thomas A. Stewart, "The Institutional Yes" (Interview with Jeffrey Bezos), *Harvard Business Review*, October 2007.

155 American consumers pocketed: There are many studies of Walmart's consumer surplus, some of which are cited in Tim Worstall, "The Waltons Deserve Their Hundred Fifty Billion; The Rest of Us Gain $5 Trillion From Walmart's Existence," *Forbes*, November 29, 2014, http://www.forbes.com/sites/timworstall/2014/11/29/the-waltons-deserve-their-hundred-fifty-billion-the-rest-of-us-gain-5-trillion-from-walmarts-existence/#25a65073e6c8, retrieved March 10, 2016.

155 visits to minute clinics: J. Scott Ashwood, Martin Gaynor, et al., "Retail Clinic Visits for Low-Acuity Conditions Increase Utilization and Spending," *Health Affairs* 35, no 3 (March 2016), http://content.healthaffairs.org/content/35/3/449.abstract, retrieved March 10, 2016.

157 "It is tempting": Abraham Maslow, *The Psychology of Science* (New York: Harper & Row, 1966).

161 When a dollar bill changes hands: D. Brockman, L. Hufnagel, and T. Geisel,

"The Scaling Laws of Human Travel," *Nature*, January 2006, http://www.nld .ds.mpg.de/downloads/publications/Brockmann2006.pdf.

161 money spent with a local business: Dan Houston, Civic Economics, "Local Works: Examining the Impact of Local Business on the Western Michigan Economy," 2002, http://bealocalist.org/sites/default/files/file/GR%20Local%20 Works%20Summary.pdf.

161 Community banks: Federal Deposit Insurance Corporation, FDIC Community Banking Study, December 2012, https://www.fdic.gov/regulations/resources/cbi/report/cbi-full.pdf, retrieved February 5, 2016.

161 "the anti-chain": Jeff Haden, "Shake Shack CEO: 'We Want to Be the Anti-Chain Chain,'" *Inc.*, July 16, 2012, http://www.inc.com/jeff-haden/shake -shack-ceo-the-anti-chain-burger-chain.html.

166 In December 2015: Sandra Pedicini, "Walt Disney World, SeaWorld, Universal Begin Using Metal Detectors at Theme Parks," *Orlando Sentinel*, December 17, 2015, http://www.orlandosentinel.com/business/tourism/os-disney-metal -detectors-security-20151217-story.html, retrieved February 29, 2016.

167 "perverse effect on strategy": Michael E. Porter, "What Is Strategy?," *Harvard Business Review*, November–December 1996.

167 Bonefish Grill: Jonathan Maze, "Bonefish Grill to Close 14 Locations," *Nation's Restaurant News*, February 17, 2016, http://nrn.com/casual-dining/ bonefish-grill-close-14-locations.

168 Its routing software: UPS data cited by *Fortune* at http://money.cnn.com/video/ news/2010/12/13/n_cs_ups_no_left_turn.fortune/, retrieved January 5, 2016.

168 UPS management realized: See Donald L. Laurie, Yves L. Doz, and Claude P. Sheer, "Creating New Growth Platforms," *Harvard Business Review*, May 2006.

169 cited Zappos as a good example: Geoff Colvin, "Bob Stoffel's UPS Green Dream," *Fortune*, April 27, 2011, http://archive.fortune.com/2010/12/16/ news/companies/csuite_ups_bob_stoffel.fortune/index.htm, retrieved January 6, 2015.

170 "The Nature of the Firm": For Coase's paper, see http://www.jstor.org/ stable/2626876?seq=1#page_scan_tab_contents; for Williamson, one might start with his Nobel Lecture, http://www.nobelprize.org/nobel_prizes/economic -sciences/laureates/2009/williamson_lecture.pdf.

170 As Geoffrey Moore says: Geoffrey A. Moore, "Strategy and Your Stronger Hand," *Harvard Business Review*, December 2005.

172 Sam Palmisano: Paul Hemp and Thomas A. Stewart, "Leading Change When Business Is Good: An Interview with Samuel J. Palmisano," *Harvard Business Review*, December 2004.

172 control more than 70 percent of the market: http://54.224.107.218/insights/ blog/blog-details/insights/2014/07/07/the-merger-of-equals-publicis-omnicom. -the-failure-and-the-aftermath, retrieved December 27, 2015.

173 A few forays into other markets: National Center for the Middle Market and Goffe, "Lessons in Innovation from the Middle Market."

173 "skill, not size": "Litigation Boutique Hot List," *National Law Journal*, February 3, 2014, http://www.nationallawjournal.com/id=1202641380425/Litigation-Boutiques-Hot-List, retrieved December 27, 2015.

173 one of the most famous Harvard Business School cases: James L. Heskett, "Shouldice Hospital Limited," Harvard Business School case, April 1983, revised June 2003, http://www.hbs.edu/faculty/Pages/item.aspx?num=21244.

175 Boston Consulting Group: For the history of BCG, see Walter Kiechel, *The Lords of Strategy: The Secret Intellectual History of the New Corporate World* (Boston: Harvard Business Press, 2010).

176 "Strategy Gallery": https://www.bcgperspectives.com/strategygallery.

176 dynamic pricing: R. Preston McAfee and Vera te Velde, "Dynamic Pricing in the Airline Industry," n.d., http://mcafee.cc/Papers/PDF/DynamicPriceDiscrimination.pdf, retrieved March 22, 2016.

176 pioneered building strong encryption: Adriene Hill, "Encryption Spreads as Apple Battles the FBI," NPR *Marketplace*, March 14, 2016, http://www.marketplace.org/2016/03/14/world/encryption-spreads-apple-battles-fbi.

177 The average price point: Katie Smith, "Zara vs. H&M—Who's in the Lead?," April 15, 2014, https://edited.com/blog/2014/04/zara-vs-hm-whos-in-the-global-lead/, retrieved March 23, 2016.

178 "lead users": E. Von Hippel, "Lead Users: A Source of Novel Product Concepts," *Management Science* 32, no. 7 (986): 791–806

178 is equally applicable to services: Florian Skiba and Cornelius Herstatt, "Users as Sources for Radical Service Innovations: Opportunities from Collaboration with Service Lead Users," *International Journal of Services Technology and Management* 12, no. 3 (2009), http://www.inderscience.com/jhome.php?jcode=ijstm.

178 Michael Jeffries: Susan Berhief and Lindsey Rupp, "Abercrombie & Fitch Chief's Ouster Shows Loafers Stopped Working: Behind the Decline of Abercrombie & Fitch and the Fall of Its CEO, Michael Jeffries," *Seattle Times*, February12, 2015, http://old.seattletimes.com/html/businesstechnology/2025687599_abercrombiefounderoutxml.html.

180 cell phone towers: "Top 100 Tower Companies in the U.S.," Wireless Estimator.com, February 8, 2016, http://wirelessestimator.com/top-100-us-tower-companies-list/, retrieved February 22, 2016.

182 Indeed, the perception: http://exstreamist.com/15-of-millennials-have-cut-the-cord-only-3-of-baby-boomers-have-done-the-same/, retrieved March 1, 2016.

182 American Customer Satisfaction Index: http://www.theacsi.org/customer-satisfaction-benchmarks/benchmarks-by-industry, retrieved February 23, 2016.

183 On-Time Guarantee: http://www.timewarnercable.com/en/support/faqs/faqs-account-and-billing/appointments/what-is-the-on-time-guarantee.html, retrieved February 23, 2016.

Chapter 10: Designing for Customer Capital Growth: When One Plus One Equals Three

185   a triad of intangible assets: Tom's *Intellectual Capital: The New Wealth of Organizations* (New York: Doubleday Currency, 1997) is, he blushes to say, considered the best book about the topic.

187   "I've tried to find": Interview with Andy Boynton, February 18, 2015.

189   *co-creation* was first used by: C. K. Prahalad and Venkatram Ramaswamy, "The Co-Creation Connection," *strategy + business*, April 9, 2002.

190   inferred that women were pregnant: Charles Duhigg, "How Companies Learn Your Secrets," *New York Times Magazine*, February 16, 2012.

190   "the world is getting increasingly transparent": Julia Kirby and Thomas A. Stewart, "The Institutional Yes [Interview with Jeffrey Bezos)," *Harvard Business Review*, October 2007.

192   "Social media and sites like": Interview with Charles McDiarmid, June 5, 2015.

192   pulsed, periodic, and persistent: See the excellent article by Christopher Meyer and Andre Schwager, "Understanding Customer Experience," *Harvard Business Review*, February 2007.

194   Some statistics show the power: "6 Reasons Why Customer Service Is the Most Powerful Word-of-Mouth Marketing Weapon," http://bright.stellaservice .com/uncategorized/have-you-heard-6-reasons-why-customer-service-is-the -most-powerful-word-of-mouth-marketing-weapon/, retrieved May 23, 2015.

195   Studies by Reevoo: Cited by Graham Charlton, "Ecommerce Consumer Reviews: Why You Need Them and How to Use Them," Econsultancy, July 8, 2015, https://econsultancy.com/blog/9366-ecommerce-consumer-reviews-why-you -need-them-and-how-to-use-them/, retrieved March 11, 2016.

196   "satisfying the control needs of the consumer": "Marketing and Customer Experience: 6 Core Emotional Needs That Shape Human Behaviour (Part 2—Control)," http://www.business2community.com/customer-experience /marketing-customer-experience-6-core-emotional-needs-shape-human -behaviour-part-2-control-0632292, retrieved October 17, 2015.

196   "When does co-creation": Interview with Francis Gouillart, CEO and cofounder of the Experience Co-Creation Partnership, January 15, 2015.

198   According to IDC: "2016—The Year of the Connected Customer," *Huffington Post*, http://www.huffingtonpost.com/vala-afshar/2016-the-year-of-connecte _b_8833496.html, retrieved December 18, 2015.

198   Swiffer: Drake Baer, "The Innovation Method Behind Swiffer Madness," *Fast Company*, March 13, 2013, http://www.fastcompany.com/3006797/inno vation-method-behind-swiffer-madness, retrieved February 16, 2016.

198   "When you talk about a triangle": Interview with Avi Steinlauf, April 22, 2015.

200   estimated at above $200 million: Jason Del Ray, "Why Sephora's Digital Boss Joined Stitch Fix, the Personal Stylist Startup That Is Growing Like Mad," *re/code*, March 22, 2015, http://recode.net/2015/03/22/why-sephoras-digital-boss

-joined-stitch-fix-the-personal-stylist-startup-thats-growing-like-mad/, retrieved February 10, 2016.

Chapter 11: The Virtuous Circle: Corporate Culture and Service Design

203 "We have a mission statement": Interview with Charles V. Firlotte, January 16, 2016.

204 "You create culture through design": Interview with Tim Brown, June 11, 2015.

205 "A culture exists to protect itself": Interview with Stan Slap, June 11, 2015.

205 "That is the product that we sell": Alex Konrad, "Salesforce Innovation Secrets: How Marc Benioff's Team Stays On Top," *Forbes*, August 20, 2014, http://www.forbes.com/sites/alexkonrad/2014/08/20/marc-benioffs-innovation-secret/#65a5cc6b1a6c, retrieved February 9, 2016.

205 "Just as you typically cannot argue": Jon R. Katzenbach and Ashley Harshak, "Stop Blaming Your Culture," *strategy + business*, Spring 2011.

206 "Culture trumps strategy": Leslie Helm, "Caffeinating the World," *Sky*, March 2014, p. 120.

206 "There are roughly 46,000": Interview with Wayne Berson, January 21, 2016.

211 "The reasons are simple": https://www.progressive.com/newsroom/article/2005/november/hurricane-damaged-cars/.

211 Angela Ahrendts: Jennifer Reingold, "What the Heck Is Angela Ahrendts Doing at Apple?," *Fortune*, September 10, 2015, http://fortune.com/2015/09/10/angela-ahrendts-apple/.

211 Circuit City: See, inter alia, Amy Hart, Erika Matulich, Kimberly Rubinsak, Kasey Sheffer, Nikol Vann, and Myriam Vidalon, "The Rise and Fall of Circuit City," *Journal of Business Cases and Applications*, n.d., http://www.aabri.com/manuscripts/121101.pdf, retrieved February 9, 2016.

213 "On the Folly of Rewarding": Steven Kerr, "On the Folly of Rewarding A, While Hoping for B," *Academy of Management Journal*, December 1975, http://www.csus.edu/indiv/s/sablynskic/documents/rewardinga.pdf.

216 "It took six months": http://www.fastcompany.com/3047019/shake-shacks-french-fry-debacle-and-how-it-recovered-from-its-biggest-mistake.

217 Ninety-nine percent of orders: Paul Leinwand and Cesare Mainardi, with Art Kleiner, *Strategy That Works: How Winning Companies Close the Strategy-to-Execution Gap* (Boston: Harvard Business Press, 2016).

Chapter 12: The Full Circle: The Service-Product Connection

219 according to the Economist Intelligence Unit: "Aiming Higher: How Manufacturers Are Adding Value to Their Business: A Report from the Economist Intelligence Unit," http://www.economistinsights.com/sites/default/files/Manufacturing%20-%20Aiming%20higher.pdf, retrieved January 18, 2016.

220 When services study manufacturing: Joel Goldhar and Daniel Berg, "Blurring the Boundary: Convergence of Factory and Service Processes," *Journal of Manufacturing Technology Management* 21, no. 3 (2010): 341–54, http://dx.doi.org/10.1108/17410381011024322.

221 A study of 348: Andreas Eggert, Christoph Thiesbrummel, and Christian Deutscher, "Hybrid Innovations: Heading for New Shores: Do Service and Hybrid Innovations Outperform Product Innovations in Industrial Companies?," *Industrial Marketing Management* (February 2015): 173–83, http://www.science direct.com/science/article/pii/S0019850115000486.

221 Schiphol Airport: Mark Faithfull, "Pay-as-You-Go Lighting Arrives at Amsterdam's Schiphol Airport," *Lux Review*, April 20, 2015, http://luxreview.com/article/2015/04/pay-as-you-go-lighting-arrives-at-amsterdam-s-schiphol-airport, retrieved January 20, 2016.

221 Caterpillar: Ann Bednarz, "Ready for a Change? IT Pros Should Be Prepared to Rethink Traditional IT Roles and Responsibilities This Year," *Network World*, January 14, 2016, http://www.networkworld.com/article/3022333/careers/shift-to-digital-business-disrupts-traditional-it.html?nsdr=true, retrieved January 21, 2016.

221 Apple Store: Phil Wahba, "Apple Extends Lead in U.S. Top 10 Retailers by Sales per Square Foot," *Fortune*, March 13, 2015, http://fortune.com/2015/03/13/apples-holiday-top-10-retailers-iphone/; Roman Loyola, "Financial history of the Apple Retail Store," *Macworld*, May 19, 2011, http://www.macworld.com/article/1159499/macs/applestoresinancials.html. Both retrieved January 19, 2016.

222 "Buying a car is no longer the worst": Cliff Edwards, "Sorry, Steve, Here's Why Apple Stores Won't Work," *BusinessWeek*, May 20, 2001, http://www.bloomberg.com/bw/stories/2001–05–20/commentary-sorry-steve-heres-why-apple-stores-wont-work, retrieved January 17, 2016.

222 Apple's 2011 Form 10K: http://investor.apple.com/secfiling.cfm?filingid=1193125–11–282113&cik=.

222 Lexus swept into: http://pressroom.lexus.com/releases/history+lexus.htm, retrieved January 5, 2016.

225 Natura's open and networked innovation: Natura Annual Report, 2014.

225 "The most important capability": Interview with Alessandro Carlucci, March 14, 2013.

225 In health care: Michael E. Porter, Stefan Larsson, and Thomas H. Lee, "Standardizing Patient Outcomes Measurement," *New England Journal of Medicine*, n.d. (2016), http://www.nejm.org/doi/full/10.1056/NEJMp1511701?query=featured_home&, retrieved February 26 2016.

226 "Performance on journeys": Alex Rawson, Ewan Duncan, and Conor Jones, "The Truth About Customer Experience: Touchpoints Matter, but It Is the Full Journey That Really Counts," *Harvard Business Review*, September 2013.

226 "if you handed an Etch-a-Sketch": Kevin Cullen, "Delivering the *Globe*, One Street at a Time," *Boston Globe*, January 3, 2016, http://www.bostonglobe.com/metro/2016/01/03/the-globe-here/m6CG7N8XTUjkdsh5GNfglN/story.html?event=event25, retrieved January 23, 2016.

227 pointed fingers:. Mark Arsenault and Dan Adams, "Globe, Distributor Trade Blame as Delivery Woes Persist," *Boston Globe*, January 4, 2016.

227 "Your carrier is": John W. Henry, "We Apologize to Our Loyal Read-

ers," *Boston Globe*, January 5, 2016, http://www.bostonglobe.com/opin ion/2016/01/05/apologize-our-loyal-readers/S0uNqQOjkx3UD7jD3WbbgL/ story.html?event=event25.

228 Xerox: Michael J. de la Merced and Leslie Pickerjan, "Xerox, in Deal with Carl Icahn, to Split Company in Two," *New York Times*, January 29, 2016, http://www.nytimes.com/2016/01/30/business/dealbook/xerox-split-icahn.html ?ref=business&_r=0.

229 "Strategy and Your Stronger Hand": Geoffrey Moore, "Strategy and Your Stronger Hand," *Harvard Business Review*, December 2005.

Chapter 13: First Steps, Next Steps

231 In 2007, the *Economist*: "Snarling All the Way to the Bank," *Economist*, August 23, 2007, http://www.economist.com/node/9681074.

231 After years of rising profits: Sean Farrell and Gwyn Topham, "Ryanair Predicts Price Falls as Profits Double," *Guardian*, February 1, 2016, http://www.theguard ian.com/business/2016/feb/01/ryanair-predicts-price-falls-as-profits-double.

231 low-cost competitor easyJet: Lizzie Porter, "Ryanair: The Truth About the Airline's Customer Services Department," *Telegraph*, August 28, 2014, http:// www.telegraph.co.uk/travel/news/ryanair/Ryanair-the-truth-about-the-airlines -customer-services-department/.

232 Jacobs told one of us: Interview with Kenny Jacobs, September 17, 2015.

239 "internal customers": For more on why and how this is a problematic, even dangerous idea, see Thomas A. Stewart, "Another Fad Worth Killing: The Idea of 'Internal Customers,'" *Fortune*, February 3, 1997.

Appendix: Tools for the Journey

260 showed that reducing customer effort: Matthew Dixon, Karen Freeman, and Nicholas Toman, "Stop Trying to Delight Your Customers," *Harvard Business Review*, July–August 2010.

260 better suited to companies: For an evaluation of CES, see Natalie Steers, "Customer Effort Score: The Truth About the Controversial Loyalty Tool," my customer.com, http://www.mycustomer.com/service/management/customer-effo rt-score-the-truth-about-the-controversial-loyalty-tool, retrieved April 12, 2016. Do not be put off by the faux sensationalism of the title.

262 omnichannel excellence: A good roundtable discussion of the differences be- tween multi- and omnichannel is "Defining the Difference Between a Multi-Chan- nel and Omnichannel Customer Experience," http://www.mycustomer.com/commu nity/blogs/customer-technology/defining-the-difference-between-a-multi -channel-and-omnichannel, retrieved April 13, 2016.

266 "DART" framework: See C. K. Prahalad and Venkat Ramaswamy, *The Future of Competition: Co-Creating Unique Value with Customers* (Boston: Har- vard Business Press, 2004).

268 "maturity model": Forrester, "An Omnichannel World: How Data and Mea- surement Are Key to Customer Engagement," Forrester Consulting Thought Leadership Paper commissioned by Neustar, August 2015.

270 according to a pair of Australian scholars: Megha Sachdeva and Renu Agarwal, "Innovation in Services and Its Measurement at Firm Level: A Literature Review," Academia.edu, https://www.academia.edu/1025338/INNOVATION_IN_SERVICES_AND_ITS_MEASUREMENTAT_FIRM_LEVEL_A_LITERATURE_REVIEW, retrieved April 16, 2016.

271 Framework for Measuring Service Innovation: Partly adapted from Soren Kaplan, "How to Measure Innovation (to Get Real Results)," *Fast Company Design*, June 16, 2014, http://www.fastcodesign.com/3031788/how-to-measure-innovation-to-get-real-results, retrieved April 16, 2016.

Index

About the Authors

THOMAS A. STEWART is a bestselling author, an authority on intellectual capital and knowledge management, and an influential thought leader on global management issues and ideas. His books include *Intellectual Capital* and *The Wealth of Knowledge*. He is the executive director of the National Center for the Middle Market at the Fisher College of Business at The Ohio State University and has served as chief marketing and knowledge officer for Booz & Company, as well as the editor and managing director of *Harvard Business Review*.

PATRICIA O'CONNELL is president of Aerten Consulting, a New York City–based firm that works with companies to devise content strategies and develop thought leadership for top management. She is the writer, with author Neil Smith, of the *New York Times* bestseller *How Excellent Companies Avoid Dumb Things*. She is also the former management editor of BloombergBusinessweek.com.